JESUS
THROUGH
MANY EYES

JESUS THROUGH MANY EYES

Introduction to the Theology
of the New Testament

STEPHEN NEILL

FORTRESS PRESS
Philadelphia

Biblical quotations from the Revised Standard Version of the Bible, copyrighted 1946, 1952, © 1971, 1973 by the Division of Christian Education of the National Council of the Churches of Christ in the U.S.A., are used by permission.
Biblical quotations from *The New English Bible*, copyrighted © 1961, 1970 by The Delegates of the Oxford University Press and The Syndics of the Cambridge University Press, are reprinted by permission.

COPYRIGHT © 1976 BY FORTRESS PRESS

Library of Congress Catalog Card Number 75–36455
ISBN 0–8006–1220–5

Second printing 1978

7353G78   Printed in the United States of America   1-1220

Contents

90320

Preface

Why another book on the theology of the New Testament, when so many excellent books are already on the market? The answer is that this book has grown out of the dilemma of a teacher.

What book should be recommended to students who come—as is often the case today—without an extensive knowledge of the Bible and without much experience in critical study; to people engaged in the delicate art of giving religious instructions in school or Sunday school who are eager to improve their qualifications; and to thoughtful laypeople—and they are many—who are prepared to go to some trouble to find out what the New Testament says and what it means? Of the existing books some make demands for a knowledge of Greek that the ordinary reader cannot meet; some are based on critical principles that are no longer wholly acceptable; several deal with a part of the New Testament only, usually Paul and John; others are so long that the reader tends to drown in them and not to swim. Inquiry has shown that I am far from being alone in experiencing this dilemma.

Would it be possible to produce a book of medium length, covering the whole of the New Testament, based on critical principles but not counting on much prior knowledge on the part of readers, while at the same time encouraging them to make their own discoveries in larger works? I have assumed throughout that the reader will turn constantly to the text of the New Testament itself, and will have or secure a concordance to the Bible—such as Young's *Analytical Concordance*—and a good introduction to the books of the New Testament.

I have included more footnotes and a longer bibliography than had been intended originally. I have been careful to include a number of works by authors whose standpoint is very different from my own. It is important that the reader understand from the start that there is hardly a single point in New Testament study on which there is one agreed view, and that it is necessary to come to the material with a critical intelligence.

Biblical quotations are in most cases from the Revised Standard Version. A few exceptions are noted as being from the Authorized

Version (AV) or from the New English Bible (NEB), or even para-phrases of the Greek.

I have to thank many friends who have helped me, notably Professor C. F. D. Moule who has commented on the whole book and, as always, saved me from a number of errors, Miss G. I. Mather who typed the first draft, and Mrs. M. Howard who typed a large part of the final draft.

Professor Henry Barclay Swete, at the end of the Preface to his masterly commentary on the Gospel of St. Mark,[1] quoted from the great Augustine some words that I would gladly make my own: "Lord God, whatever I have written in this book that comes from thee, may those also who are thine acknowledge [agnoscant]; if anything that comes from myself alone, may I be pardoned [ignosce] both by thee and by those who are thine own."[2]

---

1. *The Gospel According to St. Mark: The Greek Text with Introduction, Notes and Indices* (London: Macmillan and Co., 1898; 2d. ed., 1902).
2. *de Trinitate*, XV, 28.

Abbreviations

AV	Authorized Version (King James Version)
ICC	*International Critical Commentary*
IDB	*Interpreter's Dictionary of the Bible*
JTS	*Journal of Theological Studies*
NEB	New English Bible
NTS	*New Testament Studies*
RSV	Revised Standard Version
SCM	Student Christian Movement
SPCK	Society for Promoting Christian Knowledge
TDNT	*Theological Dictionary of the New Testament* (ed. Kittel and Friedrich)

1

On Doing New Testament Theology

To write a theology of the New Testament, a systematic and ordered presentation of its teaching, is no easy task. The whole of the New Testament is theology—that is its reason for being. The Christian church, as it grew and as the events that brought it into existence became more distant, felt the need of a collection of books in which the reasonable knowledge of God as revealed in the face of Jesus Christ would be preserved until the end of time. Through a process of selection that lasted roughly two centuries certain books were chosen and others were rejected; the New Testament was in being.[1]

Some time ago an Italian school of literary criticism set itself to distinguish between what is poetical and what is not in the writings of great poets. The attempt revealed itself in the end as ludicrous. It rested on the supposition that an exact definition of the word "poetical" is possible, and it overlooked the differences among the various kinds of poetry. In a long poem, such as an epic, lines and even whole passages may seem to lack poetic inspiration; yet they are necessary if the rise and fall of the poem are to be felt, and if its movement is to resemble the inevitability of the advance of waves upon the shore.

In the same way every attempt to separate the theology of the New Testament from the New Testament itself has been found to involve the futile enterprise of trying to separate soul from spirit. The New Testament is its theology. It is impossible to say of one passage, "this is theological," and of another, "this is not." Even in those sections that at a first reading appear to be least theological, the theology is still present and will reveal itself to the more attentive mind. Some good scholars are of the opinion that in the exciting story of Paul's voyage to Rome (Acts 27) the writer is drawing on travel tales that were current in the world of his time rather than on

1. The final definition of "the canon of the New Testament" had to wait for another two centuries.

actual memories of historical events.[2] It may well be that for some of
the nautical details he was thus indebted; but if any Greek travel tale
of the time exists, or ever existed, as heavily charged as the narrative
in Acts with the sense of divine providence, divine purpose, divine
presence, and divine protection, I have not yet encountered it.

Is it then possible to write a theology of the New Testament?

The older and traditional method was simply that of rearrangement of the materials. Rather on the method of the *Loci Communes*
of Philip Melanchthon (1521), the first work of systematic theology of
the Reformation period, the theme was divided up into topics and
headings—the divinity of Jesus Christ, the humanity of Jesus Christ,
the Holy Spirit, the church, and so on; all the relevant material was
assembled and classified, in the expectation that in this way a complete and harmonious picture of the teaching of the entire New
Testament would be arrived at. Various ingenious devices were
worked out for restoring accord if the elements brought together
appeared to be discordant. A work of this kind, *Outlines of Christian Doctrine,* was produced in 1889 by the distinguished evangelical scholar Handley Carr Glyn Moule.

All this could be useful and edifying up to a certain point. But the
effectiveness of the method depended on the acceptance of two
presuppositions—that every part of the New Testament is equally
inspired, and that, for all the variety that exists in the different parts,
they can all in the end be reduced to an undifferentiated harmony.
These are precisely the presuppositions that the theological world of
today finds it difficult to accept.

What has happened to produce a change of attitude, and to make
the former method appear antiquated?

In a variety of ways we have been rediscovering the Jesus to whom
the New Testament bears witness.

In Jesus Christ a force of inestimable magnitude began to operate
within the world of men. The movement that this Jesus initiated has
lasted through nineteen centuries, and shows no signs of diminishing or fading away. The church that bears his name has shown itself
capable of sustaining the most grievous injuries, as in the Muslim
invasions and the Russian Revolution, and of repairing what might
have been fatal losses in one direction by vast extension in another.
It has proved able to absorb into itself many different races and
cultures and to produce new syntheses of thought and conviction. It
has taken over the most varied forms of philosophical thinking and
has learned to use them for the expression of its own understanding

2. I believe that this view was first proposed by Julius Wellhausen, *Noten zur Apostelgeschichte* (Göttingen,
1907).

of the world and of man. After initial suspicion, it has adapted itself to the scientific view of the world. It has continued to inspire incomparable variety and beauty in the fields of art and literature. No power on earth seems able to stay the cataract in which literally millions of Africans are surging into the Christian church every year; there seems no limit, other than the ocean, to the possibilities of this expansion. The Christian church has produced a phenomenon previously unknown in the history of mankind—a universal and worldwide religion. Jesus Christ has influenced human history far more deeply than any other human being of whom we have record. He is still hated, reviled, and despised by those to whom his gospel is as gall and wormwood; yet he is respected and indeed revered far beyond the limits of the fellowship to which his name has been given.

At one time history tended to be written in terms of movements, and for this there is much to be said. The lives and hopes and fears of multitudes of ordinary men and women are the very stuff of which history is made. But behind every movement we are likely to find one person (or at most a small group) and we shall not fully understand the movement until we have identified and explored the nature of the person. It is impossible fully to understand Marxism without some knowledge of the life and character and even of the eccentricities of Karl Marx. It is impossible to understand Christianity without considering Jesus Christ.

Who then was this Jesus of Nazareth? It is clear that he must have been a figure of more than Napoleonic power and originality. When one of the best of the liberal lives of the human Jesus, T. R. Glover's *Jesus of History*,[3] was selling in its thousands, one not unfriendly critic was heard to say, "He does seem to make our Lord a little commonplace"—and that is the one thing that we are never allowed to do.

When a person of eminence appears, no individual will be able to apprehend that person totally. One observer will see one aspect, another observer a different aspect; and even the collection of their observations will not give us the whole person. Lord Blake has written the best biography of Benjamin Disraeli to date.[4] Yet we still have to go back to the old Monypenny and Buckle for many details; and it may be taken as certain that new perspectives will one day demand a new biography. But this is true not only of eminent persons. No one can ever know another individual completely.

3. (London: SCM Press, 1917.)
4. Robert Blake, *Disraeli* (London: Eyre and Spottiswoode, 1966).

Even after many years of happy marriage, husband and wife may suddenly discover aspects of one another's being of which, up till that moment, each had been wholly ignorant.

This being so, it is not surprising that, when that major force called Jesus of Nazareth struck human life, the fragments flew off in every direction. No single mind could encompass the whole, no single hand could draw the definitive portrait of him. Each took what he was able to grasp and recorded it in this way or in that; but each writer was sure that what was being recorded was not a matter of personal invention and creativity. A great deal of what was remembered, reported, and recorded is now irrecoverably lost to us. Some of the fragments were so far out to left or right that the church decided that they were more misleading than revealing and therefore did not merit preservation; in consequence they are known to us only through quotations in other writers, and not infrequently in the testimony of those who detested them. What we have in the New Testament is a collection of those fragments of memory and interpretation that seemed to the church to reflect Jesus as he was, and to carry with them the authentic echo of his voice. We may regret that we have no more; we may feel that at certain points the judgment of the church was at fault, both in what it retained and in what it rejected. But this is the material with which we have to work, and we must make the best of it.

When we recognize that something like this happened in the first century, certain lines of critical approach to the material, as distinct from the mere rearrangement of it, may suggest themselves to us. It may prove useful to take each of the fragments in turn, and to consider what it has to tell us of the response of men to Jesus of Nazareth. Some fragments will prove more congenial than others to the mind of the investigator; but we shall do well not to start with the assumption that there is one "right" interpretation to the exclusion of all others, and so stray into the error, condemned by every careful scholar, of selection on the basis of presuppositions formed independently of the study of the material. Only at the end, when all the material has been surveyed, shall we attempt a synthesis: What are the features common to the various fragments? Do they together present a clear picture of Jesus as he was? Do they depict one who was capable of initiating such a movement as the Christian movement over nineteen centuries has proved itself capable of becoming? Reversing the order of the New Testament, in which the Gospels stand first, our study of Jesus himself will come in the last chapter of this book, as an attempt to see that unity from which all the many interpretations found in the New Testament have moved out on their separate courses.

If this procedure is followed, three methods of approach suggest themselves as possible. The first method, a difficult one, is that of attempting to identify the different traditions that grew up in the various centers of Christian teaching. There is no reason to doubt that such differences did grow up. Shortly after the middle of the first century the great Christian centers were Jerusalem, Antioch, Ephesus, Alexandria, and Rome. Which particular emphasis found a place in the life of this community or of that would depend on a variety of circumstances: the interests of the first teacher or group of teachers and their experience of the Christian life, the pre-Christian background of the community, the proportion of Jews and Gentiles in the fellowship, and the ease of communication and exchange of ideas with other centers. What makes this approach peculiarly difficult is that few of the New Testament writings can be attached with certainty to one center rather than to another. It has generally been supposed that the "captivity" Epistles of Paul were written from Rome. But recently a number of critics have associated them with a supposed captivity of Paul in Ephesus,[5] others with the period of his imprisonment in Caesarea. Ancient tradition, accepted by many scholars today, maintained that the Gospel according to John had its origin in Ephesus. But it can hardly be maintained that this Gospel represents an especially "Ephesian" interpretation of the life of Jesus. Moreover, as we shall have occasion to note in other connections, there was far more coming and going among the Christian groups than is always allowed for, and therefore not many "pure" traditions. There were, of course, some small and isolated fellowships, largely untouched by the crosscurrents of ideas and influences, but the great churches were not among them.

The study of traditions—of their origins and the causes that led to their growth and development—is legitimate and in certain cases may prove useful. It is too uncertain and hypothetical, however, to serve as the basis for a general survey of New Testament theology.

A more useful approach may be that of considering widening circles of response to the original event. Certain periods can be seen as determined by response to what had happened in an earlier period, and as themselves preparing the way for a different kind of response in the period that was to follow. In the development of the New Testament we can identify fairly clearly five periods of response.

5. See especially George S. Duncan, *St. Paul's Ephesian Ministry* (New York: Scribner's, 1930).

There was, first, the response of the earliest disciples and of others to the message proclaimed by Jesus of Nazareth. If Jesus himself wrote anything, it has not been preserved; and, as far as we know, nothing was written down by others at that time. We are therefore wholly dependent for this period on later sources; we can do our best to work backward from the response of later times to what this response may originally have been.

Then followed, after the Resurrection, the period of oral tradition, in which the expectation of the Lord's immediate return was so vivid that it did not seem worthwhile to write anything down. This lasted for roughly twenty years, from A.D. 29 to 49. No document has come down to us entire from that period, though we know with some certainty of documents existing at that time; and, by careful use of later writings, we can discern with a high degree of probability the kind of things that were happening in that versatile and creative period in the life of the church.

Next comes the period of the Epistles, which again lasted roughly twenty years, from A.D. 49 to 69. Here the lion's share falls to Saul of Tarsus, commonly called Paul; but it is probable that other letters in the collection also belong to this period. Here we are in immediate touch with living history. Some of these letters we can date to the year, almost to the month, in which they were written. They are tingling with life and grow out of human situations, the exact nature of which we cannot always apprehend because we have too little knowledge of the background. But from these letters we can see what early Christians believed, what they found it difficult to believe, and at what points they were in danger of falling away into aberration. This is a new development of response. What had been fluid, at times almost chaotic, in the period of oral tradition is just beginning to harden into the shape of accepted doctrine. But the Christians had as yet no sacred book other than the Old Testament. The last thing that the writers thought of in connection with these often hurriedly written letters was permanence; they were written for an immediate purpose, and once that purpose was fulfilled they might be expected to disappear. It was only through a series of accidents that some of them were preserved to become in due course Holy Scripture.

Following the period of the Epistles, and in part overlapping it, comes the period of Gospel-writing. It had now become clear that the Lord might not return as soon as the earliest believers had confidently expected that he would. The first generation was rapidly dying out. To the new generation Jesus of Nazareth was only a name, a name into which content had to be put by the preservation of his words and deeds in written form. It seems that, as the churches became more settled and better organized, recitation from memory of the words and deeds of Jesus had become part of Christian worship; but aberration in memory and consequent divergence in teaching could be better guarded against if the record were preserved in written form. For a variety of reasons and in different places, four writers whom we call the Evangelists decided to set down in ordered form what a later writer, Justin Martyr (A.D. 100 to 165), called the "Memorabilia" of Jesus Christ. This period of response is marked by a new attention to what Jesus said and did, as a prelude to the central teachings concerning his death and Resurrection.

The final period, say A.D. 80 to 100, also overlaps that which preceded it and is reflected in some of the latest books of the New Testament, such as the pastoral Epistles and 2 Peter. Faith had by now become more formal than in earlier times, less enthusiastic but better regulated. The church was conscious of itself as a society, still threatened indeed by a great many dangers from external forces and from within, but consolidated and confident in its own future.

There are no absolute ends or beginnings in history but rather a process of continuous change. Some would maintain that in this fifth period of response we have already moved out of the apostolic into the subapostolic age, from the period of adventurous faith to that of conventional faith, and that we should group together with these latest books of the New Testament such works as the First Epistle of Clement and the letters of Ignatius, works which belong to the same period of development and throw some light on the transition that took place between the first and second centuries. For purposes of study there is a good deal to be said in favor of not interpreting too narrowly the idea of a canon of the New Testament, and of admitting a continuity that certainly existed.

A third method, and the one that has been most widely followed in recent years, is that of taking together certain groups of writings and elucidating their theology as central to the New Testament. The two groups that most readily suggest themselves are the Epistles of Paul, though there is not complete agreement as to which Epistles can rightly be reckoned as Pauline, and the Johannine writings, taking together at least the Gospel and the First Epistle. These two groups form so large a part of the New Testament, and are so crucial in the development of Christian thinking, that some recent continental works on the theology of the New Testament are in reality little more than dissertations on Pauline and Johannine theology;[6] a standard of orthodoxy has been set up that tends to treat other parts of the New Testament as secondary or marginal. But this will not do. The New Testament is the record of a complex and intricate process, and a true picture can be drawn only if careful attention is directed to every part of the process. There are, in fact, other groupings that we shall do well not to neglect.

In addition to the Pauline group of ten letters and the Johannine writings we must take into account the persistence of the Jewish influence as seen in the Gospel of Matthew, together with the books that are most closely related to it in spirit—the Epistle of James, the Epistle to the Hebrews, and the Revelation of John. We must also consider the more specifically Gentile point of view, as seen in the Gospel of Luke and the Acts of the Apostles, two books that stand closely together and apart from the rest of the New Testament. With the Gospel of Mark we shall take the First Epistle of Peter, for reasons that should become clear in due course as we look at the two texts in some detail. This leaves us with an appendix of five later books—the pastoral Epistles, 2 Peter, and Jude—all of which seem to belong to what was described as the final period of response.

The method to be followed in this book is a combination of the last two of these three methods. After a chapter in which we consider the life of the earliest Christians before they had any Christian literature at all, we go on to consider each of the major groups in turn; as we examine each of them, the main concern will be to determine the nature of the response to the gospel to which the writings give expression.

History and theology will be kept closely in touch with one another. History deals with people in their thoughts and ideals, their experiences and sufferings, the way they lived, the background against which they have to be seen, the way in which they helped to create new worlds out of old. But theology also deals with people, and if it is treated merely as a study and classification of ideas, it becomes desiccated and loses touch with life. The two disciplines are not the same. History deals with life in all the rich complexity of its detail and its unpredictability. Theology attempts to see patterns and to reduce the chaos of history to some kind of order. But much harm has been done to the study of both through the separation that has grown up between them. Very few theologians have had any training in the study or writing of history. Very few historians have

6. This is true of, for example, the famous work of Rudolf Bultmann, *Theology of the New Testament*, 2 vols. (London: SCM Press, 1952, 1955), and the more recent study by Werner G. Kümmel, *The Theology of the New Testament According to its Major Witnesses—Jesus, Paul, John* (Nashville: Abingdon, 1975).

turned to the study of theology. And so the dichotomy has arisen: theology has all too often been written as though it was something that grew by some spontaneous and purely intellectual process, and not directly out of the hopes and fears of men; history has been presented as a mere record of external events, without reference to any inner dynamic by which they may be controlled. We shall succeed in our enterprise only to the extent that we are able to hold the two together.

Two points remain to be considered before we turn to the New Testament itself. The first is the shortness of the period with which we are dealing. There is no convincing proof that any book of the New Testament was written later than the noncanonical First Epistle of Clement, which we can date with some confidence in the year A.D. 96. But even if we hold, as some scholars do, that some books belong to a later period, at least the greater part of our New Testament was already in existence before the first century closed. This means that a period of roughly seventy years elapsed between the beginning of the ministry of Jesus and the close of the New Testament period. So Jairus' daughter, if she survived so long, was about eighty years old when the period ended, and the young man who fled naked from the Roman soldiers (Mark 14:51) was five or six years older. The expectation of life was low in the Roman world, but this was largely due to enormous infant mortality; any child who managed to survive up to the age of five had a life expectancy not so very different from that of the modern world, and a considerable number of the survivors lived to a ripe old age. The early church seems to have laid more stress on the witness of the Spirit than on the actual testimony of eyewitnesses.[7] Yet the presence, right up to the end of the New Testament period, of a number of persons who had themselves seen and heard Jesus must have exercised a measure of control on the development of the diverse traditions.

I find it natural to stress this point, since in Kenya, where the first draft of this chapter was written, we are still as it were in our New Testament period. Everything has happened so quickly. The first Anglican baptism in the Nyanza province took place in 1909, sixty-six years ago. This means that a lady who is now eighty can remember quite clearly the days before the coming of the white man, and the manner of life of her people before Western influences began to play on them. Only in rare cases can people of that age give a coherent and ordered account of affairs; their exposition is disjointed, repetitive, and at times confused. But they really do re-

7. See three important articles by Dennis E. Nineham in *JTS*, n.s. 9 (1958): 13–25; 243–52; *JTS*, n.s. 11 (1960): 253–54.

member things that actually happened, and their evidence, rightly interpreted, is of inestimable value.   One of the major tasks of departments of history in African universities is the collection and recording of oral history before it is lost through the death of the last survivors from that period.   When we speak of the period of oral tradition in a biblical context we usually mean that early time before the New Testament books were written.   It is important not to forget that the whole of the first century was a period of oral tradition.   Just what part that tradition played in fashioning the life of the church it is not altogether easy to say; there can be no doubt that it was there, just as it is there in the life of a "younger church" today.

The second point I would make in closing this chapter has to do with what may be anticipated in the last chapter.   When we come to the end, we must come back to the beginning.   In the intervening chapters we shall have been studying results; at the end we must come back to causes.   Every theology of the New Testament must be a theology of Jesus—or it is nothing at all:

Two comments have been made so often that they have tended to be accepted as canonical and unquestionable.   The first is that the writers of the New Testament were not interested in history.   The second is that we cannot get beyond the faith of the early disciples; that is the earliest point our inquiries into the past can reach.

That the writers of the New Testament were not interested in history is in a measure true.   They were not interested in annals. Most of them showed a regrettable disregard of precise chronology, so much so that we cannot tell for certain in what year Jesus was born or in what year he died.   We do not know when Saul of Tarsus was born or in what year he was converted to the Christian faith; we have to reconstruct the events of his life as best we can from fragmentary indications.   The writers do not always make sure that their quotations from the Old Testament are correct, or attribute them to the writers who really wrote them.

All this we shall allow.   On the other hand it would be far truer to say that the only thing in which the writers of the New Testament were interested was history.   History deals not with general ideas, but with the unpredictable, the unique, and the irreversible.   The church never lost the sense of its origins, which were in a series of identifiable historical happenings.   The earliest Christian confession of faith, given to us by Paul in 1 Cor. 12:3, was "Jesus is Lord." The human name "Jesus" takes us back to a particular series of events that took place in a country that can be located on the map, and in a time frame that can be fixed with considerable accuracy though not with absolute precision.   God had acted "once for all" in one man who had lived at that particular place and time, and this action of God was something that could never be altered or withdrawn.   Christian faith has never at any time allowed itself to be detached from the events connected with that particular Jew at that particular time.   This became clearly evident in the conflict of the church with the great menace that came upon it just at the end of the New Testament period, the diverse systems called by the common name Gnosticism.[8]   Gnosticism offered a mythical redeemer who, somewhere, somehow, had appeared out of space upon earth; Christian faith countered this with the doctrine of a human and historical Savior.   Gnosticism became more and more a series of ideas and mystifications; the church met this with the recitation of historical facts, as these are found in the Creeds, including the words "crucified under Pontius Pilate."   Christianity is not a religion of ideas but of happenings—happenings in history.

Moreover, the human name "Jesus" (=Joshua, Savior) is a Jewish name and brings us immediately into contact with the whole story of the Jewish people as this is recorded for us in the Old Testament. The story of Jesus is not isolated; it stands in the historic succession of the prophets of Israel.   The Jews were perhaps the first people to write history, and they did so four centuries earlier than the Greeks. Theirs was the only religion that had found a way of escape from the twin dangers of endless repetition and mere successiveness, through the concept of a purpose in history that had a beginning and looked forward to an end.   History was bred into the blood and bones of every Jew, and Jesus of Nazareth was no exception.   If we are believers, we have been caught up into a pageant of history that began with Abraham and has lasted up to the present day: our God is the God of Abraham, Isaac, and Jacob; Abraham, Isaac, and Jacob are our ancestors.

It is also true in a sense that it is impossible to get beyond the faith of the earliest disciples.   From the hand of Jesus we have nothing. Everything that we have is the work of devout believers in him. One of the evidences for the reliability of the Gospels is that they record so accurately the accusations made against Jesus by his enemies—"This man receives sinners and eats with them" (Luke 15:2)—but we have nothing actually written by those enemies.   We do not possess the Roman protocol of the trial of Jesus of Nazareth before Pontius Pilate the governor.   The historical references to Jesus Christ outside the New Testament are few and insignificant.

8. For more on Gnosticism, see below, chap. 7.

The phenomenon that we have before us is the faith of the early believers. But to say that history cannot go beyond this and ask what it was that caused this faith is misleading. This is just what history is doing all the time—going beyond secondary evidences that are almost always partial, and to some extent distorted, in search of the undoctored incident that actually occurred. History cannot attain to the same measure of certainty as physical science; it can often establish a very strong probability. Every schoolboy knows, or knew fifty years ago, that Caesar's Commentaries are a propagandist work, the aim of which is "to malign an opponent and to glorify himself"; this does not mean that we know nothing about Julius Caesar, or about the Gauls of whom his account is partial and in part inaccurate.

It would be good if those who aspire to write on the origins of Christianity had two years' training in the parallel discipline of research into the origins of Buddhism. The resemblances between the two problems are in many ways remarkable. The Buddha himself, as far as we know, wrote nothing, but he set in motion a great wave of belief of which we have evidence in many directions. The traditions about him were carried in the memories of his disciples in many different forms. Eventually these were set down in writing. The difference is that believers in Jesus began to write within twenty years of his death, whereas probably four centuries had passed before the Tripitaka, the "three baskets," of the Pali canon reached their present form. In Buddhism, as in Christianity, the phenomenon that immediately presents itself to us is the faith of the disciples. Undeterred by the obstacles present in a confused mass of traditions, historical science has pressed on beyond this phenomenon to ask what manner of man the Buddha was and what he actually taught, and it has achieved remarkable success. Hermann Oldenberg's book, *The Buddha, His Life, His Teaching, His Company,* which was published in 1881, is a notable work of historical scholarship and has been reprinted again and again. Some critics might be inclined to say that Oldenberg is too much the captive of the Theravada or southern (Pali) tradition of Buddhism, at the expense of the Mahayana or northern (Sanskrit, Chinese) tradition. This is a matter of detail for the experts. What is significant is that Oldenberg has succeeded in producing a credible picture of Gautama Buddha as just the kind of man who might be expected to create just this kind of religious movement. He has placed him in history. He has enucleated from the traditions those elements that may reasonably be thought to go back to the founder himself. He has shown us a man, gracious, patient, considerate, serene, impress-

ing on his movement its abiding character of serenity, deeply rever-
enced by his disciples, and actually having like the Johannine Jesus
one beloved disciple.

If such an achievement is possible for historical science in a field
in which the evidences are so much more difficult to handle than
those that relate to Jesus of Nazareth, we are making no arrogant
claim if we affirm that historical inquiry not merely can, but is bound
to, press beyond the faith of the earliest disciples of Jesus to inquire
what it was, or rather who it was, that brought that faith into being—
and that in such an enterprise there is the prospect of at least limited
success.

From my window in Nairobi I can see the shadow of a tree deli-
cately etched upon the ground by the brilliant sunshine of tropical
Africa. I cannot see the tree, since there is a blank wall in front of
me. But I know my tree. It is always there when the sun shines,
which of course on the equator is most of the time. I can trace the
movement of the seasons by the way the shadow falls. I know the
time of year at which it loses its leaves and renews them. I know just
when it flowers, since I can see also the shadows of the sun-birds as
they dart from twig to twig and delight in the delicate nectar with
which my tree provides them. If a visitor were to remark, "You do
not see the tree, and therefore you are really seeing nothing," I
would be inclined to reply with Browning's Bishop Blougram, "My
shade's so much more potent than your flesh."

The application of my parable is obvious. We cannot know Jesus
Christ by direct observation. The lapse of historical time, if nothing
else, makes that impossible. We have nothing written by his hand.
We are dependent on the records and reports of others and can see
him only through their eyes. Some have drawn from this the conclusion that we can know very little if indeed anything about him;
they have tended to reduce him, in the striking phrase of Giovanni
Miegge, to the mathematical point which has position but no magnitude. Some would go even further and say it matters very little
whether we know anything about him or not: what matters is the
"that," that in Jesus Christ God encountered mankind, and not the
"what," the exact nature or content of the encounter. But this is not
what the New Testament itself affirms and claims. Luke claims to
be setting forth an orderly account "that you may know the truth
concerning the things of which you have been informed" (Luke 1:4),
and a Gospel follows. An old man, writing probably at the very end
of the New Testament period, expresses his purpose thus: "That
which was from the beginning, which we have heard, which we have

seen with our eyes, which we have looked upon and touched with our hands, concerning the word of life . . . that which we have seen and heard we proclaim also to you, so that you may have fellowship with us" (1 John 1:1, 3). The important thing was to know Christ. Those who had received this knowledge mediately through the testimony of others were not regarded as being in a position inferior to that of those who had seen with their eyes and touched with their hands; they were all one in the fellowship of an experience that was closely similar though not identical, and that experience took its origin from one man who had actually lived and died.

Anyone who sees the shadow of a tree but does not see the tree does not for that reason see nothing. It may be that in our study of New Testament theology we shall see only shadows of the Christ, but we shall not see nothing. That humble and devout scholar Robert H. Lightfoot ended his Bampton lectures, *History and Interpretation in the Gospel* (1934), with the words: "For all the inestimable value of the Gospels, they yield us little more than a whisper of his voice; we trace in them but the outskirts of his ways." Lightfoot was dismayed by the misunderstanding that arose from these words. He had miscalculated in supposing that his readers would know the Book of Job as well as he knew it himself, and that they would complete the quotation for themselves. The words that he expected them to be able to supply were these: "The thunder of his power who can understand?" (Job 26:14).

2

The Earliest Church

The church of Jesus Christ began, we are told, with a group of frightened men and women in an upper room in Jerusalem (Acts 1:12–14). They were all Jews, and they were all frightened—and not without reason.

We do well to learn as much as we can about this group, since they were the acorn out of which grew the stately oak that we see today. But it is not easy to come into direct contact with them. They have left no written record of their own. Our principal authority is the earlier chapters of the Acts of the Apostles, a work supposed to have been written by that Luke who had been a traveling companion of the apostle Paul. We shall have occasion to note from time to time the astonishing brilliance of Luke as a historian, and his accuracy in detail where this can be tested. But Luke was writing, in all probability, more than fifty years after the events he was describing. There were many people still living who could guide him with their recollections, especially if he was actually the Luke who had spent two years in Caesarea with Paul. Yet we cannot rule out the possibility that he is to some extent idealizing that primitive church, and presenting a portrait rather than aiming at exact photographic accuracy in every detail. So we shall treat Luke's evidence with a certain amount of caution. We are able to check it at certain points from the references in the Epistles of Paul, who had contact from time to time with the church in Jerusalem. We can see those early days dimly through the researches of scholars who are trying to get behind the written documents of the New Testament to that period in which the earliest traditions of the church were taking shape.[1] And we now know a great deal more than we ever knew before about Judaism in what we call the first century A.D. and about the life of the

---

1. This is the method of study known in English by the rather clumsy title, "Form Criticism." The first three practitioners of this craft were Karl Ludwig Schmidt, Rudolf Bultmann, and Martin Dibelius. One of the first expositions of the method in English (not altogether friendly) was Vincent Taylor, *The Formation of the Gospel Tradition*, 2nd ed. (London: Macmillan & Co., 1942). For a useful guide to the method see Edgar V. McKnight, *What is Form Criticism?* (Philadelphia: Fortress Press, 1969).

Jewish people in that period.   It is against this background that we have to attempt to reconstruct the convictions of the earliest group of believers.

A critical study of such evidence as we have leads us to the conclusion that the Christian experience of this group can be summed up in three words: resurrection, Spirit, and reconciliation.

What distinguished the Christians from the other inhabitants of Jerusalem was their conviction that Jesus of Nazareth, who had been crucified by the authorities, was alive.   The Resurrection was the burden of their proclamation in the earliest days.

We have been so much influenced by the Greek tradition, in which body and spirit appear as separate, and separable, constituents of human nature, that it is difficult for us to think ourselves back into the unitary Jewish concept of human nature.   According to that view, man is alive only when what we call body and soul, or body and spirit, are united.   If he has no body, he is a ghost, an inhabitant of Sheol, very much like those "strengthless heads of the dead" whom Odysseus saw in his pilgrimage to the netherworld.   Very few Jews believed in the total extermination of a human being at death; perhaps even fewer believed in anything that could be called *life* on the other side of the grave.   Those who, in the time of the Maccabean troubles (second century B.C.), came to believe in the new doctrine of resurrection seem to have thought that the faithful Jews who had died in the time of persecution would be called out of their graves to live again a physical life on earth in the kingdom of God.[2]

Some students of the New Testament have thought that the earliest Christians were content with the idea of a spiritual resurrection, but later, in the desire to reinforce their preaching, added the stories of the empty tomb and of those physical appearances of Jesus that are recorded in the Gospels.   But this view involves a serious misunderstanding of the Old Testament, and an almost total disregard of the evidence that we have.   Paul's discussion of the Resurrection in 1 Corinthians 15 (the earliest written evidence for the Resurrection that we possess) will yield us clues of the greatest value.   The whole burden of the Corinthians' questions is this (v. 35): "Someone will ask, How are the dead raised? *With what kind of body* do they come?"   Paul takes it for granted that resurrection implies a body, and that, if the dead are raised at all, they will have what he calls, without explaining his words in detail, a spiritual body.   And he defends this doctrine by analogy with the Resurrection of Jesus Christ; this he could not have done unless he believed that the

2. See especially 2 Macc. 12:43–45.

Resurrection of the Lord was a total resurrection, in which the whole personality including the body was involved.

It was Christian preaching of the Resurrection that aroused the anger and hostility of the Jewish authorities. That some Jews should proclaim the absurdity that a man who was known to have been crucified and killed was still alive was bad enough. That they should go on to affirm that one whom the Jewish authorities had rejected and who had become accursed by being hanged on a tree (Gal. 3:13; Deut. 21:23) was in reality the chosen one of God, that his Resurrection was God's vindication of his righteousness as against the baseless charges made by his accusers, and that he would come again to establish the kingdom of God on earth—all this was intolerable.

Unless the body of Jesus had been surreptitiously removed, as was suspected by some (Matt. 28:13),[3] the Jews had in their hands the perfect instrument for putting a stop to the babbling of the Christian believers. All they had to do was to open the tomb in which Jesus had been buried and show his body in an advanced state of decay. There could have been no difficulty about identification. As recent discoveries have shown us, the skeleton of a crucified man is easily identifiable as such after nineteen centuries.[4] If this had been done, it is likely that the believers in Jesus would have contrived to preach *some* doctrine of resurrection, but they could not have gone on preaching *that* doctrine of resurrection which all the evidence combines to show they did actually preach. There is no evidence that the Jewish authorities ever took this simple step to put an end to the Christian preaching. It is at least possible that they did not do so because they did not know where the body of Jesus was.

The second major doctrine proclaimed by the first Christians was that the Spirit of God had come to men in a new and universal fashion. Every good Jew knew about the Spirit as portrayed in the Old Testament. The Spirit was a manifest and exceptional power, which came upon specially selected people to enable them to do certain things that would be beyond the limits of unaided human capacity. This could be manifested as sheer spiritual strength, as in the case of Samson (Judg. 14:19; 15:14); it could be the power that enabled the prophet to say, "Thus saith the Lord" (Mic. 3:8); in Isa. 61:1–4, the claim of the anointed one that the Spirit of the Lord was upon him to proclaim the year of the Lord's favor comes near to the

---

3. Joachim Jeremias seriously discusses this possibility in his *New Testament Theology* (London: SCM Press, 1963), 1:305ff.

4. A good account of these discoveries is in J. H. Charlesworth, "Jesus and Jehohanan: an Archaeological Note on Crucifixion," *The Expository Times*, February 1973, pp. 147–51.

New Testament usage of the term.   The Spirit could come and go; it could be fitful in its operations.   But throughout the Old Testament this gift is one that is limited in its extent; God could take some of the Spirit that he had granted to Moses and distribute it among seventy of the elders of the people of Israel, with startling effects (Num. 11:16–30); but there is no suggestion that the desire of Moses that the Lord would put his Spirit upon all his people ever became a reality (Num. 11:29).

We may be inclined to think that the elegant speech recorded in Acts 2 represents not so much the extemporary utterance of Peter in a moment of great excitement as a condensation of innumerable Christian sermons, as these took shape in the experience of Christian living and through the minute study of the Old Testament Scriptures in the light of the revelation in Christ.   But whether the speaker was Peter or another, the believers soon came to grasp the significance of the new dispensation, and found in the Old Testament the proof text that would guarantee the correctness of their understanding.   The prophet Joel had foretold in the name of the Lord, "I will pour out my Spirit on all flesh" (Joel 2:28; Acts 2:17).[5]   On the basis of this and other prophecies some of the Jewish interpreters had declared that one of the signs of the messianic age would be the universal distribution of the Spirit.   To the early Christians it was self-evident that this was what had occurred; the prophecy had been fulfilled.

It is not easy to determine exactly what happened on the first day of Pentecost after the death of Jesus, for knowledge of which we are wholly dependent on Luke and the narrative of Acts 2.   Luke, as is his way, has painted a highly artistic picture in which the events of that day are represented as the reversal of the curse of Babel in Genesis (11:1–9).   There the false unity that man had attempted to engineer through his own ingenuity had been condemned by God, and had ended in frustration and misunderstanding.   Now had come the true unity of all men, planned and intended by God.   Luke is careful to arrange the representatives of the nations under the three Old Testament groups of the sons of Noah—Shem, Ham, and Japheth—in order to emphasize the universality of the gift of the Spirit on this occasion (see Gen. 10:1 ff.).   The traditional interpretation has been that the apostles were then given the power to speak in many diverse languages in order that the gospel of Jesus might go out into all the world.   This is reflected in the Proper Preface for Whitsunday in the Anglican Book of Common Prayer: "giving them both

5. The NEB "upon everyone" avoids the awkward Hebraism, "upon all flesh," but is too weak: the phrase means "upon the whole human race."

the gift of diverse languages, and also boldness with fervent zeal constantly to preach the Gospel unto all nations." But in point of fact those who came from all these geographical areas would speak or understand one or more of three languages—Latin, Greek, and Aramaic; if the disjointed utterances of the apostles had been expressed in these three languages, almost all of those present would have been able to understand something of what was being said.

Details are perplexing. The central argument is clear. The conviction that runs through the whole New Testament, and not merely through the Acts of the Apostles, is that the promise of the messianic age has been fulfilled; all who by faith in Jesus Christ have entered into that new age have received the Spirit, who is now known as the Spirit of the living Christ. To be a Christian is to have received the Spirit. Moreover, that gift is not a presence that may come and go, like the Spirit that came intermittently on Samson and then again left him; it is a permanent reality by which the life of the believer is at every point conditioned.[6] Of the many gifts ascribed in the Old Testament to the Spirit, those most stressed in the early church were understanding and power (e.g., Isa. 11:2). The believer was now in a position to understand the whole counsel of God, including the mystery of that Providence that had permitted the death of the Messiah at the hands of the chosen people. To be an inhabitant of a new world demanded a new manner of living, the pattern of which had been seen in the life of Jesus Christ; the believers discovered in themselves a mysterious power that made it possible for them to live this new life—including the willingness to die—and they identified this power with the Spirit.

This is not to say that all this was evident to the believers in the first days and weeks after the Resurrection. All theology is a matter of slow growth; the church does certain things, and then retrospectively discovers the reasons for doing them. What experience of the Spirit meant to the earliest Christian believers has to some extent to be inferred from the rest of the New Testament. But when Paul and John and later writers set forth the nature of life in the Spirit, they claim not to be adding anything new but to be expounding and elucidating that which had been accepted and believed from the beginning, and in favor of which no special argument needed to be adduced.

The third pillar of the faith, reconciliation, is slightly less easy to identify in the earliest traditions. The early Christians continued to

6. There are, of course, other references to the coming of the Spirit with power on those who had already received him, e.g., Acts 4:31; 13:9.

attend the temple, in which the offering of the lamb daily in the morning and "between the two evenings" continued for another thirty years. They seem not yet to have affirmed that, since the perfect sacrifice had been offered, all other sacrifices, including the daily reminder of God's covenant with his people, had been reduced to insignificance. The traditions of the church, as we find them reflected in the earliest Christian worship, drew more on the synagogue than on the temple. Here was the regular round of Scripture-reading, exposition, and prayer, and these were combined with certain specifically Christian elements. But Jesus himself had added a new dimension of intimacy to the old tradition of worship. He addressed God as *Abba*, "Father," and this our best authorities tell us was something new in the Jewish approach to God. He bade his disciples address God in the same way. The Jewish religion, as it existed in the first century A.D., was one of barriers and of exclusion.[7] As the Epistle to the Hebrews reminds us (7:11–14), since Jesus belonged to the tribe of Judah and not to the tribe of Levi he would have had no access at all to the earthly sanctuary. But this made no difference at all to his approach to God; he passed always as through an open door. The believer knew from experience that his fellowship with Jesus was unbroken, and therefore for him the direct approach to God "through Jesus Christ our Lord" became the determining reality of life. Jesus was reported as having spoken, at the Last Supper, of a covenant, or a new covenant, in his blood. Long before the Epistle to the Hebrews was written, devout believers must have discovered that covenant in Jeremiah 31, where it is written, "They shall all know me, from the least of them to the greatest, says the Lord; for I will forgive their iniquity, and I will remember their sin no more" (v. 34). Forgiveness comes to be one of the great words in the Christian proclamation.

There were Christians in places other than Jerusalem. In Galilee there must have been many who had been witnesses of the ministry of Jesus and had believed. But Jerusalem was the center of the civic as well as the religious life of the Jews; as the environment of the early Christians, it played so important a part that some attention must be paid to the city and to its life.

I had long tried to work out what the population of Jerusalem might have been in the days of Jesus, and, on the basis of the slender evidence available to me, had reached the figure of thirty thousand as being at least probable. Since then Joachim Jeremias has

---

7. A plan of the temple in the days of Jesus makes plain the limitations of access for different classes of people—Gentiles, women, Israelites, priests, and the high priest. Details are found in Joachim Jeremias, *Jerusalem in the Time of Jesus* (Philadelphia: Fortress Press, 1969), pp. 79ff.

confirmed my estimate on the basis of far more extensive learning.[8] This means that the Jerusalem of those days would rank today as a fair-sized town; and as ancient cities were always, like the old City of London, close-packed and crowded, no one would live far from the center of affairs or far beyond the sound of the temple trumpets.

Although isolated on its hills from the main highways, Jerusalem was a cosmopolitan town. Here were the palaces of the Herods, unoccupied for the greater part of the year, but bringing in from time to time with the multitude of servants and retainers a strong breath of another and non-Jewish world. These Herods were an international family, some of whom maintained intimate relations with the ruling family in Rome (one of them had actually been for a number of years a hostage there) and spoke Greek among themselves.[9] The Roman colonial power, with a tact that might have been more extensively used, had arranged that Caesarea and not Jerusalem should be the ordinary residence of the governor. But the Antonia Tower was in Jerusalem, and Roman soldiers, who were not likely at that stage of imperial history to be Italian in origin, were part of the life of the city. It would seem hardly possible for anyone living in Jerusalem to be wholly ignorant of Greek. But even in a cosmopolitan community it is possible for certain people, on aristocratic or sectarian grounds, to keep themselves separate from the life that is going on around them. Certain Europeans, after fifty years of residence in Kenya, boast that they do not know a single word of Swahili, the lingua franca. In the same way, some of the more fanatical Jewish sects may have cut themselves off from the life around them and limited themselves to Hebrew and one of the Aramaic dialects. But this must not be regarded as typical. Many of the early Christians were Galileans, whose attitude to the outside world was more open than that of Judean tradition. The Acts of the Apostles tells us (chapter 6) that a number of the believers belonged to the Diaspora groups which spoke Greek at home, and to which Hebrew was a foreign and largely incomprehensible language.

Jerusalem was a city actively engaged in trade and therefore directly aware of the wider world outside Palestine. But what kept it constantly in touch with the whole of the ancient world was the fact of pilgrimage. According to the Jewish Law all the males of the people of Israel were to present themselves before the Lord three times a year at the great annual festivals (Deut. 16:16). Once Israel

8. Ibid., p. 84.
9. On the complicated family history of the Herods see the accurate study by Arnold H. M. Jones, *The Herods of Judea* (Oxford: Clarendon Press, 1938). More popularly, Stewart H. Perowne, *Life and Times of Herod the Great* (London: Hodder and Stoughton, 1956) and *The Later Herods: The Political Background of the New Testament* (London: Hodder and Stoughton, 1958). See also Harold W. Hoehner, *Herod Antipas* (Cambridge, 1972).

had become settled in the land of promise it became plain that this command could not be fulfilled by every adult male in the population. But the practice of pilgrimage never died out, and the New Testament is not our only evidence that in the time of Jesus and later it played a considerable part in the life of the Jews, as it has in the life of the Muslims since the days of the prophet Muhammad. The majority of the pilgrims no doubt came from the land of Palestine, but Simon of Cyrene was far from being the only pious Jew who had made the long journey at least once in a lifetime in order to present himself to the Lord of hosts in his sanctuary (Ps. 84:5–7).

For many years I had wondered whether it was possible to determine the number of pilgrims who assembled every year, or three times a year, in the Holy City. As far as I know, the only evidence in ancient literature comes from the Jewish historian Josephus (A.D. c. 37–c. 100), who reckons the number of those sharing in the Passover meal at 2.7 million.[10]   This is obviously absurd. Our debt to Josephus is great, since without his *Histories* we would know little of the Herods or of that calamitous war against the Romans in which Jerusalem was destroyed and burned. But this statement should serve as a warning as to the critical care that we have to exercise before accepting anything that Josephus tells us. It is reckoned that at the great Kumbh Mela, observed once every twelve years in India at the junction of the Ganges and the Jumna, sometimes a million pilgrims assemble, to the great distress of the police who are always anxious about the spread of epidemics. The area of the Kumbh Mela, however, is the vast sandy expanse exposed when the waters of the rivers have fallen to their lowest level. The rocky heights of Judea, with their inhospitable crags and declivities, are as different as could well be imagined from the plains of India. Josephus was using a reckless imagination rather than the sober caution of the historian.

Working on slender evidence, I had come to the conclusion that, when the flood of pilgrims was at its highest, the population of Jerusalem might treble, and that this would be likely to occur at the annual celebration of the Passover. Thus an influx of more than sixty thousand pilgrims at any one time would not be expected. Professor Jeremias puts the figure considerably higher, but recognizes that his is a maximum estimate.

10. *Bella Judorum* 6. 9. 3, quoted by Emil Schürer, *The Jewish People in the Time of Jesus Christ*, rev. ed., edited by Gezá Vermés and Fergus Millar (Naperville: Allenson, 1973), 2:291. Schürer remarks correctly that "there was nothing that contributed so much to cement the bond of union between the dispersions and the mother country as the regular pilgrimages which Jews from all quarters of the world were in the habit of making to Jerusalem on festival occasions." See Henry St. John Thackeray, trans., *Josephus*, vol. 3, *The Jewish War Books IV–VIII*, The Loeb Classical Library (London: William Heinemann, 1928), p. 499. Thackeray corrects the arithmetic of Josephus and points out that the total should be 2,556,000.

Clearly this fact of pilgrimage was of the greatest importance for the early Christians, although, being generally taken for granted, it is hardly referred to in our sources. The picture of the Jerusalem church as an isolated group, almost completely out of touch with the Gentile world, does not correspond to the facts. The real picture of that first century is one of ceaseless coming and going between all parts of the Roman Empire, which stretched from Britain to the Euphrates and Tigris, and of an intricately interwoven network of relationships. Luke gives us an account of one day of Pentecost, but there were thirty-seven other days of Pentecost before the outbreak of the Jewish war brought pilgrimage to an end.

Accurate calculation is impossible. But if we take it that on an average no more than sixty thousand persons came to Jerusalem each year, of whom two-thirds were inhabitants of Palestine, and that each of those who came from outside Palestine made the pilgrimage on an average twice, we find that every year a minimum of ten thousand strangers made their appearance in Jerusalem, for a total of three hundred and seventy thousand in the years between the death of Jesus and the outbreak of the war. Almost all of these would have heard something of the new messianic movement in Israel, though the majority probably remained skeptical or uninterested. But some at least are likely to have gone back to their distant homes as believers in Jesus. Others may have come to Jerusalem as believers, to renew their faith at the original source of inspiration. The leaders of the Jerusalem church, so far from being an isolated body, were in constant and living touch with every part of the Roman Empire and with all the main centers in which the Christian faith had taken root.

Internally the Judaism of the days of the apostles was far from being as rigidly monolithic as accounts of it have often implied. It was in fact a forum of vivid and lively discussion, and many and varying points of view could be maintained within the overarching unity of the Jewish faith.

Best known of all the Jewish sects at the time of Jesus[11] are, naturally, the Pharisees—through the not very favorable picture of them familiar to everyone from the Gospels. It is possible that at one time the Pharisees had hoped to capture the prophetic zeal of Jesus of Nazareth for their own movement. Disappointed in this expectation, they had turned against him; yet there was much in the austere earnestness of their understanding of the Law, as well as

11. One of the disciples of Jesus is specifically said, by Luke alone, to have belonged to the extreme nationalist sect of the Zealots. It is debatable whether "Zelotes" is correctly rendered as "the Zealot," and the attempt of Samuel G. F. Brandon, in *Jesus and the Zealots* (New York: Scribner's, 1968) to connect the Christian movement closely with that of the Zealots has not met with general acceptance.

their belief in the resurrection of the faithful, that might have led them into sympathy with the comparable earnestness of the new faith.[12]

It was less likely that the Christian cause would find sympathy in the ruling and priestly caste of the Sadducees. This was the group that was bound to experience profound anxiety as to the possible political repercussions of the new movement. The modern reader is not likely to find much that is attractive in the picture of the cool, calculating, worldly-minded Sadducee, or in the foxlike prudence and cunning of Caiaphas (John 11:49–50). Yet these conservatives, with their rejection of what they regarded as later and apocryphal additions to the ancient Law, could put in a good claim to being the true Israelites, the only trustworthy supporters of the traditions of the fathers.

Our awareness of the breadth of the possibilities that lay before a pious Jew in the days of the apostles has been considerably extended by the discoveries at Qumran of what are commonly called the Dead Sea Scrolls. If the members of the monastic community at Qumran were in fact Essenes, we now know a great deal more about the Essene tradition than we did before. Living not very far from Jerusalem, this monastic and ascetic group, with its own rigid rules of order and discipline and a highly independent attitude toward the Old Testament, had hardly been known until the new flood of discoveries began in 1947. Certain early hopes that the new documents would brightly illuminate the rise and early history of Christianity have not been fulfilled. We have indeed learned that even the strictly traditional Judaism of Jerusalem was much less impervious to Hellenistic influences than we had supposed—some of the phrases in the Fourth Gospel that had been regarded by scholars as unmistakably Hellenistic have now been found in the Dead Sea Scrolls. It is possible that John the Baptist had to some extent come under Essene influences before he began his independent ministry; but this is no more than a possibility. There is a remote possibility that Jesus of Nazareth at some stage of his career had some contact with the Qumran group, but the differences between his convictions and theirs are so great that it is impossible to demonstrate any deep influence of the Essene movement upon him.

Then there were the Hellenists. In the sober words of Bishop A. C. Headlam,[13] Judaism had need of Hellenism, and this need was

---

12. Luke describes the Pharisees at a later date as having had a measure of sympathy for Paul (Acts 23:6–10). Note also the attitude of Gamaliel the Pharisee as reported in Acts 5:33–39.

13. See his excellent article on the Herod family in James Hastings, ed., *A Dictionary of the Bible Dealing with its Language, Literature and Contents including the Biblical Theology* (Edinburgh: T. and T. Clark, 1898; 2d. ed., 1908). The article includes a useful table of the complicated genealogy of the Herods.

met in the days of Jesus by the influence of the Herods. This does not mean that all Hellenists among the Jews in Palestine were "Herodians" in the sense in which that term is used in the Gospels. But the Hellenistic Jews spoke Greek among themselves, almost certainly read the Old Testament in Greek in their synagogues, and could be relied on to take a less rigid view of the traditions of the men of old time than that held by their brethren who lived their lives mainly in the Aramaic-speaking world.

All, or almost all, these varieties of Jewish faith and practice were to be found also among the early Christians. There were undoubtedly some who had simply added belief in Jesus as Messiah to their strict Jewish faith. It was to them inconceivable that any jot or tittle of the Law should fall to the ground. Salvation was from the Jews (John 4:22), and within the walls of the Jewish faith it must forever remain.

The majority of Christian Jews seem to have accepted the permanent validity of the covenant made by God with Abraham and Moses, but to have been more aware than their conservative brethren of the difference that the acceptance of the Christian message had made to their ancestral traditions. The special gatherings of the Christians for worship came to mean more to them than the temple ritual; "Christ our paschal lamb" (1 Cor. 5:7) came to be more significant than the actual lamb of the Passover festival. The earliest Christians were all connected by birth or personal adherence with the Law of Moses and with the life of the Jewish community, and the question of the admission of Gentiles to the church did not immediately arise; but it was likely that, when the time came, the Gentile applicant would get a better hearing from the less rigidly traditional group than from those who held that every item in the long catalogue of the Laws of Moses was binding on every single believer.[14]

It is not surprising that Hellenists were to be found also among the Christian believers. Some among those Jews who had returned to Jerusalem from the Diaspora, the scattered world of Jews in the Roman Empire, were among the earliest hearers of the gospel. Those who are familiar with the problems of a multilingual church today will find nothing strange in the account given in Acts 6 of the dispute between the Jews who spoke Aramaic and those who spoke Greek, and the very sensible arrangements made by the church to avoid friction and dissension in the future. Luke, with his usual minute care in the use of titles, nowhere uses the term "deacon" in

14. We may see here evidence of the continuing influence of Galilean Christianity on the life of the early church. Leonard E. Elliott-Binns argues strongly for this continuing influence in *Galilaean Christianity*, Studies in Biblical Theology (London: SCM Press, 1956).

connection with the newly appointed officers; but such secular functions as they were appointed to carry out present themselves, at an early stage of development in every church, as a necessary part of Christian organization.

And then there is Stephen. His name is Greek, and he is presented as belonging to the Greek-speaking faction. But he seems also to have been able to speak fluent Aramaic, and there is no single trait in what we are told of his teaching that can be specifically described as Hellenistic. He is by all accounts a perplexing figure. What in the world is the intention of Luke in introducing Stephen, and devoting to him so much of his precious space? Various answers have been given.

Some interpreters have seen in Stephen the great forerunner of Paul. Professor William Manson, among others, has made out a carefully argued but not altogether convincing case for seeing a connection between Stephen's teaching and that of the Epistle to the Hebrews.[15] A wide range of other suggestions has been made.

The great classical scholar and poet A. E. Housman was once heard to remark that Stephen, having made the worst speech on record (Acts 7), was then very deservedly stoned to death. Many readers may have shared this view, though they may not have been inclined to express it so irreverently.

Stephen's speech seems to be no more than a boring summary of Old Testament history. But here again we do well to take warning from Luke's subtle and unemphatic way of writing history; he never tells you what he is doing, and he sometimes hides in a parenthesis what he regards as really important. A careful reading of Stephen's speech shows that he was making three points, each of which represented an essential element in his defense. The orthodox Jews attached immense importance to the land, the revelation (or the messenger), and the temple. Stephen shows conclusively that the most important revelations had been given outside and not within the limits of the Holy Land; that the Jews had always rejected and persecuted the messengers sent to them, even Moses, the greatest of them all; and that the temple was an afterthought, which God was inclined to despise as soon as it had been built. The speech shows itself, on investigation, to be a brilliant piece of theological argument. Luke, writing fifty years later, must either have had good sources on which to draw, or have been gifted with an almost unparalleled inventive capacity.

15. *The Epistle to the Hebrews an Historical and Theological Reconsideration* (London: Hodder and Stoughton, 1951).

Marcel Simon[16] thinks it more than probable that there were groups in Jerusalem that looked back (like the writer to the Hebrews) to the tabernacle rather than to the temple, and found the golden age of Israel in the wilderness period rather than in the time of either David or Solomon. Such groups might well have been readily attracted to the Christian fellowship. A more recent investigator, Martin Scharlemann, is inclined to link Stephen with the Samaritans, who had their rival temple on Mount Gerizim and among whom Christian work was to start immediately after the martyrdom of Stephen.[17] This, if it could be demonstrated, would be extremely interesting. Both Luke and the writer of the Fourth Gospel show special interest in, and indeed partiality for, the Samaritans. The theology of that strange people, the descendants of whom still exist at Nablus, is gradually emerging from the mists of the centuries,[18] and we find them not to have been a band of almost illiterate sectaries but a thoughtful people, with their own understanding of the Law and a profound devotion to the traditions as they had received them. In view of the intense bitterness that characterized Jewish relations with the Samaritans (John 4:9) any suggestion of Samaritan influence or sympathies within the holy people of God would be quite sufficient to account for the violence of the accusations made against Stephen, and, together with the vigor of his counterattack, for the precipitate and illegal execution that was its consequence.

We do well not to forget the remarkable variety of elements out of which the earliest Christian communities were being built up. But on one point they were all unanimous—the major home industry of the early Christians was combing the Old Testament in search of passages that could be christologically interpreted. It is possible that within the New Testament period itself a beginning was made with the collections of these testimonies into a single volume.[19] Finding references in a parchment or papyrus roll is always a tedious process; how much more convenient to have all the relevant passages collected and ready to hand for use in controversy with the Jews. In the appeal to Old Testament Scripture there was no difference between the Jewish churches and those of Gentile origin.

Some stress has to be laid on this point, since a rather different view of early Christian history has been put forward and is still held in some parts of the Christian world. It is believed that there were

16. Marcel Simon, *St. Stephen and the Hellenists in the Primitive Church* (New York: Longmans Green, 1958).

17. Martin H. Scharlemann, *Stephen: A Singular Saint* (Rome: Pontifical Biblical Institute, 1968).

18. A comprehensive survey of Samaritan research and its results is to be found in John Macdonald, *The Theology of the Samaritans* (London: SCM Press, 1964).

19. The existence of such collections of *Testimonia* among the Qumran groups renders this conjecture quite probable. See C. H. Dodd's letter to T. F. Glasson in *The Expository Times*, October 1975, pp. 21-22.

in existence very early, pre-Pauline groups of Gentile believers who had developed their theology largely in independence of the old tradition, and in a much closer relationship to the ideas and beliefs of their non-Christian neighbors.[20]

Kyrios, "Lord," was a title commonly used in the Hellenistic world for deities of various kinds, though it is doubtful if any of the occurrences of the term in extant texts is actually earlier in date than the New Testament documents. (We may note, however, that Paul does refer in 1 Cor. 8:5 to many gods and many lords.) Gentile Christians who made the confession "Jesus is Lord" may have used the words in a sense rather different from that attributed to them by their Jewish brethren. Moreover, many of these Hellenistic gods were dying and rising gods—gods who died with the onset of winter and rose again with the coming of spring. J. G. Frazer in his first great work, *Adonis, Attis, Osiris* (1890), collected many of these myths and put them together in most attractive form. Would it not be likely that these Gentile Christians, surrounded by this world of thought and imagery, would insert Jesus into the category of such dying and rising gods and interpret their faith in him and their participation in his risen life in terms and thought-forms derived from these mystery religions? The parallels are close enough to lend plausibility to this point of view.

There are, however, also grave objections. In the first place, no instance can be quoted, from the literature of the times, of the application of the idea of a dying and rising god to a known historical figure.[21] If the believers did put Jesus among the gods of the mystery religions, they were not following a well-established pattern but were doing something no one had ever done before. It is not impossible that they did so; but it must be judged unlikely.

Secondly, the use of terms derived from one world of ideas does not necessarily imply acceptance of those ideas. The mystery religions certainly existed, and became increasingly popular in the second century of our era. They were remarkably successful in keeping their secrets from the ears of the uninitiated, so much so that we can only conjecture what those secrets actually were. But no doubt words used in that connection had become widely known, and some may have passed into common currency. Christians in Mediterranean cities would almost certainly have picked up some of

---

20. The lead was taken in this interpretation by the so-called history-of-religions school, building on the work of Wilhelm Bousset's notable *Kyrios Christos* which is at last available in English (Nashville: Abingdon, 1970). Unfortunately the very important work of Carsten Colpe of Berlin on the work and history of this school, *Die Religionsgeschichtliche Schule*, has not yet been translated into English.

21. The custom known from various parts of the Mediterranean world of worshipping certain deceased heroes (e.g., the Spartan general Brasidas) as demigods throws no light on the problem we are discussing.

these phrases, just as today we readily speak of "escalation" or of "being with it" without necessarily being aware that these are recent additions to our language, and without knowledge of the sources from which they are derived. The use of a "mystery" term does not necessarily mean that Christians learned the term from a "mystery" source, still less that the term would have the same significance for a Christian as for the initiate in one of the mystery cults. At a rather later date (Justin Martyr, A.D. c. 150) "enlightenment" has become almost a technical term for baptism. Light plays a very important part in mystery and Gnostic writings. Yet it is at least possible that it came into Christian language by way of "light" sayings in the Old Testament—as for instance Ps. 36:9, "in thy light we are bathed with light" (NEB)—rather than borrowed from a "mystery" source.

The strongest argument of all against the influence of the mystery religions is that there is no direct evidence for the existence of such Gentile and Hellenistic churches, developing on their own and with little or no contact with the Jewish and Jerusalem tradition. All the evidence that we have points in exactly the opposite direction; what we know of Gentile churches suggests that they too had an almost excessive regard for the Old Testament, and shared with their Jewish Christian brethren the interest in finding foreshadowings of the new revelation in the old.

We have, in point of fact, a remarkably clear picture of a Gentile church in the later chapters of the Epistle to the Romans. It is probable that there were some Jewish Christians in Rome,[22] but their number is likely to have been small. Paul throughout addresses the Roman Christians as Gentiles (1:13; 11:13; etc.) and assumes that their point of view will be determined by their background. Here, just as in any other Epistle, he bases his argument on the Old Testament and assumes that his readers will have sufficient knowledge of the Jewish Scriptures to enable them to pick up his allusions and to follow the course of his argument. We have no trace anywhere of any early Christian congregation of which the same would not be true.

There were, of course, differences between Palestine and the rest of the Mediterranean world. Jerusalem Christians tended to think of Jesus as the one who had gone away into heaven and would one day come again to rejoin the friends who had not forgotten him, whereas the Gentile Christians experienced more vividly the presence of the risen Christ through the Holy Spirit in their assemblies.

---

22. Romans 16 presents a difficult critical problem. Was it part of the Epistle to the Romans as sent by Paul? Or did it originally belong to an Epistle written to some other church? On this question critical opinion is still divided, as can be learned from recent commentaries on the Epistle.

But for this there is surely a natural explanation: those who had seen Jesus in the flesh and now saw him no more would think of him in one way; those who had never seen him and had received only the charismatic experience of the Spirit would think of him in another way. But Jewish Christians were not unaware of the continuing presence of Jesus in their midst, and Gentile Christians shared with their Jewish friends the expectation of the return of Christ in glory. Of this close connection between the two nothing is more striking than the adoption by Gentile Christians of some of the Aramaic phrases that were current in the Palestinian churches. The Romans said *Abba* when they prayed (Rom. 8:15). The Corinthians seem to have opened their Eucharistic worship with the phrase *Maranatha*, "our Lord, come," just as Syriac-speaking Christians today are bidden in their liturgy, *Stomen Kalos*, "let us stand in order due," though none of them knows a single word of Greek. Incidentally, the almost accidental preservation of the phrase *Maranatha* by Paul in 1 Cor. 16:23 reveals to us that the Palestinian Christians had at a very early date begun to use the expression "our Lord" of Jesus Christ, and that the declaration, also preserved by Paul in 1 Cor. 12:3, "Jesus is Lord," is not so purely Hellenistic as we might otherwise have thought.

That there were differences among various Christian communities in different parts of the Roman world, and beyond it in Mesopotamia, no one would be inclined to deny. Yet the similarities are more striking than the differences.

All Christian communities everywhere in the ancient world had adopted baptism with water as the sign of admission into the new kingdom, which, though hidden, was the great reality brought by Jesus Christ into the world. We have no knowledge of the way in which this universal acceptance had come about, unless we take Matt. 28:19 as expressing exactly a command of the Lord himself. The baptism of John was not accepted as equivalent to Christian baptism; that had been an admission by repentance into the hope of a kingdom yet to come; Christian baptism was incorporation into One who was already a King, though the final manifestation of his kingdom was to take place at some undefined date in the future. Had the disciples themselves received this incorporation into Christ through baptism? If so, how and when? To this question the evidence available to us gives no answer. In what name was baptism administered? There is some reason to think that in the beginning baptism was given simply in the name of the Lord Jesus (Acts 19:5); but when Matthew's Gospel was written some fifty years later, the use of the threefold name of Father, Son, and Holy Spirit appears to have been accepted as axiomatic. Writing about twenty-five years after the Resurrection, Paul (in Romans 6) can regard baptism and faith as almost identical—if you believe, you will be baptized; you are not likely to be baptized unless you have really believed. But baptism in the New Testament is always the transition from the world that is under the power of the evil one to the world that has been redeemed by Christ; there is no clear reference to the baptism of those who have been born within the Christian fellowship. Believers in infant baptism and protagonists of believers' baptism alike quote the New Testament in support of their arguments;[23] but neither group has as yet been able to persuade the other that the evidence of the New Testament is convincing.

Baptism was the first of the ceremonies that have come to be known in the church as sacraments. What of the second, commonly called the Holy Communion or Eucharist?

It is a good illustration of the dangers of the argument from silence that, if Paul's first letter to the Corinthians had failed to survive, we should have no evidence at all that the Pauline churches observed the Lord's Supper; we should also be without our earliest account of what was said and done by Jesus at the Last Supper,[24] words and acts that Paul cites as the authority for continuing to observe this rite. Moreover, Paul claims that what he had delivered to the Corinthians he had received from the Lord himself (1 Cor. 11:28). This need not be taken to mean that he had learned these truths by special revelation; the word in the Greek seems to indicate rather a tradition that went back to the Lord himself and that had been duly passed on to Paul by those who had been in Christ before him. We need not be disturbed by the silence of the other Epistles. No one writes about what is taken for granted by everyone; Paul deals with the matter only because of the irregularities that had grown up in public worship in the Corinthian church. It is significant that in his warnings and instructions to the Corinthians he so exactly confirms the succinct and perhaps in some ways idealized account of life in the early church that is given us by Luke (Acts 2:42–47).

This was the new thing in Christian worship; a meal such as was regularly observed among the Christians found no place in the regular routine of either temple or synagogue. And yet in one sense what the Christians did was already very old. Almost certainly the cus-

23. John Calvin laid great stress on Acts 2:39, "the promise is to you and to your children." The argument may be theologically sound; nevertheless it is based on a mistranslation. "Children" means "descendants," and has nothing whatever to do with infants.

24. The reader may need a reminder that all our existing Gospels were written later than the Pauline Epistles.

tom had been established that on special occasions, if not every day, the head of the family would break bread and distribute it to all those present, and after blessing God over the cup, would pass it around the circle. It may well be that the very prayers Jesus used have been in part preserved to this day in the Jewish prayers for the Sabbath. What was new was the significance that Jesus read into the ancient acts and words. The early tradition that came to Paul emphasized the covenant element in the feast: "This cup is the new covenant in my blood" (1 Cor. 11:25). Yet the principal emphasis of the Eucharist seems in early times to have lain elsewhere. The Christians knew themselves to be living in an interim; the feast that Jesus celebrated with his disciples led their thoughts to that other and greater feast to which he had referred when he had spoken of drinking of the fruit of the vine new with them in the Kingdom of God (Matt. 26:29); that feast to which every pious Jew looked forward, which at the end of the days the Lord would make for all the nations on the mountains (Isa. 25:6). So sorrowful recollection was more than swallowed up in joyful anticipation. In later liturgies this note of eschatological expectation has been almost wholly lost.

All the earliest churches, Jewish or Gentile, labored under three major theological misunderstandings, out of which they had gradually to make their way. This is clear evidence that Jesus, after having communicated to them certain fundamental ideas, then left it to the Holy Spirit to lead them gradually into all truth (John 16:13). This may be encouraging to those of a much later date who find a great deal in Christian theology perplexing. Moreover, we should bear in mind that this is a process that has not yet come to an end; in the words of John Robinson (1575–1625): "God hath much light and truth yet to break forth from his holy Word."

The first error was a miscalculation on the time scale. They all thought that the Lord would come back very soon, perhaps in a matter of weeks or months, or, as the period lengthened and immediate expectation was seen to be disappointed, at least within the lifetime of those who had believed. This was what Paul had taught to his friends; hence the exceeding dismay (1 Thess. 4:13) of the Thessalonians over the death of one or two of their members in the brief period between the departure of Paul and the composition of his first letter to them. How were those who had died to have a share in the joyful inauguration of the kingdom at the coming of the Lord?

This foreshortening of the time of the church was the accepted view of the Christians for a considerable period. Robert Browning depicts it as still warmly alive at the time of the death of the last survivor among the apostles:

Nay, should his coming be delayed a while,
Say, ten years longer (twelve years, some compute)
See if, for every finger of thy hands
There be not found, that day the world shall end,
Hundreds of souls, each holding by Christ's word
That he will grow incorporate with all,
With me as Pamphylax, with him as John,
Groom for each bride! Can a mere man do this?[25]

There was no awareness of the long pilgrimage that the church would have to accomplish in time, no thought that the period of the church might be even longer than that long epoch of preparation that stretched from the days of father Abraham to the days of Messiah. It is not easy for us who look back on the many centuries of Christian witness to penetrate even in imagination the minds of whose who, as they looked forward, seemed to see the dawning just below the horizon of their days. Yet the effort must be made, since that atmosphere of joyful exhilaration provides us with the explanation for many things in the New Testament that would otherwise be obscure. It explains, in the first place, why Christians took so little interest in the organization of their fellowship; why organize what is already in the process of passing away? The early church seems to have taken over parts of the system that prevailed in the Jewish communities, and for the rest to have left things very much to chance. It was the second century, not the first, that brought about uniformity in the appearance and the life of the Christian groups. The expected shortness of the interval also accounts for the failure of the first generation to set down in writing any account of its experiences. The Jews, in any case, attached greater importance to the spoken than to the written word (except for the inspired words of the Law); and, when there was a vigorous oral tradition at the center of affairs and it was expected that the Lord would come back before the first witnesses had died,[26] what need was there for anything beyond the words of living testimony and exhortation?

The second error was the expectation that, with the coming again of Messiah as unmistakably the Anointed of the Lord, the whole people of Israel would believe, and would become again what they were always intended to be—the people of God. The death of Jesus, if not at the hands of his own people at least with their consent, was a grave perplexity to the believers. How could it come about that the rulers in Israel, with their deep knowledge of the Law and the

---

25. "A Death in the Desert." No better brief statement has ever been penned of the sense in which Christians believe Jesus of Nazareth to be the Son of God.

26. John 21 seems to make it clear that a tradition had lingered on, at least in some Christian circles, that the Lord would come before the last of the eyewitnesses had died.

prophecies, should fail to recognize the One who came to fulfill them all and to set the seal on all God's promises? With their profound belief in the providence of God, the Christian teachers were bound to acknowledge that the death of Christ had a place in God's plan for the deliverance of his people; they do not seem at that earliest stage of Christian thinking to have recognized in that death the central act of God in the reconciliation of the world to himself. The Crucifixion appeared to them as a kind of mistake, a momentary blindness during which the people and their rulers had betrayed the One whom they should have adored. But the time would come when this blindness would be taken away, and the whole people would become the people of the new covenant.[27]

The hope of the early Christians was not unreasonable. Occasional outbursts of fanaticism such as that which caused the death of Stephen were to be expected; but otherwise the Jerusalem church had managed to adapt itself fairly well to the situation.[28] The Christians did not openly violate the Jewish laws. They had their own convictions as to the Messiahship of Jesus, and their own special prayers and ceremonies; but a Jewish world that could include the Qumran community may have found no great difficulty in finding a place also for the Christians. It is clear that Christian preaching had had considerable success. We have no means of knowing how many Christians there were in Jerusalem; but the influence that community exercised on the whole Christian world suggests that the number must have been considerable;[29] and Jews of the Diaspora were likely to be more open to the new ideas than their more conservative brethren in Palestine.

The hopes and expectations of the conversion of Israel were to be entirely frustrated. We shall have occasion to deal elsewhere with the contention that arose as to the conditions on which the Gentiles might be admitted to the Christian fellowship. Apart from this major controversy, there was a hardening on both sides. Christians were dismayed by the obstinacy of the Jews in refusing to accept the Messiah, and in certain cases by their instigating persecution against his followers. The Jews came more and more to regard the Christians as renegades who could no longer be accepted as forming part of the house of Israel. The church and the synagogue were moving on increasingly divergent paths, and in time the separation was to become complete. The *Dialogue of Justin Martyr with Trypho, the*

---

27. This is easier to understand, if, after the persecution that followed the death of Stephen, the Hellenistic element in the Christian community in Jerusalem was greatly reduced.

28. In the speeches in Acts 2 to 5 the apostles seem almost to be apologizing on behalf of the rulers and the people for the error that they had committed.

29. Note the remarkable statement in Acts 6:7 that "a great many of the priests were obedient to the faith."

Jew (A.D. c. 150) shows that, even a hundred years later than the time of which we are writing, it was possible for Jews and Christians to meet on terms of mutual respect and courtesy.   But this was the exception; animosity was the rule.

It has been suggested, not without plausibility, that Jesus had been declared formally excommunicate from the synagogue (John 9:18–23).   Jewish custom, taken over also by the eastern Christian Churches, was that the name of an excommunicate person was never pronounced.   So it has come about that, in spite of the strength of the Christian movement, the name of Jesus of Nazareth occurs far less often than we might have expected in the extensive Jewish literature of the early Christian centuries.   It has been observed that in the Fourth Gospel the Jews never once mention the name of Jesus; he is always referred to simply as *houtos*, "this man."   Conversely, by the time that this Gospel was written, "the Jews" are unmistakably the enemy; the term is no longer simply racial or national, it has acquired a theological tinge.

This is the great impoverishment that has befallen us.   We cannot live fully as Christians without the help of our Jewish brethren. Some of them have found faith in Christ, and we owe a great debt to the insights that they have brought with them.   But for the vast majority the veil is not yet taken away (2 Cor. 3:14); Jesus of Nazareth may be the friend, even, as Martin Buber expressed it, "the elder brother"; he is not yet the Anointed One of God, the Savior of the world.[30]

We come now to the third misapprehension.   The first Christians devoutly believed that Jerusalem, the City of David, would become the religious capital of the world.   For this they could find support in the prophecies of the Old Testament.   Isaiah had heard the nations saying

> Come, let us go up to the mountain of the Lord,
>   to the house of the God of Jacob,
>   that he may teach us his ways,
>   and that we may walk in his paths. (Isa. 2:3)

Zechariah equally had foreseen that "many people and strong nations shall come to seek the Lord of hosts in Jerusalem and to entreat the favor of the Lord; ten men shall take hold of the robe of a Jew and say, "Let us go with you, for we have heard that God is with you," (Zech. 8:22–23).   The Christians could not but observe the steady

---

30. For an impressive presentation of the changed attitude of the Jewish world to Jesus as seen in school textbooks and similar literature, see Pinchas Lapide, "Learning About Jesus in Israel," *The Christian Century*, March 7, 1973, pp. 285–89.

stream of pilgrims who came to Jerusalem from every part of the known world. The majority of these came only to hear the words of the old covenant. But if Jesus came again and was visibly reigning in the Holy City, surely the eyes of all men would turn to him; the Gentiles also would find their place within the new covenant, and there would be one people as there was one God.

This belief was to go down in final and shattering disappointment. Jesus had looked into the future and had seen what was bound to come when the unyielding obstinacy of the Jews encountered the hard rock of the Roman power. Ill-led and divided as they were, the Jews for almost four years resisted all the might of Rome in one of the most famous sieges of history. The Jewish war made heavy demands on the resources of the Roman Empire, at a time at which that empire was gravely weakened by inner dissension. But there could be only one end to the struggle. Jerusalem was captured, with horrifying loss of life. The temple was burned, and the requirements of the Law could no longer be fulfilled. The civil organization and national existence of the Jews came to an end, and were not to be restored for nearly nineteen centuries.

The effect of the destruction of Jerusalem on the Christians was naturally less momentous than its impact on the life of the Jewish people. Yet an event so portentous could not fail to have consequences even for those less directly affected by it than the Jews of Palestine.[31] The churches in other parts of the Roman Empire, especially those founded by Paul, had never submitted to dictation from the church in Jerusalem. Yet this was the mother church to which all turned in veneration and affection. Above all, this was the repository of the true tradition about Jesus, against which all other churches could test and verify their traditions. Now the center had been destroyed; there was no visible focus of unity for the scattered limbs of the body.

Many of the Christians in Jerusalem fled across the Jordan to Pella and there reorganized their lives. There seems to have been an attempt, similar to that made after the death of the prophet Muhammad, to organize a kind of caliphate in the family of Jesus.[32] This was perhaps a natural step in view of the special position held by James the brother of the Lord, who had kept the Jerusalem church together for thirty years, until his assassination in an outburst of Jewish fanaticism in A.D. 62. It is not easy to define the position held

---

31. See Samuel G. F. Brandon, *The Fall of Jerusalem and the Christian Church*, rev. ed. (Naperville: Allenson, 1957).

32. Eusebius (*Historia Ecclesiastica*, IV, 22. 4) reports that, after the death of James, the church in Pella chose Symeon as bishop, who, as a son of Clopas, was a cousin of the Lord. He adds that Symeon guided the church until his death as a martyr at some date after A.D. 100.

by James; like so many things in the early church this appears to have been something that grew rather than was defined. James was always there. Others came and went on their apostolic journeys—so we may infer from Paul's statement that, when he went up to Jerusalem "after three years," he saw none of the apostles except Cephas and James the Lord's brother (Gal. 1:19). There was always there one central figure, deeply respected by all; it was probably in large part due to the simple Jewish piety of James that the Christians were able for the most part to live undisturbed in the Jewish milieu. But this was a personal position, and one that could not be transferred to any other.

It is tempting to think that Mark, writing not very long after the death of James, includes in his Gospel the striking saying of Jesus, "Whoever does the will of God is my brother, and sister, and mother" (Mark 3:35), precisely to exclude the idea that the family of Jesus had any claim to a special position in the church. The church as a whole would have been willing to echo the words of Paul, "though we have known Christ after the flesh, yet now henceforth know we him no more" (2 Cor. 5:16 AV). The idea of a caliphate never had a chance of acceptance in the wider church, in which the lordship of the Spirit was increasingly becoming the dominant element as the earthly life of Jesus faded into memory. We are told by the Christian historian Hegesippus that the emperor Domitian, hearing of some Jews who claimed some kind of a shadowy kingdom (they were, in fact, grandsons of Jude, the brother of the Lord), summoned them to his presence, but finding them to be simple and undistinguished men, sent them away without taking any action against them.[33]

Christians were never completely excluded by the Romans from the Holy City as were Jews after the defeat of Bar Cochba in A.D. 132. Christians continued to regard Jerusalem with affection and interest, and the habit of Christian pilgrimage seems to have established itself long before the days of the Lady Egeria in the fourth century.[34] But Jerusalem was not destined to play forever the part of the mother church; after A.D. 70 the church never again had one focal point to which all Christians turned their faces. The great centers of thought and activity were Antioch, Alexandria, and Rome, to which in the course of time Carthage, the first great center of Latin-speaking Christianity, and Constantinople, the new Rome, came to

---

33. Eusebius, who quotes Hegesippus, adds that "they governed the churches, both as martyrs and relatives of the Lord, and, peace being restored to the Church, they lived until the reign of Trajan" (*Historia Ecclesiastica*, III, 20. 1–6).

34. On this see Henry Chadwick and Hans von Campenhausen, *Jerusalem and Rome* (Philadelphia: Fortress Press, 1966). Egeria or Etheria left an account of her travels that is a mine of information on the life of the church in Jerusalem in her day (Eng. trans. by J. Wilkinson in 1971).

be added.   Judeo-Christianity continued to exist for a considerable period, and in certain of its forms manifested an almost pathological hatred for Paul and all his works.   But all this belongs to the history of the early church, and not to the theology of the New Testament. As soon as Jerusalem fell, it became clear that the future of Christianity was to lie in the Gentile and not in the Jewish world.

3

The Pauline Corpus

Roughly a quarter of the New Testament has passed for many centuries under the name of the apostle Paul, who had in earlier life been known as Saul of Tarsus.

That so much of the New Testament comes to us from the hand of one man we owe to accident, or, as Christians might be inclined to say, to Providence. When and how and by whom the collection was made we cannot say with certainty, but we can infer a good deal. After the destruction of Jerusalem the church came more and more to depend on written documents; the central fount of tradition had dried up and the original witnesses were dying off one by one. It occurred to someone[1] that there must be a great deal of material of the highest value lying about in the records of the churches. He set himself to collect it, and to make it available for permanent use.

The task was formidable. Paul's surviving letters were all occasional missives, written to meet a particular need. No doubt the churches that had received these letters read them again and again over a certain period, but then they seem to have fallen out of use—there is singularly little sign of any Pauline influence in the later writings of the New Testament.

The early churches, meeting secretly in the house of one of the wealthier members of a group, had no facilities for storing documents. Some of them may have had a room, somewhat like the Genizah of a Jewish synagogue, in which were preserved worn-out copies of the Scriptures, too holy to be destroyed but no longer serviceable in worship.[2] Some of Paul's letters had been copied and exchanged among different churches, but the life of others must

---

1. The name of Onesimus is sometimes mentioned in this connection. We know that there was in the early second century a bishop of Ephesus named Onesimus, who may be the same as the runaway slave known to us through the Epistle to Philemon. The connection is possible but not certain. Luke the beloved physician is also mentioned as one who could be credited with the compilation of the Pauline corpus.

2. In modern times the opening of the Genizah of the ancient synagogue at Cairo has revealed to us treasures, which the labors of Professor P. Kahle over many years have made available to the world of scholarship.

have depended on a single copy. Moreover, papyrus is a brittle
material unlikely to survive long in a damp climate. Much must
have irretrievably perished, being reduced to a pile of fragments
of which no further use could be made.

And yet our "Onesimus" had remarkable success. At the end of
his labors he had recovered letters addressed to seven churches.
Two churches had received two letters each, and the collector added
the little private letter to Philemon in which he may have had a
special personal interest; thus the number of letters included in the
collection amounted to ten. What we know as the pastoral Epistles
never formed part of this collection; the Epistle to the Hebrews,
though deeply Pauline in much of its thinking, belongs to a different
section of the New Testament. Our collector may have made mis-
takes. Faced with not easily identifiable fragments, he may have
combined together sections that really belong to different Epistles.
In the case of 2 Corinthians there are strong reasons for thinking that
this is what happened. Some scholars believe that the same is true
of 1 Thessalonians and Philippians.[3] We cannot exclude the possibility that in some cases the fragments have been arranged in the
wrong order. But on the whole the collector has done a marvelous
job; this apostle is a man whom we can come to know; he speaks to us
directly across the interval of nineteen centuries.

The existence of the collection, as we have it in the New Testament, does not mean that we can immediately make use of it to write
our chapter on the theology of the apostle Paul.

Is it possible to regard all the ten letters as wholly and reliably
Pauline? Ancient scholarship answered unhesitatingly, Yes; modern scholarship tends to give a much more cautious and restrained
reply. A century ago the famous German scholar Ferdinand Christian Baur (1792-1860) maintained that only four letters—Romans,
Galatians, and the two letters to the Corinthians—could be accepted
as genuine. This view, once widely held in Germany, is not now
generally accepted; most scholars today would agree that Baur rejected much that can confidently be accepted as genuine Pauline
material. Hardly anyone today doubts the authenticity of 1 Thessalonians; this is important, since this letter, small as it is but perhaps
the earliest of all the New Testament books, contains unique and
indispensable information. Most scholars accept Philippians as
Pauline, though some doubt the unity of the letter, and many are
puzzled over where it should be fitted into the chronology of Paul's
life. It would be difficult to imagine anyone taking the trouble to

---

3. E.g., Francis W. Beare, *Epistle to the Philippians*, 2nd ed. (Naperville: Allenson, 1969).

forge the letter to Philemon; in any case, a forger who managed to produce so delicate and exquisite an Epistle must have been a genius of the same stature as the apostle himself. The letter to Philemon seems to carry with it the genuineness of the letter to the Colossians; some are not yet convinced; but the number of those who hold Colossians to be authentically Pauline appears to be on the increase.[4]

That leaves us with only 2 Thessalonians and Ephesians as still subject to serious doubt. Even those who feel that the differences between 1 and 2 Thessalonians are so great as to exclude the possibility of actual Pauline authorship of the latter would agree that the supposed unknown writer had learned a great deal from Paul and departs only at certain points from what we know to have been Pauline doctrine. Ephesians, which seems to have been a circular letter rather than an Epistle directed to a single church, may have been written by a follower deeply versed in Pauline doctrine as an introduction to the collection of writings, which at that time was about to be made available to the Christian world.[5]

So, even if we accept as valid the doubts expressed by a number of critical scholars, we still have eight letters, written over a period of perhaps ten to twelve years, which we can use in our attempt to make the acquaintance of the apostle and of his thought. One more reservation needs to be expressed. The Acts of the Apostles includes much material on the life and work of Paul. But this is a source that we shall use with a measure of caution, recognizing that as compared with Paul's own writings it is a secondary and not a primary source.

Who then is this Saul of Tarsus, better known as Paul, and what are we to make of him? The most casual reading of the Epistles will make us aware that we have to deal with one who was a great man, a great thinker, and a great writer.

Paul reveals himself as very human—in his fears and anxieties, in his distress over criticism, his impatience, and his scorn of those whom he finds unworthy of his respect. But there is nothing petty about the apostle. He must have been endowed with extraordinary courage and physical toughness to have endured the sufferings he details for us in 2 Corinthians 11, and to have retained any kind of equanimity. Yet he shows himself to be also a man of the most exquisite sensibility, capable of profound and unwavering affection

4. See Charles F. D. Moule, *Epistles of Paul to the Colossians and Philemon* (Cambridge, 1959), and Werner G. Kümmel, *The Theology of the New Testament According to its Major Witnesses—Jesus, Paul, John* (Nashville: Abingdon, 1975), p. 141.

5. Of course there are still defenders of the view that Ephesians is Pauline in the sense of having been written by the apostle himself. This view was defended in what is still the outstanding commentary on the Epistle, that by J. Armitage Robinson, *The Epistle to the Ephesians* (London: Macmillan & Co., 1922). See also Bibliography, below.

for his friends. Above all he is a man whose whole being is unified by the power of a single passion, by intense concentration on a single theme. When he writes to the Philippians (3:13) "One thing I do," he is telling the truth. When earlier in the same Epistle he writes "as it is my eager expectation and hope that I shall not be at all ashamed, but that . . . Christ will be honored in my body, whether by life or by death" (1:20), words written with a sentence of death hanging over him, he reveals the nature of that passion.

A great thinker, Paul can be and often is abominably difficult. But he is not intentionally difficult. Again and again he is trying to say things that had never been said before and for which he has no vocabulary ready to hand. "Voyaging through strange seas of thought alone," he takes what instruments of language he can find, and the problem of communication is not always solved. In a particularly difficult passage, Rom. 5:13–22, he is wrestling with the idea that in Christ a new humanity has come into being; but what is the relationship between this new humanity and the old, between the inheritance of disobedience in the first Adam and the glorious consequences of obedience in the One whom elsewhere he calls the last Adam (1 Cor. 15:45)? It often happens that when Paul is most difficult, he is also most original, and the perplexing passages are those that may offer the greatest reward to the student who is not deterred by the difficulties, but will gird himself to the task of finding out what it is that the apostle is really trying to say.

A great writer. Only one non-Christian writer of the first few centuries can be compared with Paul for intensity of thought and vigor of expression, the neo-Platonist Plotinus. Of the Christians only Tertullian and St. Augustine come near him in this respect. Paul was obviously a Jew, trained in all the intricacies of the Rabbinic tradition. But he never writes translation Greek, as we may sometimes suspect the writer of the Fourth Gospel of doing. His Greek is his own. It is not classical, but Paul never makes a grammatical mistake, and, though his use of prepositions has been the despair of pedants from the days of the apostle to our own, this is due not to ignorance but to a great writer's indifference to the straitjacket of overprecise grammatical rules. His vocabulary is wide and in part unique; when he has difficulty in expressing himself, this is due to the complexity of his thought and not to any lack of fluency in Greek.

The variety of styles he commands is truly astonishing. Within the comparatively few pages that have survived, we pass from the arid scholasticism of the argument about the two covenants in Gal.

4:21–31, to the almost feminine tenderness of the pastor caring for his flock in Thessalonica (1 Thess. 2:7–8), to the vigorous rhetoric of his self-defense against his opponents in Corinth, to the architectonic splendor of the sustained argument in Romans 5 to 8, to the pure lyricism of the hymn to love in 1 Corinthians 13.

It is this variety that makes it so difficult to give a general account of the theology of Paul. It is reported that when Sir William Orpen was confronted with the task of painting the portrait of Cosmo Gordon Lang, then Archbishop of York, he said, "I see seven archbishops; which of them do you wish that I should paint?"[6] So with the apostle. We all have our favorite passages; we all tend to emphasize one aspect at the expense of others. From the time of Luther onward it has been almost impossible for anyone steeped in the Lutheran tradition to understand Paul fully, since one key only, justification by faith, has been taken as the clue to interpretation, and this is not a key that will open all locks   The only way to guard against this one-sidedness is to read and reread all the Epistles that we have felt able with some confidence to ascribe to the apostle himself, and as far as possible to free ourselves from all prejudices and let the writings make their own impression on our minds.[7]

Who, then, is this man? He tells us a good deal about himself. He was a Jew, of the tribe of Benjamin, brought up in the strict tradition of the Pharisees, zealous beyond all his contemporaries in the Jewish faith with a zeal that led him to persecute the new Christian movement (Gal. 1:11–14). But then everything was changed for him by an experience which he nowhere describes in detail, but to which he is almost certainly alluding when he writes, "Have I not seen Jesus Christ?" (1 Cor. 9:1). For the details of the experience we are dependent on the writer of the Acts of the Apostles, who describes it no less than three times with slightly different emphases. Nothing that Luke writes is contradicted by anything in the Epistles, but the details of the narrative receive no confirmation from the scanty evidence provided by Paul. On the essential point there is no difference between the two sources—it was the conviction that Jesus of Nazareth had really risen from the dead, was alive and was accessible, that changed the whole world for Saul of Tarsus and compelled him "to burn what he had adored and to adore what he had burned." The intensity of his devotion to his new Lord, his emphasis on being "in Christ," on "Christ in you," has led some scholars to write of the

6. What he did actually produce was described by the subject of it as "pompous, proud and prelatical."
7. This is a much less formidable task than might be supposed. The whole collection can be read through in four hours. The Epistle to the Romans can be read without haste in twenty-five minutes. It is impossible to become acquainted with Paul by reading him in snippets, as is all too often done.

mysticism of the apostle Paul;[8] but the term is not appropriate. In mysticism, in any strict sense of the term, the "I-thou" relationship ceases to exist; in Paul it is never forgotten.

We may infer that Saul of Tarsus was born about A.D. 10 and that his conversion took place about A.D. 35. The chronological indications are thin;[9] but we must reckon with an interval between the death of Jesus and the conversion of Paul sufficient to allow for the Christian movement's growing to a point at which it could be seen as a threat to the existence of the Jewish organization of religion. Then followed a long period of ten to fourteen years, of which, apart from the mention of one or two visits to Jerusalem, we know absolutely nothing except that they were passed in the regions of Syria and Cilicia (Gal. 1:21). So, when somewhere about the year 50 Paul sat down to write the first of the Epistles that have been preserved to us, he was already a mature man and a missionary of wide experience. During these years of obscurity, when he was no more than a lone preacher on the frontiers of the Christian world, his thought was slowly maturing, and he was gaining that inner power that made of him the first great theologian of the Christian church.

A little light is thrown on these years by the list of his sufferings which Paul gives us in 2 Corinthians 11. Though he was later to be known as the apostle of the Gentiles, and he himself recognized this as the peculiar vocation that had been given him by Christ, the implication is that a great part of his time was spent as a missionary to the Jews. "Five times I have received at the hands of the Jews the forty lashes less one" (2 Cor. 11:24). Why was Paul so often subjected by the Jews to this extremely painful and unpleasant, but only in rare cases dangerous, form of punishment? The most probable explanation is supplied to us in Acts. The rulers of the Jews "charged them not to speak or teach at all in the name of Jesus" (4:18). When the apostles disregarded the prohibition and continued to proclaim salvation in the name of the One who had been crucified, the rulers again summoned the apostles and subjected them to the same punishment that was later so often to be inflicted on Paul (Acts 5:40). To proclaim salvation in the name of One who had been condemned and rejected by the leaders in Israel now constituted a crime, which would bring the offender within the reach of severe disciplinary action. That synagogue authorities in comparatively remote Jewish communities followed the same

---

8. Albert Schweitzer wrote a notable book with the title *The Mysticism of Paul the Apostle* (London: A. & C. Black, 1931). See also Schweitzer's *Paul and His Interpreters* (London: A. & C. Black, 1912).

9. For an original reconstruction of the life of Paul, see John Knox, *Chapters in a Life of Paul* (Nashville: Abingdon, 1954); the chronology is dealt with in chaps. 3, 4, and 5. George Ogg, *The Chronology of the Life of St. Paul* (London: Epworth Press, 1968) is a careful and thorough study.

practice as their leaders in Jerusalem suggests that these leaders in Jerusalem exercised more authority over the whole of Jewry than has sometimes been admitted.

The second great crisis in Paul's career came when, at the end of the hidden years, he was called to take part in the notable movement at Antioch, which had led to the proclamation of the gospel to Gentiles who had never been influenced by the Jewish Law, and to the admission of uncircumcised believers into the full fellowship of the Christian church (Acts 11:25–26). From this time onward Paul was at the very center of the controversies that for a time threatened to break up permanently the unity of the Christian community; he became at once the best loved and the best hated man in the Christian world.

The next ten years, covering roughly the period A.D. 48 to A.D. 58, were spent in ceaseless journeyings. At some time in this period, and probably early rather than late, Paul became convinced that the gospel must be preached in Rome itself, and that, when he had fulfilled his task in the imperial city, he must press on to Spain, which in his day represented the limit of the known world (Rom. 15:28). Things did not work out in the way that he had expected. A visit to Jerusalem somewhere in the year A.D. 56[10] led to his arrest by the Romans. Long imprisonment in Palestine and Rome awaited him. It is possible, though doubtful, that another period of liberty was granted him after the years of captivity. But there is no reason to doubt the tradition that he died as a martyr in Rome in the days of Nero, perhaps in the great persecution of A.D. 65, perhaps rather earlier. There are a great many things in the story of the apostle's life that we would like to know, and that we must be content at least for the time being not to know. Much of the background against which the Epistles were written must remain permanently obscure to us. Yet to one who reads them with sympathy they gradually yield the portrait of a most remarkable man and the outlines of a most remarkable theology.

A careful study of the Epistles may bring us to the conclusion that the whole of the Pauline theology depends upon three great terms or ideas: resurrection, Spirit, and reconciliation.

On the basis of these three, almost the whole of Paul's teaching can be brought into coherence. The conclusion reached through our detective work on the beliefs of the earliest Christians was that precisely these three terms provide the essential key to their understanding of the Christian faith. The element of sheer creative origi-

---

10. John Knox places this in A.D. 53 or 54 (*Chapters in a Life of Paul*, p. 85), but I think this is too early.

nality in Paul must never be underestimated. But this correspondence at the central points of the faith suggests that the differences between Paul and the Jerusalem tradition were less radical than has at times been suggested.[11]

Resurrection

Paul's whole outlook was changed by the conviction that Jesus Christ was alive, and that God had decisively vindicated the one who had been rejected and condemned by the chosen people. This was the starting point of his Christian thinking; to this he ceaselessly returned.

Paul recalled to the memory of the Corinthians the methods of his first preaching among them: "I delivered to you as of first importance what I also received, that Christ . . . was raised on the third day in accordance with the Scriptures" (1 Cor. 15:3–4). A variant translation is "first of all"; but this variation makes hardly any difference to the theological significance of the passage. What the Corinthians had to learn from Paul, as Paul had learned it from Christ himself, was that "Christ has been raised from the dead, the first fruits of those who have fallen asleep" (15:20). If this had failed to get across, then the apostle's preaching would have been in vain.

The First Epistle to the Thessalonians, which is thought by some to be the earliest of all the New Testament writings, gives an invaluable summary of the teaching as Paul gave it to a Gentile audience. When speaking in the synagogue to Jews or Gentiles already influenced by the Law, he would speak in one way: belief in God could be taken for granted; the message would be primarily about Jesus of Nazareth and about the claim that he was the destined Messiah, liberally supported by quotations from the Old Testament. In speaking to Gentiles untouched by the Law, none of the same assumptions could be made; the message would have to be primarily about God, and this is exactly what Paul tells us it was: "You turned from idols, to serve a living and true God, and to wait for his Son from heaven, whom he raised from the dead, Jesus who delivers us from the wrath to come" (1 Thess. 1:9–10). This passage is so central for our understanding of Paul that it may be beneficial to set out the points contained in it which are (1) the folly of idolatry; (2) the nature of a living God; (3) the necessity of "conversion"—"You turned"; (4) the historic connection with Jesus of Nazareth; (5) the death of Jesus; (6) the Resurrection of Jesus; (7) eschatological expectation; and (8) the certainty of judgment, from which, however, the Christian is exempt (cf. Rom. 8:1).

11. A careful, rather conservative analysis of this relationship was provided by Wilfred L. Knox in *St. Paul and the Church of Jerusalem* (Cambridge, 1925)

We have interesting confirmation of this method from a rather unexpected source. In Acts 17 it is recorded that shortly after leaving Thessalonica Paul reached Athens. To this he himself makes reference in 1 Thess. 3:1: "We thought it good to be left at Athens alone." The ancient but not always reliable tradition preserved in the footnotes to the two Thessalonian Epistles states that each of them was written from Athens. Just at the time at which Paul was engaged in writing 1 Thessalonians, he was called, according to Acts, to bear witness before an audience very different from that of the dockers and petty tradesmen of Thessalonica—the very Areopagus itself, the assembly of the learned men of Athens. Paul's speech to this venerable company, as recorded in Acts, is a piece of accomplished and well-turned rhetoric. It is unlikely that it is an exact summary of what Paul said on that occasion. The striking thing is that the contents reflect precisely Paul's contemporary summary of his teaching at Thessalonica. They proclaim (1) the folly of idolatry; (2) the nature of a living and true God in creation and providence; (3) the call to repentance (or conversion); (4) the certainty of judgment; (5) the identification of human destiny with one historical individual (not here named); and (6) the sign of the Resurrection, by which the authority of the appointed judge is guaranteed.

These coincidences cannot be accidental. This really is the way in which Paul preached to a Gentile audience. A good deal of what he said can be paralleled from Jewish propaganda in favor of monotheism. The distinctive element in this Christian preaching was the doctrine of resurrection to which every sermon inevitably led up—the doctrine that called forth the mockery of the intelligentsia of Athens (Acts 17:32), but at the same time led others to faith and membership in the new community.[12]

There can be no doubt that Paul understood the Resurrection as an event that had actually taken place in history; not an idea, a doctrine, an emotional experience, but an actual event, which had changed the whole course of human history and brought into being the new creation (2 Cor. 5:17). But this event became effective for the believer only insofar as he himself had died and risen again with Christ. The Resurrection is understood not just as an event in the past, but as a permanently creative power, the nature of which the believer cannot understand until he has felt its operation within himself. Paul expresses this truth in the most dramatic form possible, when he writes in Gal. 2:20, "I have been crucified with Christ;

12. It should be noted that some scholars hold that both Paul and the writer of Acts were drawing on an earlier and pre-Pauline summary of the faith, which may have had its origin in the mission to Jews rather than in the mission to Gentiles. See Ernest E. Best, *The First and Second Epistles to the Thessalonians* (New York: Harper & Row, 1973) pp. 85–87, with extensive references to other works.

it is no longer I who live, but Christ who lives in me." Of the life of the believer in Christ, he writes, "that as Christ was raised from the dead by the glory of the Father, we too might walk in newness of life" (Rom. 6:4 AV). In baptism both Christ's death and Christ's Resurrection become part of the experience of the believer (cf. Col. 3:1–4).

Spirit

Of all the many services that Paul rendered to the nascent Church of Christ, none was greater than his elucidation of the nature of the Spirit as the Spirit of the risen and living Christ.

The early Christians still lived very much in the atmosphere of the Old Testament. There the Spirit had manifested itself as an overwhelming, divine, irrational afflatus, which it was impossible to resist, which would overrule for the time being the natural capacities of the human spirit, and then might depart as suddenly as it had come. This understanding of the Spirit had been reinforced by those startling experiences that were not limited to the day of Pentecost, and are grouped together under the convenient modern term *glossolalia*, "speaking with tongues."

Interest in this phenomenon has been renewed by its appearance, from the beginning of the twentieth century, in the groups that are known as Pentecostal and in the movements that call themselves charismatic. Within a somewhat wide range of variations, the phenomena seem to be everywhere much the same. The subject finds himself speaking words that he himself may not understand, but that give a sense of release and of a peculiarly intimate fellowship with the risen Christ. Occasionally the words spoken have been identified by those who hear as belonging to a language that the subject has no recollection of ever having heard or learned. But more often the sounds are unintelligible, "the tongues of angels" of 1 Cor. 13:1. Some claim to be able to interpret these sounds; when an interpretation has been given, it has in most cases conveyed familiar truths of the Christian faith rather than new insights or "revelation." Danger arises when this special manifestation is regarded as the only sign of the coming of the Spirit, and when those who have received it place themselves in a superior class, from which they can look down on those in the fellowship to whom this special sign has not been granted.

The expression "Do not quench the spirit" in 1 Thess. 5:19 shows that the leaders of that congregation had tried, with less than perfect success, to control what seemed to them aberrant and possibly dangerous tendencies; the balancing phrase, "do not despise prophesying," seems to present the view of the young people who found the more conventional sermons of the elders less interesting than the excited utterances of those on whom the Spirit had fallen.[13]   It was in Corinth, however, that these manifestations of the Spirit had reached a point at which they threatened to disrupt the whole order of the Christian community.   Those who had received the afflatus declared that, when the inspiration was upon them, they could not control themselves but must speak, with the result that three or four would be speaking together and the assembly would resemble bedlam rather than a congregation of the God who is a God of order (1 Cor. 14).

Paul's handling of the situation in Corinth is strictly practical, but, as in so many other cases, he uses practical problems as the occasion for some of his profoundest theological affirmations.

He does not condemn or reject these special manifestations.   In fact he claims himself to have spoken in tongues more than any of them (1 Cor. 14:18)—an unexpected utterance that reminds us how little we really know of this many-sided apostle.

But he claims that all Christian life is life in the Spirit, and that the operation of the Spirit is to be seen in every Christian activity and in every operation, however routine and monotonous, which contributes to the building up of the Christian fellowship (1 Cor. 12: 27–30).

Among these many gifts, glossolalia (the gift of tongues) must be regarded as rather inferior, since it is an individual gift that makes little, if any, contribution to "edification," to the instruction and strengthening of the Christian fellowship.   Prophecy, the inspired exegesis of the Old Testament that played such a large part in Christian worship, is greatly to be preferred to speaking in tongues.

God is not honored by paroxysms of emotion, in which the believer claims to be in the grip of a power too strong for him to control.   "The spirits of prophets are subject to prophets" (1 Cor. 14:32)—and the spirits of charismatics are to be subject to charismatics.

What matters far more than anything else is the love that binds Christians to their Lord and to one another.   If love is present, the self-giving love of which alone the term *agape* is used in the New Testament, we may infer the presence of the Spirit; if it is absent, whatever pretensions may be put forward on behalf of those who claim to be spiritual, the spirit that is in them is not the Spirit of the risen Jesus.

It is this relating of the Spirit to ethical transformation, and not

13. For a different view of the nature of prophesying, see ibid., p. 239.

simply to sudden and passing phenomena, that is Paul's abiding and masterly contribution in this field. At an even earlier date he had set forth the fruit of the Spirit as "love, joy, peace, longsuffering, gentleness, generosity, meekness, reliability, self-control" (Gal. 5:22). Here the spirit seems to be directly connected with Jesus of Nazareth, and with the ideal life as this had been seen in him. Paul refers elsewhere to the meekness and gentleness of Christ (2 Cor. 10:1); he refers to his generosity (2 Cor. 8:9). Christ is to Paul "the Son of God who loved me and gave himself for me" (Gal. 2:20).

The exact relationship of Paul to Jesus of Nazareth is a complex question that has been endlessly debated, and for the full discussion of which a separate treatise would be needed. To some the connection has seemed so tenuous as hardly to exist at all. This view seems to rest on a misunderstanding of the situation. Paul does not exist in a timeless world, in which he worships a timeless Redeemer. He never shows any tendency to separate his gospel from the historical happenings associated with Jesus of Nazareth. He is not entirely consistent in his use of the titles Jesus, Christ, Lord; and our problem is additionally complicated by the tendency of those who in early days copied the manuscripts of the New Testament to confuse and conflate different readings. Yet, as a general rule, when Paul uses the simple personal name "Jesus," he is consciously referring to a definite historical period and to the events that took place within it. The most striking example is to be found in 2 Corinthians 4, in which the repeated use of the name "Jesus" indicates that Paul is deliberately and formally presenting a parallel between his own sufferings, which his enemies tended to regard as a judgment of God on a false apostle, and the sufferings endured less than a quarter of a century before by the actual Man who had lived and died in Palestine.

When Paul was writing, no Gospel had as yet been written, and he, like other contemporaries, was dependent on oral tradition. We have seen that at two crucial points he refers to a tradition that had come to him from the Lord himself. He quotes a word of the Lord as having final authority (1 Cor. 7:10), and contrasts this with his own inspired judgment, which yet does not have the same authority as an actual dominical word.

It is true that Paul twice refers almost contemptuously to "knowing Christ after the flesh" (2 Cor. 5:16 AV).[14] It is impossible to preach or to live as though the Resurrection had not occurred; there is to be no archaeological hankering after days that have been but are no more. This consideration leads us on to Paul's central theo-

---

14. At this point the RSV paraphrases "we once regarded Christ from a human point of view."

logical discovery about the nature of the Spirit. He would not for a moment deny the continuity of the Spirit that he has known with the Spirit as manifested in the Old Testament. But every time a Christian uses the word Spirit, he uses it in a sense in which it could not have been used in the Old Testament, since that Spirit is now the Spirit of the risen Jesus. What does the Spirit do? He makes Jesus the living contemporary of every man, everywhere, and permanently available to all. Christian life is life transformed by the Spirit, not by adherence to a set of rules or by following some vague spiritual ideal, but according to the lineaments of One who had lived not so long ago and about whom manifold traditions were now circulating in all the churches.

It has been thought by some that Paul identifies the Spirit with the living Christ. It is true that at times he seems to come very near doing so. In Rom. 8:9–11, "if in fact the Spirit of God dwells in you" is followed immediately by "But if Christ is in you," and that again by "if the Spirit of him who raised up Jesus from the dead dwells in you." We seem to be not far from the identification of the one with the other.

Yet there is always a difference. We are never told to be like the Spirit. We are constantly told to be like Jesus Christ. Paul can boldly say "Be imitators of me, as I am of Christ" (1 Cor. 11:1). He tells his Philippian friends to have in themselves that mind which was also in Christ Jesus (Phil. 2:5), or, more exactly, "let your way of thinking be the same as that which you have seen manifested in Christ Jesus."[15] The image of God (Gen. 1:26) had been lost by the first Adam; it has been restored in the last Adam; Christians, having been set free from the old, "have put on the new nature, which is being renewed in knowledge after the image of its creator" (Col. 3:9–10). The difference, to use a more modern idiom, is that between the static and dynamic elements in the life of the church; there must be a fixed point of reference, and there must also be a place for movement and change.

A great truth is enshrined in the old evangelical phrase, "the finished work of Christ." At a certain point the earthly career of Jesus of Nazareth came to an end; what he has done has been done, and need never be done again. To what he has done he cannot and will not add anything *in the same way*. But with God every end is a

15. The translation, "Have that same mind among yourselves as you have in Christ Jesus," which has found its way into a number of modern translations, including the RSV, seems to me erroneous. It postulates a very odd use by Paul of the Greek language. It involves dichotomy between "the mind which you have among yourselves" and "the mind which you have in Christ Jesus"—a dichotomy I do not believe that any writer of the New Testament was likely to make. Moreover, the traditional translation fits the context far better than that which has been so recently invented.

new beginning. The end of Christ known after the flesh is the beginning of Christ known after the Spirit. It is to this living Christ that Paul wishes to introduce those to whom he preaches; but it never occurs to him that this heavenly Christ, encountered through the living Spirit, is other than the Man whose risen form he had seen in the vision that made him a Christian.

Reconciliation

"Reconciliation" is the comprehensive term that Paul uses when he has in mind the whole plan of salvation, God's purpose for his human creatures in its totality. The ministry that has been committed to the apostle is the ministry of reconciliation; as an ambassador of Christ he pleads with men in winning words to be reconciled to God (2 Cor. 5:20). It is implied that by being reconciled to God men will also be reconciled to one another. This is not stated by Paul in so many words, but is worked out logically in his teaching on the church as the body of Christ.

Reconciliation always implies two-way traffic; there must be a giver and a receiver. But Paul everywhere makes it plain that in this process the initiative has always been with God and never with men. It is God who in Christ is reconciling the world to himself (2 Cor. 5:19).[16] The Anglican Thirty-nine Articles declare that Christ died to reconcile his Father to us. This is perhaps the one serious theological error in that generally admirable document. Paul has no doubt that judgment rests in the hands of God. He can declare uncompromisingly that "the wrath of God is revealed from heaven" (Rom. 1:18), and no attempt to make the words mean something other than what they obviously mean is likely to be successful. This is not the capricious anger of an irresponsible tyrant; it is the implacable hostility of God to everything that is evil. Yet Paul does not represent God as the angry father who must in some way be placated. It is He who takes the initiative in providing in Christ the means of reconciliation. Man can do nothing to save himself; all that he need do is to allow himself to be saved.

It is the world that God is reconciling to himself. In Rom. 8:21 Paul passes beyond the bounds of our ordinary thinking, and looks forward to the time when the whole creation will be delivered from bondage to corruption into the liberty of the glory of the children of God. How this will come about and what exactly it will mean he does not define. The words stand as a reminder that the redemption wrought in Christ was far greater than our finite minds will ever be

---

16. This is the correct translation; the familiar "God was in Christ" of the AV is misleading. The RSV gives the correct translation in the margin.

able to grasp. We may recall the word of the Fourth Gospel that "God so loved *the world*" that he gave his Son (John 3:16)—one of those unplanned coincidences between Paul and the Johannine writings reminding us that the unity of the New Testament is something that can be traced in every part of it, but cannot be summed up in a few sentences.

While Paul was engaged in this work of proclaiming the all-sufficiency of Christ, he received the alarming tidings that the whole of his work was being placed in jeopardy by a rival form of teaching. Among the Galatians a group of teachers was proclaiming that, though salvation was through Christ, this salvation was available only to those who through circumcision had entered into the old covenant and by this act of obedience had linked themselves directly to Abraham as their ancestor. Paul recognized at once that this was no secondary matter; it went to the very heart of his doctrine. He was compelled to rethink the whole of his teaching on reconciliation, and found the solution by working out that doctrine of justification by faith, which many modern readers find extremely difficult to understand. He deals with this theme at length in the Epistle to the Galatians and more succinctly in the Epistle to the Romans.

Here we have to pause for a moment to consider a question related to the complex problem of the chronology of the life of Paul. On the traditional reckoning Paul first met the Galatians on what is commonly called his second missionary journey. If that were so, the letter to the Galatians would be brought close in time to the great trilogy, Romans and 1 and 2 Corinthians. The wise historian never uses the word "impossible"; he has seen too many improbabilities establish themselves as undoubted fact. Yet even the cautious historian must admit it to be extremely unlikely that the same writer could treat a controversial subject such as circumcision so differently in two nearly contemporary writings as Paul does in Galatians and Romans. In Galatians the tone is passionate and impetuous; circumcision or noncircumcision presents itself as a question literally of life or death for the church. In Romans circumcision is no longer a matter of controversy; it is a theological problem that can be calmly and dispassionately discussed. It would seem that something must have happened to account for the remarkable change in tone between the two Epistles. One event would provide a perfect explanation for the change—a formal decision by the leaders of the church that for Gentile Christians circumcision was unnecessary. In Acts 15 Luke tells us that exactly such a decision was made, at what is commonly called the Council of Jerusalem. Some of the strict

Jewish party had been saying, "Unless you are circumcised according to the custom of Moses, you cannot be saved" (Acts 15:1), a brief
and clear summary of the problem that Paul had had to face in
Galatia; circumcision is related to salvation and not to ritual conformity.   In the letter sent out to the churches, as recorded by Luke,
circumcision is mentioned and then brushed to one side; the requirements laid on the Gentiles are limited to a few ceremonial rules
such as would make it possible for Jews and Gentiles to participate
together in a common meal.

Why does Paul not refer to the Council in the Epistle to the
Galatians? Because the Council had not yet taken place. Why does
he not refer to the Council in the Epistle to the Romans? Because
the decision of the Council had become immediately effective, and
the demand that Gentile believers should be circumcised had never
again been raised.[17]

Once it is realized that Galatians must have been written before
the Council met, many of the pieces of the jigsaw puzzle begin to fall
into place.

Not all problems are solved. Who were the Galatians? Sir William
Ramsay put forward the view that they were the Christians of Derbe
and Lystra and other cities visited by Paul on his first missionary
journey—Galatians as inhabitants of the Roman province of Galatia,
but Lycaonians and so on by race.   There are a number of difficulties
in the way of acceptance of this view.   It may well be that Paul is
here dealing with one of the Christian groups that had come into
being under his ministry during the long silent period to which we
have referred.   The phrase "You know it was because of a bodily
ailment that I preached the gospel to you at first" (Gal. 4:13) at least
opens up the possibility of several visits, and suggests that Paul's first
visit was not of quite recent date.

Nor can we identify certainly the false teachers who were the
cause of all the trouble in Galatia. They may have been emissaries
of the strict Jewish party in Jerusalem; but this is nowhere stated by
Paul.   It is at least as likely that they were local believers who in
their study of the Old Testament had reached the conclusion that the
covenant of circumcision was of permanent obligation, and that Paul
had deceived them by passing on to them a partial and imperfect
Christianity, which must now be supplemented by obedience to the

17. It has been maintained that if the Council had met and passed such a decision as has been recorded by Luke,
Paul in dealing in 1 Corinthians 8 with the question of "eating things sacrificed to idols" could not have failed to
refer to this decision.   But this view rests on a careless reading of the Epistle; the two situations are entirely
different.   The Council was regulating the relationship between Jewish and Gentile Christians in a mixed
congregation; Paul was dealing with the problems of Gentile Christians living in a particularly wicked and
dissolute city; how far could they rightly go in association with their non-Christian relations and friends?   It must
be admitted, however, that none of the proposed solutions is entirely successful in reconciling the account in Acts
15 with what we can gather from the Pauline Epistles.

binding precepts of the old covenant. We can however reconstruct with some confidence the main outlines of the story.

Paul had been for some time engaged in fostering the remarkable new Christian movement in the great eastern city of Antioch. There, as it seems, for the first time Christian evangelists had directly approached Gentiles who had never been influenced by the Jewish Law, and some of these had believed and been baptized.[18] In the relaxed atmosphere of that cosmopolitan city the barriers created by the Jewish Law had been allowed to fall, and Jewish and Gentile Christians had joined without mutual suspicion in the common meal.

The leaders of the movement, however, were aware that they were being watched with suspicion by some of the stricter party in Jerusalem. It was therefore decided to take advantage of a visit of Paul and Barnabas to Jerusalem in another connection to hold a full discussion with the leaders of the Jerusalem church, and to make sure that the very real danger of the splitting of the church into a Jewish and a Gentile wing should be finally averted.

All went well. There was no public debate. This Paul specially stresses in the words "privately before those who were of repute" (Gal. 2:2). The discussions seem to have been lengthy and to have ranged over the whole field of Christian doctrine and practice. But in the end the three great leaders, James, Peter, and John, were satisfied that in all essentials the gospel as preached by Paul was the same as that which they were engaged in preaching; they recognized that there would be differences between the mission to Israel and the mission to the Gentiles, but such differences did not amount to division between those who had been made one in Christ.

There had been, however, one unfortunate contretemps, which was to cause Paul acute and unforeseen embarrassment. He was accompanied by a young Gentile Christian named Titus. During the days in Jerusalem he allowed himself to be persuaded that it would be better that Titus should be circumcised. As a Gentile Titus could not accompany his fellow-Christians when they went up to the temple—even the suspicion that a Gentile had entered the sacred courts was sufficient, at a later date, to provoke a dangerous riot (Acts 21). He would not be admitted to any of the fellowship meals of the Christians; he was no more than an outsider and a hanger-on.

---

18. I think that in Acts 11:20 *Hellenas* must be the correct reading, though the weight of textual evidence is against it. Luke clearly intends the reader to see in this something of a revolution—and preaching to *Hellenistas*, Greek-speaking Jews, would have been in no way revolutionary.

Paul seems to have accepted the advice of his Jewish companions that all inconveniences could be gotten out of the way by the simple step of having Titus circumcised. By doing so, Paul at once exposed himself to the charge of inconsistency: with one voice he declared the superfluity of circumcision; with another he arranged for the circumcision of a Gentile believer. It is not surprising that his opponents in Galatia took the maximum advantage of this event as supporting evidence for the charge that they laid against Paul of inconsistency and timeserving.[19]

Controversy lay in the future; for the time being the work went on prosperously in Antioch, apparently with the blessing of the Jewish wing of the church. A second crisis arose with the visit of Peter to Antioch. At first he entered without hesitation into the life of this unusual community and participated in the common meals. But later a group arrived in Antioch claiming to represent the stricter party in Jerusalem, and persuaded Peter that his action was imprudent to the point of folly. It is easy to infer the kind of arguments that they are likely to have used. In India to this day a high-caste convert to Christianity who eats with low-caste fellow-Christians will find himself ejected from the family home and unable to bear any kind of Christian witness to his relations. Would it not be wise for Peter, for the sake of the gospel, to avoid such contamination? If it became known in Jerusalem that Peter had been eating with uncircumcised Gentiles, he might well find himself excommunicated by the mother church; at best he would have disqualified himself for any further activity in the mission to Israel. Peter and Barnabas both yielded to these plausible arguments. Paul, still an almost unknown missionary on the frontiers of the church, with astonishing courage stood up to the great leader of the apostles and rebuked him to his face (Gal. 2:11–16). How far his intervention was successful we are not told.

Just as this crisis had been surmounted, the evil tidings from Galatia arrived. It was clear that the arrangement privately reached by Paul with the leaders in Jerusalem had now so many holes in it as to be completely ineffective; something far more public and official was needed, if the sorely tried church of Jesus Christ was to be rescued from being permanently divided in two. It may well have been at this moment of supreme anxiety that Paul dashed off the letter to the Galatians, in which he expressed both his passionate

---

19. It seems clear to me that Titus was circumcised. If not, what reason could there be for the extreme embarrassment under which Paul is clearly suffering as he pens the confused passage, Gal. 2:1–10? And what other ground could there be for the charge made against him by his enemies that he was still pleasing men (Gal. 1:10) or still preaching circumcision (5:11)? This view is supported by the "Western" reading in the difficult passage, Gal. 2:1–10; this gives the sense, "We did yield for a brief moment," i.e., in one particular case, and as a defense of the Gentile mission in one situation of particular difficulty. See Frederick J. Foakes Jackson and Kirsopp Lake, eds., *The Beginnings of Christianity*, 5 vols. (London: Macmillan & Co., 1933), 5:197–99.

anxiety for his beloved converts and his passionate concern that the gospel as he had preached it should be neither diminished nor impugned.

The Council was held. We are not bound to accept as historical every single detail of the account given by Luke in Acts 15; but the general account of the events seems to be reliable.[20] The privileged position of the Jews, as the recipients of the oracles of God and as the first to hear the word of the new covenant from the lips of Jesus himself, was not denied. But it was made clear that circumcision was a disciplinary regulation that Jewish Christians might maintain in force if they wished; and that the Mosaic Law was binding on Gentiles only insofar as it helped to remove obstacles in the way of Jews and Gentiles sharing equally in the common life. The victory of the more liberal party was almost complete; the unity of the church had been maintained.

We must now turn to consider, against this background, the two Epistles in which Paul treats of this crisis in Jewish-Gentile relationships.

The Epistle to the Galatians shows many signs of haste in composition, and some confusion in argument. But one central idea runs through it. The key word is "promise." There was a period of promise long ago, when God spoke to Abraham and showed him the coming of "the seed" in whom all the promises were to be fulfilled (Gal. 3:16–17). Then Jesus came, and the epoch of promise was resumed. What then of the Law, which played so large a part in the experience and the imagination of the Jew? It was simply an interim inserted to fill in the gap between the two periods of promise (3:19). The Law did, indeed, fulfill an important function in increasing the awareness of sin; but it had nothing to do with salvation. The Law was like the slave-guardian[21] to whom the children of free men might be committed (3:24); but, when Christ came, it lost its validity, since the time of maturity had come and such tutelage was no longer necessary (4:1–7). This is a brilliant reconstruction of salvation history; it shows how far Saul the Pharisee had departed from the traditions in which he had been deeply schooled.

Abraham is the link between this sketch of a theology of history and the doctrine of justification by faith, to which we must now turn. "Abraham believed God, and it was reckoned to him as righteousness" (Gen. 15:6; Gal. 3:6).

---

20. The apostolic injunctions to the Gentiles are given in the manuscripts in a number of different forms. On this, see any recent commentary on Acts.

21. RSV translates "custodian"; this is better than the "schoolmaster" of the AV, but does not make clear that the "pedagogue" would almost certainly be a slave, and thus misses a not unimportant point in Paul's argument.

This doctrine is difficult for us to understand, since it is expressed in language that is unfamiliar to us, and draws on legal, or forensic, concepts that we find hard to associate with religion. Moreover, the interpretations given by theologians at various periods have perhaps made it more, rather than less, difficult to understand.

In the sixteenth century the doctrine became involved in the tedious controversy between Protestants and Roman Catholics as to whether the righteousness of Christ is imputed to us or imparted to us, and as to the place of good works in relation to salvation. Luther did at times make clear that the faith of which he spoke was not to be identified with mere intellectual assent, but must be understood in terms of total self-surrender to the mercy of God revealed in Christ. Also, he declared on many occasions that he had never condemned good works as such; he had only been anxious to make it clear that good works are not those performed by a seeker after salvation in order to merit the favor of God (as in the medieval play *Everyman*) but are those that a believing Christian cannot refrain from putting into execution in gratitude for the salvation that he has already received. Almost the whole of Luther's genuine rediscovery of Paul was lost in the Lutheran orthodoxy that began to harden in about 1560.[22]

Understanding of the doctrine has been made more difficult for the English reader by the introduction in recent times of a most unfortunate mistranslation. Fifty years ago Dr. James Moffatt, in his widely popular version of the New Testament in modern English, wishing to avoid the word "justify," which is not in use in ordinary parlance, translated the Greek word *dikaioun* by the English "acquit." The disease has spread and has made its way even into the New English Bible. This is not simply a change in words; it involves a complete change in meaning. To acquit an accused person is to declare that that person has not committed the offense with which he has been charged and is therefore innocent. If God could acquit the sinner and declare the guilty innocent, the whole of our salvation would be based on a lie, and Christianity would be as immoral as the Hindu supposes it to be. In the Hindu understanding of the universe, everything is held together by *Ṛta*, the inexorable principle of order, rather like the *Anangke*, the "necessity" of the Greeks, which cannot be violated even by the gods themselves. If Christianity refuses to

22. The best account of Lutheran orthodoxy known to me is that in Charles Beard's still invaluable Hibbert Lectures (originally delivered in 1883), Lecture 8, "The Rise of Protestant Scholasticism." See Beard, *The Reformation of the Sixteenth Century in its Relation to Modern Thought and Knowledge*, reprint ed. (Ann Arbor: University of Michigan Press, 1962).

recognize the inexorable as inexorable, it thereby reveals itself to the Hindu mind as being an inferior kind of religion.

We must turn back to Scripture and see what it actually says. Paul, challenged by the existence of the Law, has two problems to face. How can man who by sinning has lost his right relationship to God put himself back into that right relationship? How can a righteous God accept sinners? The dilemma is real. Paul finds the answer in the doctrine of justification by faith.

His argument is what is known as forensic, that is to say, it is couched in terms of the law courts and of a formal trial, and to most Christians this is an unfamiliar manner of speaking and thinking about God. But perhaps the difficulty is not as great as it has sometimes been made out to be. Even in a court of law, acquittal and condemnation are not the only two possibilities; in almost every country in the world there is also the possibility of a pardon. The word "pardon" is frequently used simply as synonymous with forgiveness, and its strict legal sense is overlooked. Here there is no subterfuge; there is no question of declaring a criminal innocent. His guilt has been proved and is fully recognized; but the sovereign, if it seems good to him, may intervene and declare that the offender has been pardoned, that is, restored to his rights within the community, his guilt being as though it had never been and as something that can never again be quoted against him.

In this procedure a number of points have to be carefully noted. No judge as such can issue a pardon. This is a prerogative only of the sovereign power. The initiative can be taken only by the sovereign, in an action to which the term "grace" can appropriately be applied. No man can ever claim a pardon. An innocent man may claim that the court should recognize his innocence and declare him free from the charge that has been laid against him. A criminal may claim fair trial and proper sentence if he is found guilty. Beyond that neither can go. A pardon is a royal act, and always has in it an element of the unexpected and of surprise. The one who is pardoned can do nothing to earn the gift. He should freely recognize the fault that he has committed and make no concealment of it. He should recognize to the full the generosity with which he has been treated and see that this generosity springs only from the good will of the sovereign and from no other source. He should feel himself bound to accept the gift with deep gratitude and to regard himself as forever beholden to the sovereign who has shown him grace. From the other side, if the pardoned criminal shows a proper sense of his own condition, and of the new condition into which he has been transported by the gift of pardon, the sovereign may feel that he has "done the right thing." Through recognition by the one pardoned both of guilt and of liberation, he has put himself once again into a right relationship with authority, the law, and society.

We shall not find all these ideas in Paul. Yet they do introduce us to the area with which the apostle is dealing in his teaching about justification by faith. The man who is justified is neither good nor righteous in the ordinary sense of the term; but he has put himself into what in the circumstances is the right relationship with God, through a complete and honest recognition of what he has done and failed to do, and through his admission that he is dependent only on the goodness of God and on nothing whatever that he can do himself for the gift of life and favor. How is it possible to believe that one who takes up this attitude can be acceptable to God? Paul's answer is that this becomes possible only through the initiative that God has already taken in Jesus Christ. To believe is to see that God in Christ has moved toward the sinner before the sinner began to move toward God, to know oneself to be accepted in him without regard to any question of virtue or of compensation for the wrong done. Such knowledge must result in a deep and permanent sense of indebtedness and of gratitude for the immensity of the favor conferred.

Great harm has been done by interpretations of the doctrine of justification that present it as an almost mechanical transaction unrelated to the dark and personal realities of the situation. Forgiveness is never something that can be lightheartedly claimed and granted. It is always a very serious matter. Paul would have commended Anselm for writing: "You have not yet considered of how serious a weight sin is." When wrong has been done, there is a price to be paid before reconciliation can take place. Since it is impossible for the one who has done the wrong to pay the price, in the mystery of God's economy the One who has been wronged elects himself to pay the price and to open the road to forgiveness. In the Hindu system the ineluctable order of the world says: You sin; you pay. In the Christian mystery of grace, God says: You sin; I pay.

We have to be careful in our use of such terms as "ransom," "price," and so forth, lest we confuse a personal with a commercial transaction, as Anselm tends to do. But have we any other language in which to express what we want to say? In the simple words of the hymn,

> There was no other good enough
>   To pay the price of sin.
> He only could unlock the gate
>   Of heaven and let us in.

Simplicity of language is matched by profundity of thought. When we look upon the cross of Christ, we know that this is true, though the plummet of our thought may be unable to sound the depths of the goodness and mercy of God.

But justification is by faith. In Paul the word "faith" almost always implies total self-abandonment to the love of God revealed in Jesus Christ our Lord, total abandonment of any attempt to establish a claim upon God by any supposed righteousness of our own, and an unconditional acceptance of what God in Christ is willing to give. But this involves a kind of death, and therefore this word "faith" nearly always has in Paul's writings the undertone of death and the overtone of resurrection. If the case is to be transferred from the court of law to the court of grace, from the court of rejection to the court of gracious acceptance, the old self must die. The sinner who has accepted the righteous sentence of death upon himself knows that he can live only by the life of the one who died and rose again. And that old self, once dead, must make no further attempt to set itself up as god in its own world.

Justification establishes a new and permanent relationship between God and men. The sinner knows that he will never be able to claim any righteousness of his own; never will he be able to appear in the presence of God, here or hereafter, except inasmuch as he has been incorporated into the life of Jesus Christ. It is true that Paul writes, "Whom he justified he also glorified" (Rom. 8:30). But this glory is always derived and never intrinsic.

The Reformers of the sixteenth century were so concerned to exclude every possibility of "work-righteousness" and of a return to the idea of human merit that they did not find it easy always to recognize that justification by faith is only the beginning of Christian life and does not include the whole of it. But the first eight chapters of the Epistle to the Romans are to be read as a single whole. In a brief passage (Rom. 3:21–31) Paul sets out the general principle of justification. He then goes on to answer the objection that such rebirth as is implied in justification (cf. John 3:1–16) is impossible by dealing at length with the faith of Abraham and the birth of Isaac. The birth of a son to a man a hundred years old was no doubt physically impossible and so is the rebirth of a sinner into new life. But neither is impossible to a God who calls the dead back into life, and speaks of things that are not as though they already were (Rom. 4:17). That birth happened long ago; the new birth in Christ can happen and does happen today.

Paul then passes on in Romans to an impressive panorama of the Christian life under the category of the four freedoms:

This great passage of sustained eloquence begins with "Since we are justified by faith, we have peace with God through our Lord Jesus Christ" (5:1)[23] and ends with "nothing shall be able to separate us from the love of God, which is in Christ Jesus our Lord" (8:39 AV). Later theological reflection has added little to what Paul has set forth in these great chapters.

If we accept Philippians and Colossians as genuine Epistles of Paul, and Ephesians as setting forth a recognizably Pauline theology, we shall observe a distinct shift in his theology, a shift that may be described as a movement of his thought away from the central idea of redemption to a new interest in the church and life in the church. Of course the church had always been present to the mind of Paul; had he not written to a number of churches? But nowhere in the earlier letters do we find the almost mystical fervor of such an expression as: "and gave him to be head over all things to the Church, which is his body, the fullness of him who all in all is being fulfilled" (Eph. 1:22–23 par.). It is this shift, in point of fact, that has led a number of scholars to class these later Epistles as deutero-Pauline rather than Pauline, and to doubt whether they can have come directly from the hand of the apostle himself. Since Paul as a writer is so versatile both in thought and in expression, such a conclusion must not be arrived at hastily and unadvisedly. And here, as before, we cannot hope to understand the theology unless we make use of what we can learn of the life of the apostle and of the circumstances out of which that theology arose.

Paul had wrestled long and intensively with the problem of the unbelief of Israel. How had it come about that a people of God, so long and so carefully prepared by the Law, by the words of the prophets and the worship in temple and synagogue, had failed to recognize the Messiah when he came, and for the most part had persisted in that hardness of heart that made them refuse to admit the vindication of the claims of Jesus granted by God in the great sign of the Resurrection? Paul has set out for us his perplexity in detail in the Epistle to the Romans, 9–11.

Romans, like all the other letters of Paul, really is a letter; understanding of it has been made more difficult by the tendency to

---

23. The alternative reading found in some manuscripts, "let us have peace with God," has nothing to commend it, though it has found acceptance in some modern translations.

concentrate on chapters 1–8 as though these constituted a treatise in dogmatic theology, and to let the rest of the Epistle look after itself. The reality is quite otherwise. Careful study of the concluding chapters will make plain the situation in which the apostle is writing; and this in turn explains the method he follows in the construction of this great Epistle.

The church in Rome was a Gentile church. There may have been, indeed almost certainly were, some Jewish Christians in that church, but Paul consistently addresses his readers as Gentiles, and we may suppose that his arguments would have been differently constructed if they had not been addressed to Gentile Christians. The Roman church was perplexed by the existence within it of three different groups: those who by circumcision had become Jews, and felt themselves bound to the observance of considerable parts of the Jewish Law; those who had attended the synagogue as "learners" or "God-fearers," who had been attracted by the high ethical quality of the Jewish faith but had not accepted its ceremonial requirements;[24] and those who had come into the church straight from the Gentile world, and to whom therefore the Jewish Law meant nothing—they felt entitled to esteem all days alike (Rom. 14:5) and could see no point in the observance of the Jewish festivals. How were the three groups to coexist without friction, and in that unity they had been taught was one of the signs of the fellowship of Christ's people into which they had been brought? Paul is the recognized authority on all such questions; the perplexed Christians have sent a message to him asking for guidance, and the Epistle to the Romans is the result.[25]

If the gospel is all that matters, what is the significance of the continued existence of Israel? Has Israel any significance at all, or can we simply conclude that God has cast off his ancient people and that his concern now is only for the believers in Jesus?

This is a conclusion that Paul is wholly unwilling to accept: "God has not rejected his people whom he foreknew" (Rom. 11:2). The gospel must still be preached "to the Jew first and also to the Gentile" (1:16). To be a Jew is an immense privilege of which Paul himself is proud. And the hardening of Israel can be providentially explained; it is this hardening that has made possible the coming of the time of the Gentiles, in which the Christians in Rome have been brought into the fellowship of believers. But Israel is still the root of the tree, and that root is holy; it was into this tree that the Gentiles had been grafted: "it is not you that support the root, but the root

---

24. There are many references in the Acts of the Apostles to hearers of this class, e.g., 16:14; 17:17; 18:7.
25. This is not definitely stated, but seems to be a legitimate inference from the Epistle itself.

that supports you" (Rom. 11:18). We are all by faith the children of Abraham. But, when the fullness of the Gentiles has come, a strange thing will happen. Israel, seeing that which cannot be denied, and recognizing that the signs of the messianic kingdom are unmistakably present among the Gentiles, will be challenged to think again, and to realize that the Messiah has really come. "And so all Israel will be saved" (Rom. 11:26).

"All Israel will be saved." Paul shared the belief of the early Christians that the blindness that had befallen the people of Israel and their rulers was only a temporary phenomenon, and that when the appointed time had come unbelief would give place to acceptance and adoration. He added two points to the general expectation—the view that the conversion of the Gentiles would be the lever that would effect the great change, and the conviction that the conversion of the Jews would be not the consequence of the coming again of the Messiah in glory but the final preparation for that climactic event. In this conviction Paul had also reached the conclusion that he himself was the instrument through which this challenge was to be presented to Israel in Jerusalem, the very sanctuary of its faith.

Much of Paul's time during the closing years of his ministry in freedom was taken up with the collection for the poor saints in Jerusalem (Rom. 15:25–26). It is generally assumed that the recipients of the generosity of the Gentiles would be poor Christians only, and there are strong grounds for accepting this view. But would that limited object account for the magnitude of the operation undertaken by Paul? We are hampered in answering that question by lack of information as to the number of poor believers. But if we can hazard the guess that 10 percent of the inhabitants of Jerusalem were believers and that all of them were indigent, that would involve only about eight hundred families. Was the poverty of so small a group sufficient ground for the appeal made by Paul to all the Gentile churches, in which there were a number of affluent members, over a number of years to collect money to be sent to Jerusalem? It is clear, from the minutely careful arrangements made by Paul as described in 2 Corinthians 8 and 9, that he expected the sum to be considerable. Is it possible that the hint given in Acts 24:17, "after some years I came to bring to my nation alms and offerings," is correct, and that the purpose of the collection was to bring relief to the poor in Jerusalem, without distinction between Jewish believers and Christian believers? If this were so, it would account for the magnitude of the enterprise. Whom was Paul so anxious to reconcile? Those who picture the early church as the scene of internecine warfare between the Jerusalem church and the followers of Paul take it for granted that the collection was to serve as an olive branch held out by Gentile to Jewish Christians. But all the evidence in Paul's writings points to the fact that it was to the Jewish people as a whole that he intended to direct his appeal. To whom is Paul referring when he writes: "For if the Gentiles have come to share in their spiritual blessings, they ought also to be of service to them in material blessings" (Rom. 15:27)? The Gentiles had received no benefits from the Jewish Christians in Jerusalem; Paul ceaselessly maintains that his ministry came to him directly from Jesus Christ and that he and the churches that he had founded were in no way dependent on the Jerusalem church and its apostles. The whole argument of chapters 9–11 is that the Gentile Christians are directly related to Israel as a nation; Israel is the root, and the Gentile Christians are the wild-olive branches that, contrary to nature, have been grafted into Israel, the true olive tree, of which the stump remains, though some of the natural branches have been broken off (Rom. 11:17–24).

Evidently Paul had planned his last journey to Jerusalem as a deliberate challenge to the Jewish people and to its chiefs. He would bring with him converted Gentiles as proof of the sovereign power of God and of the extension of his covenant to those who had never known him; he would bring the gifts of the Gentile churches as proof of the solidarity that these Gentile Christians now felt with the descendants of Abraham, Isaac, and Jacob. In a moment of aberration the chief priests and rulers had rejected the Messiah, who had come to them in the guise of a village carpenter; surely they would not reject the servant, when he came with the first fruits of the gospel and the plain evidence that the illimitable power of God was now at work through the preaching of the Resurrection of Jesus of Nazareth.

The leaders of the Jews who thirty years earlier had rejected the Master showed that they were equally capable of rejecting the servant. Paul's journey to Jerusalem, intended as a journey of reconciliation, ended in riot and tumult. He was destined to reach Rome, but as a prisoner and not as a free man. To one so passionately and tenderly devoted to his own people as Paul was (Rom. 9:1–5), this rejection must have come as a great and grievous shock. When he had written "and so all Israel will be saved," he was not giving expression to some vague eschatological hope for an unimaginable future. He was writing about something that, like the return of the Lord, he confidently expected to take place in his own lifetime.

Now he had ruefully to recognize that this would not happen; Israel had been hardened in unbelief, and, though there would always be Israelites who like himself would come to believe in Jesus as Messiah, these would be no more than a small minority. Israel could no longer play the same part in his theology as it had in earlier days. In Galatians he had written, "Peace and mercy be on all who walk by this rule, upon the Israel of God" (6:16). He would write such words no more. A gap had been left in his theology; how was it to be filled?

It was natural that he should turn to that new reality that had come to be known as the church (*ekklesia*) of Jesus Christ.

The word *ekklesia* has in itself no theological connotation whatever.[26] It can be used in Greek to denote almost any assembly, even a session in a teacher's classroom. It is one of the words used in the Greek Old Testament, though rather inconsistently, to designate the assembly of the people of Israel.[27] But no one can say why this word came to be used to denote Christian gatherings, and why it so caught on as to become the regular term by which both local assemblies and the worldwide fellowship of Christian believers are designated. The most probable explanation, and also the most prosaic, is that because the Jews had chosen one of the available synonymous words, *synagoge*, for their assemblies, the Christians deliberately, and to avoid confusion, rejected the term adopted by the Jews and chose the other.[28]

Naturally Paul had taken over this term, as he took over so much else, from those who were in Christ before him. All his great letters are addressed to churches. He uses the term in the singular for each separate local church, or in the plural (1 Cor. 11:16) for the churches as a collectivity in which a common faith and a common order prevail. These are churches of Jesus Christ; it is this that makes them distinct from any other body; their life is derived from him and to him they look as Lord, as example, and as Savior.[29]

Among the characteristics of the church, that which Paul values above all others is unity. Where this is threatened, as in Corinth and in Rome (1 Cor. 1:11; 11:18; etc.), he writes in moving and some-

---

26. The word is related to *ekkalein*, "to call out," and innumerable edifying sermons have been preached on the theme that God has called the church out from the world. The theology is excellent, the philology is poor. The word *ek-*, "out from," seems to refer to no more than the fact that in Athens the official messengers called the citizens *out* from their houses to attend their common assembly.

27. See the classic and authoritative article by J. Y. Campbell, "The Origin and Meaning of the Christian Use of the Word *Ekklesia*," *JTS* 49 (1948): 130ff., reprinted in idem., *Three New Testament Studies* (Leiden: Brill, 1965) pp. 41ff.

28. Nevertheless, in that highly independent work, the Epistle of James (2:2), we do find the word *synagoge* used to denote the Christian assembly.

29. The term "Savior" is used only rarely in the New Testament, perhaps because the term was used too freely of emperors and other benefactors. See the article by Werner Foerster in Gerhard Kittel and Gerhard Friedrich, eds., *TDNT*, trans. Geoffrey W. Bromiley (Grand Rapids: Eerdmans, 1971), 7:1003–21. Professor Foerster's is an exceptionally valuable study of the use of the term Savior in the Hellenistic world.

times indignant tones to his fellow-Christians to recall them to their own true nature and duty. For this purpose his favorite metaphor is that of the body, the various limbs of which have different functions, each of which finds its place and meaning only in the unity of the body itself. This is set forth at greatest length in 1 Corinthians 12; the life of this body is the Spirit who distributes special gifts to the members as he wills; but in the pregnant expression, "so also is Christ" (1 Cor. 12:12 AV), the body is identified as in a special way related to Christ who is its Lord (12:5). The same thought recurs more briefly in the almost contemporary Epistle to the Romans (12:4–5), with much the same significance. Here the reference is to unity in Christ—"so we, though many, are one body in Christ, and individually members one of another" (12:5). Stress is laid on the corporate unity of believers, and on their mutual dependence, under Christ, upon one another. This is a unity that must be visible to the eyes of the world.

In the Epistle to the Colossians (and still more in that to the Ephesians, of which we shall make less use, since it is held by many to be post-Pauline), a new dimension has come in. The Man of Galilee is now seen as the center not only of the history of the church but of the history of humanity as a whole, and indeed of the universe. This sense of Christ as the head over all things has already found expression in the great hymn in Phil. 2:10; at his name things in heaven and things on earth and things under the earth are to bow. But this thought is far more explicit in Colossians, and for a reason that is not far to seek. Like others before and after them, the Colossians had been perplexed about the relationship between the infinite God and this finite world. Jewish speculation, to be later taken up and elaborated in Christian thought (Dionysius the Areopagite; sixth century), and even more wildly elaborated in the Gnostic systems of the second century, had been inclined to find "that which fills the gap" (the *pleroma*) in hierarchies of angelic beings. Paul will have none of this. "You look for something to fill the gap? Why, in Jesus Christ the gap is completely filled; in him it was God's will that the *pleroma* in its fullness should dwell in bodily form. You need no other heavenly power—thrones, dominions, principalities" (Col. 1:17–20, paraphrase). The work of Christ is now seen in its cosmic dimensions; it was the Father's will to reconcile all things to himself through Christ and his death. This idea is already familiar to us from earlier Epistles, but here it is treated with greater amplitude; it is made clear that it is through the church that this immense operation is being carried through to its fulfillment. Hence the centrality of the idea of the church in Paul's theology at this later stage of his development.

At this point the relation between the head and the members assumes a new importance. The church *is* the body of Christ, and he *is* the head in which the body finds its unity and its source of fulfillment. Israel has receded into the background, and for Jew and Gentile alike the central question is that of this new and living relationship to Jesus Christ. We have had hints of this already in the Epistle to the Romans; God is the God also of the Gentiles, who will save the Jew by faith and the Gentile through faith (3:30). In Colossians, and still more fully in Ephesians, this idea is worked out in detail; the admission of the Gentiles to faith is not a kind of afterthought; they have been there in God's purpose from the very beginning, elect in him before the foundation of the world (Eph. 1:4). The total removal in Christ of the barrier, the wall of separation between Jew and Gentile, leads in Ephesians to a triumphant cry of rejoicing over the mystery of God's purpose, now at length revealed to his saints (Eph. 3:14–21).

It is often stated that, the nature of the church being entirely spiritual, Paul is little interested in organization. Service in the early church is to be understood in terms of function, not of office, a distinction it is difficult to maintain, since every regular performance of a function implies some kind of authority, some official commission without which its performance would be impossible. It is true that there are few traces in the New Testament of the rigid forms of organization that began to grow up in the second century; but even in the earliest Epistles there are evidences that the Christian groups of that time were not chaotic but had within themselves principles of order, as was to be expected in view of the close dependence of these early groups on Jewish tradition and practice. As early as 1 Thess. 5:12, Paul refers to "those who are over you in the Lord," a phrase which, though it can hardly be regarded as a formal title, does suggest some regular authorization. It was presumably these authorities who, in the name of order, were trying to "quench the spirit" (5:19). Paul always stresses both the variety of gifts and graces of the Spirit, and the need for humility, modesty, and mutual service (notably in Romans 12 and 1 Corinthians 12). There is no sharp distinction between "clergy" and "laity," yet there is no necessary cleavage between spontaneity and the beginnings of established order.

In Philippians (1:1) Paul greets the overseers (*episkopoi*) and servants (*diakonoi*) without specifying the functions and duties to be

carried out by each. Those who object to the later development of
the episcopate are happy to note that the term is in the plural, and
that there is no trace here of the "monarchical" episcopate as it began
to manifest itself in the second century.[30]   In the Epistle that deals
most fully with the life of the church in fellowship, 1 Corinthians,
Paul nowhere uses the term "presbyter," found frequently in other
parts of the New Testament.   But this ceases to be remarkable if, as
there are good grounds for thinking, this letter was actually addressed to the presbyters in Corinth, who, like Clement of Rome
at a later date, were carrying on the correspondence on behalf of the
church as a whole.   When Paul writes that "you can all prophesy
one by one" (1 Cor. 14:31), it is unlikely that he is according this
permission to every individual member of the congregation, especially when we take account of his views as to the proper demean-
or of women in church.

At the very end of our period, in the enumeration in Eph. 4:11 of
"apostles, prophets, evangelists, pastors and teachers," we see the
beginnings of a distinction between the itinerant and the local ministry, which was to take shape in the difference between the bishop
who cared for a city and its surrounding country, and the presbyter
who was attached to a single worshipping group.   This distinction
had, in fact, been there from the beginning.   Paul did not regard
himself as a pastor—"Christ did not send me to baptize" (1 Cor.
1:17); and so baptism, a ceremony that Paul regarded as both obliga-
tory and supremely important, he seems to have handed over either
to other members of his entourage or to that local ministry that was
already coming into being.

To many questions we can give no clear answer.   Every Christian
denomination today likes to find its own lineaments in the pages of
the New Testament, and none can do so with perfect success, since
we live not in the first but in the twentieth century.   But one thing
we can say with certainty—and this is confirmed by the observation
of contemporary societies: no society has ever managed to exist
without officers, and without some, perhaps rudimentary, organization.   The Pentecostalists have been described, not without reason,
as "the early Christians of the twentieth century."   There is a moving quality in the story of the early days of this movement, in which
believers formed groups as and where they were able, meeting in
whatever buildings became available, where every man testified as
the Spirit gave him utterance and all things were bathed in the glow

---

30. The term "monarchical" has given rise to much misunderstanding. It has nothing to do with any prelatical
autocracy; it simply means that for the future there is to be one bishop in one place.

of a vivid spontaneity.[31]   But as the movement grew, the situation changed. Regular ordination gradually took the place of the unorganized "ordination of the pierced hands"; the need for a trained and full-time ministry came to make itself felt. There is little to choose today in the matter of organization between a Pentecostal church and one of the "left-wing" free churches of the "main-line" tradition. This process may shed light on similar processes that may have been going on in New Testament times.

To what is all this leading?   There is a purpose of God; in what will it find its consummation?

Paul shared the belief of his fellow-Christians that the Lord would return within the lifetime of at least the majority of those living at the time at which he was writing. Many attempts have been made to show that his later eschatological teaching is different from his earlier teaching. Of course there is development; but this is rather a change of emphasis and expression than a radical abandonment of positions earlier held. Yet Paul is always an independent thinker, and is never content simply to repeat traditional formulae.

Jewish messianic expectation, in at least some circles, included belief in an earthly kingdom, with a view to participation in which faithful Jews would be raised from their graves in their earthly bodies. From the beginning Paul rejects this idea. Already in 1 Thessalonians we are told that when the Lord comes, living believers will be caught up to meet the Lord in the air (4:17); this is not an earthly kingdom, but one that will be realized in another sphere, the nature of which we can at the present time no more than dimly perceive. More important than such details is the central affirmation—"so we shall always be with the Lord" (1 Thess. 4:17). This refrain runs throughout the Epistles; to depart from this life is "to depart and be with Christ, for that is far better" (Phil. 1:23 AV). To be absent from the body is to be present with the Lord (2 Cor. 5:8). Paul's eschatological expectation is wholly centered in Christ. Hope to him is never mere optimism; it is the "joyful expectation of good things to come, based on the experience of God's faithfulness in the past." But this Lord who will come again is always the Jesus who lived and died for us that we might live with him.

This kingdom is spiritual, and yet at the same time it is a kingdom in which the body will play a part. This is difficult for us to grasp, since "body" to us is a merely material entity, from which we hope

31. The best account of this period is in Nils Bloch-Hoell, *The Pentecostal Movement: Its Origin, Development, and Distinctive Character* (Oslo: Universitetforlaget, 1964), pp. 1–65.

one day to be delivered. But to Paul the term *soma*, "body" (which in some contexts we may render as "organism," and almost as "personality"), speaks of fellowship, communication, and activity. A spirit without a body would be a ghost—isolated, weak, ineffective, not really alive at all. But this body will be a spiritual body—"flesh and blood cannot inherit the kingdom of God" (1 Cor. 15:50). Therefore the thought throughout is that of transformation; "we shall all be changed" (1 Cor. 15:51). The Lord will descend to transform the body of our humiliation after the likeness of the body of his glory (Phil. 3:20). And so we shall enter into the fullness of fellowship with one another and with the Lord.

At certain points the mind of Paul reaches out in bold speculations in which it is difficult for us to follow him. Christ is the cosmic Christ, in whom the whole universe is held together and finds its meaning (Col. 1:19). The whole universe shall be delivered from the bondage of corruption into the liberty of the glory of the children of God (Rom. 8:21). And then comes the astonishing climax: Christ, having fulfilled his task as Christ, having gathered to himself a people, so that he is now *totus Christus*, the head and the body inseparably joined together, will surrender his kingdom to God the Father that God may be all in all (1 Cor. 15:24). This sense of ultimate triumph runs through the entire Pauline corpus and gives to his messages the notes of joy, confidence, and hope. The life of the apostle was one of ceaseless toil, anxiety, and suffering. Yet he can regard all this as the light affliction of a moment in comparison with the eternal weight of glory that is to be revealed (2 Cor. 4:17).

So Paul finishes his work and lays down his pen. It is surprising that there is so little evidence in early Christian sources outside the New Testament of a continuing influence of his work and writings. Paul plays such a large part in our New Testament, and has exercised such profound influence over the whole life of the church, that it is only with an effort we recall that in the first century there were many types of Christian faith other than the Pauline. For a period, before the letters were collected, he was almost unknown, and even in those churches to which he had written he was known only in partial and fragmentary form. When the Epistles as we have them became available, the church seems to have experienced great difficulty in understanding them. The problems with which Paul dealt were no longer problems; the atmosphere of the times was different, spontaneity having been replaced by a more formal, almost legalistic type of faith and church observance, the exuberance of new faith by the sobriety of longer experience. The excellent and devout Clement of

Rome would have been quite at home in the church of the eighteenth century.   The depth and sobriety of Paul contrast strangely with the extravagances of the Epistle of Barnabas and the naïveté of the *Didache,* the "Teaching of the Twelve Apostles."   Among the earlier fathers of the church, only Tertullian among the Latins and Basil the Great among the Greeks can establish a claim to be regarded as Pauline figures.   John Chrysostom writes of him with enthusiasm, but perhaps shared with the whole Eastern tradition a failure quite to grasp the essentials of the Pauline message.   It is only when we come to Augustine of Hippo (A.D. 354 to 429) that we find a kindred spirit who could write of Paul from within and from personal experience of those two worlds that Paul so vividly delineates.

A rediscovery of Paul has again and again been synonymous with the renewal of the life of the church.   Both Martin Luther and John Wesley were kindled to passionate Christian activity by a new awareness of the meaning of justification by faith.   Yet each of these rediscoveries seems to have been partial, and not to have embraced the whole width of the apostle's teaching.   Paul Tillich has made the acute remark that the felt needs of men, and therefore their responses to the gospel, have varied from age to age.   In the ancient world men were obsessed by the sense of *phthora,* "decay," and longed for the security of incorruption.   In the Middle Ages men were burdened with a sense of guilt and the fear of damnation; their quest was for forgiveness and freedom.   In our troubled age the nightmare of man is the feeling of meaninglessness; there is a desperate search for meaning in life.   So the Greek living in the decaying world of the late Roman Empire found consolation in Paul's doctrine of transformation and incorruption.   The Reformers found the answer to their complaints in the doctrine of justification by faith, often too narrowly interpreted in forensic and legal terms, yet bringing a real deliverance, since now in Christ it would be possible for sinful men to stand without fear in the presence of a holy God.   In our own age of anxiety, in a world that is being remorselessly unified yet contains within itself the seeds of ever more rancorous hostility, it seems that the Epistle to the Ephesians, the ecumenical Epistle, truly Pauline even if not entirely from the hand of Paul, with its sense of the unity of all things in Christ and of a purpose that runs continuously from the beginning to the end, may provide the torch to lead us out of the fog of meaninglessness into the clear light of meaning and purpose in Christ.

Yet, when we have done our best, we shall always find that the apostle goes beyond us.   When we think that we have caught him, like Proteus he escapes from our grasp. There are aspects of his thought that we have overlooked, heights that we have not scaled, depths that we have not plumbed. Herein lies the fascination and the frustration in the endless task of trying to expound and to systematize the thought of one who, even at his most systematic, breaks through the system that he is trying to construct. We know that we shall always fail. And therefore the best service the expositor can render to the reader is to send him back to the apostle himself, to make his own discoveries, and perhaps to stumble upon truths that have remained undiscovered by his guide.

4

The Beginning of the Gospel

Why should anyone want to write a gospel?

The question can hardly have arisen in the earliest days of the church. When the oral tradition was so much alive, so rich and varied, when it was expected that the Lord would come back very soon, why write anything down? The writing of four Gospels, and perhaps others that have not survived, can be accounted for only by a change or changes in the situation of the church—at every point the New Testament grows out of history. We may specify three changes that had certainly taken place, and that may in part account for the beginnings of Gospel-writing.

The older generation of Christians was beginning to die out, and still the Lord had not come back. If Josephus is to be relied on, James the brother of the Lord had been done to death in A.D. 62.[1] It is probable, though not certain, that both Paul and Peter died in the first great persecution in Rome, somewhere about A.D. 64 or 65. The early Christians did not feel themselves tied to the word of eyewitnesses; they laid equal stress on the testimony of the Spirit. Yet something faded out of the life of the church as the original hearers died and disappeared.

It became clear that the somber forebodings of Jesus about Jerusalem and the Jews were going to be fulfilled. Jewish hostility to the power of Rome had been steadily growing. The moderating influence of the more sober elements was weakening, and fanaticism was coming into its own. One result of this threatening atmosphere and of the beginning of commotions seems to have been a renewal of eschatological expectation; the dangers of such excitement had already been seen in Thessalonica, where Paul had had to intervene

---

1. Josephus, *Antiquities of the Jews*, XX, 9. 1, 199. The other James, the son of Zebedee, had been put to death by Herod at a much earlier date, almost certainly in A.D. 41.

and check what might have developed into a total disruption of the social life of the Christian community. A return to the actual words spoken by Jesus was desirable, and especially a reminder of the warning he had given that "the end is not yet."

There was a developing danger from "heresy." The church was growing with great rapidity, spreading mainly through the testimony of Christians who had received no training for the work such as Paul supplied to the group of young men by whom he was constantly surrounded. Some of these witnesses had had only marginal contact with the apostolic message. Some were deliberately preaching "another gospel" (Gal. 1:6 AV), though even of these Paul in his all-embracing charity could declare that, in one way or another, it is Christ who is being preached (Phil. 1:18), and that therefore he rejoiced. A greater danger arose, perhaps, from the zeal of those who preached sincerely what they believed, but with imperfect knowledge, and therefore with a tendency to aberration and to a detachment of the faith from its historic origins in the life and teaching of Jesus of Nazareth. A century later the church in Rome, faced with the perils arising from Gnosticism, affirmed its sturdy adherence to the historical character of the faith by inserting in its creed the name of Pontius Pilate, thus making of an obscure Roman governor the second most famous man in human history. Similarly, some in the second generation of Christians felt that the best corrective to aberration was a plain setting forth of "those things which are most surely believed among us" (Luke 1:1 AV) in the form of a selective recital of the things that concerned the life, ministry, death, and Resurrection of Jesus Christ. Such a book in the hands of preachers would give them the minimum of what they must teach if they were to be true to the gospel of Jesus Christ; and at the same time, by reference back to the words and works of Jesus, would warn them of the kind of questions that they would be asked by Jews and Gentiles and provide the kind of answers that they should give. Three of our four Gospels stand in a clear relationship to the evangelistic work of the church.

It is possible that the work we know as the Gospel according to Mark was actually the first work of its kind ever to be written. Notes and jottings of sayings and works of Jesus may have been circulating in the churches at an earlier date. There appears to have been a collection of the sayings of Jesus, which in one form or another was available to Matthew and Luke, though today we do not suppose that we know so much about a document to which the scholars have given the apellation Q (from *Quelle*, the German word for source) as men did in the days when the great German New Testament scholar Adolf von Harnack (1851–1930) thought that he could reconstruct Q entire.[2] It is practically certain that the story of the passion existed before the time Mark wrote as the one continuous narrative that was widely current among Christians. And Mark almost certainly had access to many oral traditions beyond those he found it possible to use in a small work, the limits of which were determined by what could be included in a single papyrus roll. So there was plenty of material on which a self-chosen Evangelist could work. But the material awaited that genius who would be inspired to weave all the most relevant parts of it into a unity in the form of a story that begins with the witness of John the Baptist and ends with the Resurrection of Jesus Christ. The author of our Second Gospel may well have been that genius; we do hear of other Gospels, but we have no evidence of a work of this kind with an earlier date than that at which Mark was likely to be writing. We may have before us the very earliest specimen of this type of book.

Mark's Gospel is difficult to handle theologically, since it is mutilated both at the beginning and at the end. It is clear that the conventional ending, Mark 16:9–20, is a later addition. It is not to be found in the best and oldest manuscripts; moreover, it is little more than a summary of events that are referred to in the other three Gospels.[3] Two views are held as to how the Gospel originally ended. The majority are of the opinion that at a very early date the conclusion of the Gospel was lost through an accident that befell the manuscript. A minority hold that the Gospel was intended to end at 16:8, "for they were afraid," and that Mark wrote no account of the Resurrection appearances of Jesus.

This second view, which has been accepted by a number of reputable scholars, deserves careful consideration; but the difficulties in the way of accepting it are considerable. It is not impossible that a book in the Greek language should end with the word gar, "for," but it is unlikely in the highest degree.[4] Far more formidable is the objection that, in view of the central place played by the Resurrection appearances in early Christian preaching, for which we have the unimpeachable evidence of Paul, it is scarcely credible that anyone

2. Harnack's book appeared in English translation in 1908 (The Sayings of Jesus: The Second Source of St. Matthew and St. Luke, trans. J. R. Wilkinson [New York: G. P. Putnam's Sons, 1908]). Some scholars have gone so far as to doubt whether there ever was a Q at all; others who would not go quite as far as this would not commit themselves beyond the point of affirming that there was a fairly solid and well-authenticated body of tradition that may have been passed on in oral rather than in written form.

3. There are in the manuscripts a number of different endings to the Gospel and this fact adds to the probability that the original ending is missing. For details the reader may refer to any good introduction to the New Testament, or to any commentary on Mark's Gospel.

4. Diligent search has produced a number of parallels, but none of these can be considered a close parallel; the weight of the evidence is as I have stated it.

as concerned as Mark was with the *preaching* of the gospel would
have passed over in silence so essential a part of that preaching. Not
all the brilliant argumentation of that devout and sensitive scholar R.
H. Lightfoot has availed to convince me that such a solution of the
problem is possible.[5] If we inquire as to the place in which we
should look for evidence as to the lost ending of Mark, we need look
no further than Matthew 28, where we shall see that what changed
the stunned amazement of the women into joy and liberty of proclamation was an actual meeting with the risen Lord.[6] "They were
afraid" is a misleading translation of the Greek word; it is constantly
used to describe the religious awe that comes upon a man when in
the presence of a great supernatural reality.[7] This would be the
natural reaction of the women when it dawned upon them that the
Lord might be alive. This is the first reaction of the convert today;
but, when the first amazement has passed off, his immediate impulse
is to share the glorious news with all his friends.

I have long held that the beginning of Mark's Gospel is missing no
less than the end. It is just credible that a book might end in the
middle of a sentence; it is hardly credible that the same work would
also begin in the middle of a sentence. The difficulties attendant on
this view have largely been dissolved by the discovery that the
codex, the flat book of the kind to which we are accustomed, came
into existence much earlier than was previously supposed. From
careful study of the papyrus fragments in Egypt, it is now known that
the codex was extremely popular among the Christians, who from an
early date were passionately interested in Bible-reading, and may
even have invented this kind of book—so much more convenient for
frequent use than the papyrus roll. There is no reason to date the
change from roll to codex later than A.D. 130; it may have begun to
take place as early as A.D. 70.[8] If one end of a papyrus roll is
damaged, there is no reason why the other end should be damaged
also. But if the last leaf of a codex has been torn off, there is at least a
possibility that the first leaf also will have disappeared. This is what
seems to have happened to Mark's Gospel.

Many difficulties disappear when we realize that the first verse of

---

5. Robert H. Lightfoot's *Gospel Message of St. Mark* (Oxford, 1950), pp. 80–97, seems to me to be still the best
exposition of this view in English. There are a number of other studies in works translated from the German, for
instance, the work of Willi Marxsen, *Introduction to the New Testament: An Approach to its Problems* (Philadelphia: Fortress Press, 1968) and *Mark the Evangelist* (Nashville: Abingdon, 1969).

6. Of course Matthew has rewritten the story in his own special style; he marks his sense of the overwhelming
power of the Resurrection by bringing in convulsions in the natural order as evidence of it. But Matthew has been
following Mark closely, and there is no reason to suppose that he suddenly deserts him at this point.

7. As in Mark's narrative of the transfiguration, 9:8, "They were exceedingly afraid."

8. On all this see a fascinating chapter by Colin H. Roberts in *Cambridge History of the Bible*, ed. Stanley L.
Greenslade, 3 vols. (Cambridge, 1963–70), 1:48–60, in which all the latest information is carefully set out and
analyzed.

the Gospel, "the beginning of the Gospel of Jesus Christ the Son of God," is not from the original writer of the Gospel but is a scribal annotation. Henry Barclay Swete, in his superb commentary on the Gospel,[9] realized that this must be so, but could not explain how it had come about. The word *evangelion*, "gospel," is nowhere used in the New Testament to denote a book; it always refers to proclamation. Here the reference is to a book; attempts to find any different meaning remain unconvincing. The manuscripts are at this point deeply divided, some reading "Jesus Christ," others reading "Jesus Christ the Son of God." Cuthbert H. Turner has given convincing reasons for holding that the longer reading is to be preferred.[10] The expression "Jesus Christ the Son of God" is not wholly without parallel in the New Testament; but it is more like the language of the second century than that of the first.

We can begin to piece together what happened. For some years Mark's Gospel enjoyed immense popularity—no other book of its kind existed. Within a few years it came to the notice of both Matthew and Luke, and this is evidence of wide and early diffusion. Each of them, recognizing the merit of the work, took it over almost entire for incorporation into his own Gospel. The result was the beginning of that neglect from which Mark suffered through many generations until the nineteenth century brought rehabilitation. The two more complete Gospels had immediately replaced Mark in popularity and almost brought about the complete disappearance of that Gospel; why preserve so imperfect a document when two far more adequate accounts of the life and times of Jesus were already available? So it came about that when a copyist was combining into one codex the four Gospels recognized by the church, the only copy of Mark that he could find was one that had been mutilated; accordingly he inserted the brief note, "This is where a new Gospel begins." It is possible that the same copyist, recognizing the abruptness of the ending in his copy, inserted what may be called the conventional ending, combining details from the other sources available to him.

Nothing much is gained by speculating on the possible contents of the missing first page. If we compare Mark's account of the temptation of Jesus (1:12–13) with those found in Matthew and Luke, we may infer that there was a similarly brief account of the lineage and birth of Jesus, and something to lead up to the abrupt appearance of

9. *The Gospel According to St. Mark: The Greek Text with Introduction, Notes and Indices* (London: Macmillan and Co., 1898).
10. "A Textual Commentary on St. Mark I," *JTS*, January 1927, pp. 150ff.

John the Baptist, introduced in Mark 1:2 by the second half of a
sentence of which the first half is missing.

What theology of Jesus of Nazareth is presented by this great and
original author, writing probably a little more than a generation after
the events he records? One of the great gains in recent critical study
of the New Testament, in what has come to be known by the awkward term "Redaction Criticism," has been the recognition that each
of the four Evangelists is a powerful and original theologian in his
own right; far from being simply collectors of scraps and patches of
tradition, each of the Evangelists has his own purpose, his own
understanding of the facts, and his own appropriate method of pre-
sentment. By careful study of the text it should be possible to arrive
at an assessment of the theological presentation, and, by a second
stage in inference, at a judgment as to the kind of situation in which
such a presentation would have been found necessary and acceptable.[11]

Mark's Gospel is a drama. This stands out clearly if the Gospel is
read without a pause from start to finish. It is written throughout
from the point of view of those who lived through the actual events
without foreknowledge of how they were to end. The only word of
Jesus from the cross recorded by Mark is the word of dereliction,
"My God, my God, why hast thou forsaken me?" (15:34). Jesus does
indeed speak of his Resurrection, but such words seem to have
produced perplexity rather than encouragement in the minds of the
disciples (9:10). The light of the Resurrection is not thrown back
into the narratives preceding the story of the passion. This is a book
of conflict and tension. As the events of the passion draw near, the
strain reaches an almost unbearable level of intensity. Only in this
Gospel do we find the menacing introduction to the passion story:
"And they were in the way going up to Jerusalem; and Jesus went
before them; and they were amazed; and as they followed they were
afraid" (10:32 AV).[12] Only in this Gospel do we find, in the account
of Gethsemane, the very strong expression, he "began to be greatly
distressed and troubled. And he said to them, 'My soul is very
sorrowful, even to death'" (14:33–34).

For a writer who knows how the story is going to end to write as

---

11. In this and the following sections we are not dealing with the historical reliability of Mark and the other
Evangelists, the relationship between their accounts and the events as they actually happened. That problem will
be considered in the last chapter of this book. Here we are considering simply what types of theology were
developing in the Gospel-writing period, roughly between A.D. 65 and 90.

12. I find myself in agreement with the judgment of Cuthbert H. Turner that this is one of the passages in which no
single Greek manuscript has preserved for us the true reading; this should be "*he* was amazed," i.e., "he entered
into deep distress," or as Turner translates it, "he was overcome with consternation." See *A New Commentary on
Holy Scripture Including the Apocrypha*, ed. Charles Gore, Henry Leighton Goudge, and Alfred Guillaume (New
York: Macmillan Co., 1928), vol. 2, p. 90.

though he did not know demands an immense effort of historical imagination. Those of us who are older can recall experiences of the period of World War II. I can remember exactly my feelings when in 1939 I heard over the radio the news of Hitler's pact with Stalin; the words that formed themselves in my mind were, "Does this mean that we now have to fight another Hundred Years' War?" Again and again in the years 1940, 1941, and 1942, in spite of Mr. Churchill, we felt it impossible that Germany would not win the war. Yet if I were to sit down and write a book about that war, would I be able to keep from my mind as I wrote the knowledge of how it did actually end? This is just what has been achieved in Mark's Gospel. If the writer was, as tradition has affirmed, the John Mark whom we encounter in various passages in the New Testament, he had lived through the period of the ministry of Jesus, though marginally rather than centrally, and may have had some recollections of his own. At least it is likely that he had talked to some who could recapture the atmosphere of those times. The connection of Peter with this Gospel, which began to be asserted as early as the second century A.D., cannot be proved; at least Peter's connection cannot be dismissed as fanciful.

Mark lays stress on the inability of the first disciples to grasp the meaning of the teaching of their Master. In one passage, to which there is no exact parallel in any of the other Gospels, he reproaches them sadly with their obtuseness: "Having eyes do you not see? and having ears do you not hear? and do you not remember? . . . And he said unto them, Do you not yet understand?" (8:17–21). Those who hold that there was continuing tension between Paul and the original apostles in Jerusalem tend to interpret such passages as polemical, claiming that the true understanding of the gospel came through the Pauline and Gentile traditions, rather than through those who had so long and so strangely shown themselves insensitive to the meaning of the teaching. This is not impossible. It is equally possible that Mark is recording things exactly as they were. We are so familiar with the teaching of Jesus that we often fail to recognize its original, indeed its revolutionary, quality. George Moore's *The Brook Kerith* hardly qualifies as a manual of theological truth; yet its picture of the rather stupid, puzzled, quarrelsome group of disciples may be a good deal nearer to reality than the romanticized picture of the apostles that has often been passed off as history. Even with the shadow of the cross falling directly upon them, they were still thinking in terms of an earthly kingdom, in which some would be allotted more prominent places than others (Mark 10:35–45).

In another way also the Gospel is intensely dramatic. Everything turns on the correct answer to the question, Who is Jesus? At the beginning of this century William Wrede, in a book called *Das Messiasgeheimnis in den Evangelien* (1901),[13] raised the fundamental question—Why was the life of Jesus so unmessianic? Wrede's answer is that the idea that Jesus was Messiah dawned on the minds of the disciples only after the Resurrection, and that from that vantage point they read back the idea of messiahship into the period of the earthly life; but, since it was impossible to do this too extensively without disrupting the entire tradition of the life of Jesus as it had come down to them, they introduced the messianic idea as a secret that could not be disclosed until Jesus was risen from the dead; in the Gospel it is, as it were, a sound heard off the stage but never openly proclaimed.

Wrede was nearly right but not quite. He raised some most important questions, but the answers he himself put forward have been subjected to formidable and perhaps unanswerable criticism.[14]

There were very good reasons why Jesus should not put himself forward as the Messiah. Indeed, one of the main problems of his ministry was the choice of words in which to express the message he had come to bring. Every word drawn from the Old Testament was weighed down by associations that ran counter to almost everything that Jesus desired to express. The most problematical of all these words was precisely the word "Messiah." Jesus had the utmost difficulty in convincing the disciples that the kingdom he had come to bring would not fit into any of the categories with which they were familiar. To have proclaimed himself openly as Messiah could only have deepened misunderstanding. There was a reason other than the possibility of misunderstanding that made any messianic proclamation impossible. Such a proclamation would have run directly contrary to the whole method and message of Jesus. He presents himself to the people in the full three-dimensional activities of a man—eating and drinking, acting and speaking—and so submits himself to their judgment. It is they who must find out for themselves the answer to the question, Who is Jesus? At this point Mark comes very near to that Gospel which in other ways his least resembles, the Gospel according to John. There too we find the same refusal to speak plainly ("So the Jews gathered round him and said to him, How long will you keep us in suspense? If you are the

13. "The Messiah-secret in the Gospels," which has at last been translated into English under the title *The Messianic Secret* (Naperville: Allenson, 1972).
14. Among those who have questioned Wrede is Albert Schweitzer in the concluding chapter of his *Quest of the Historical Jesus*, reprint (New York: Macmillan Co., 1968).

Christ, tell us plainly" [John 10:24]), the same demand that men should think for themselves, and the consequent disputes and dissensions among the people. The dramatic structure of the two Gospels is remarkably similar. With that frankness that is an engaging characteristic of all the Gospels, neither Mark nor John makes any attempt to conceal the unfavorable answers that were given to the question. Each presents us with a picture of the parallel growth of faith and unbelief. It is instructive to look at some of the answers that, according to Mark, were actually given.

Those of Jesus' own circle reached the conclusion that he was beside himself, that fanatic enthusiasm had turned his brain (Mark 3:21; 3:31–35), a not unnatural attitude on the part of relatives or friends when one member of the family moves out of the familiar routine and gets himself widely talked about. They have had their followers in modern times among those who have discussed "the sanity of the eschatological Jesus."[15]

The general opinion among the people seems to have been that Jesus was a prophet, like one of the prophets of old (Mark 8:28). We are so accustomed to thinking of a prophet as a man of words that it does not occur to us immediately to think of a prophet as a man of action. But the thoughts of the men of the time of Jesus would naturally turn to Elijah and Elisha, who were men of few words and of many mighty actions. There are remarkable parallels between the works of Jesus and the works of the prophets of old. Jesus healed a leper, but so had Elisha healed Naaman the Syrian (2 Kings 5). Jesus fed people in the wilderness; but Elisha had also fed a hundred men with the scant provision made by the man from Baal-Shalisha (2 Kings 4:42–44). Jesus had raised to life a child apparently dead; both Elijah (1 Kings 17) and Elisha (2 Kings 4) had done the same. It was natural for the people to think that the old times had come again. But if they put the question at all, they were more likely to think that Jesus was the prophet who had come to prepare the way for the Messiah than that he was himself the Anointed One of God.

The enemies of Jesus frankly said that he was in league with evil powers and derived his power from them: "He is possessed by Beelzebul, and by the prince of demons he casts out the demons" (Mark 3:22). What was the source of this intense hostility to Jesus on the part of influential sections of the population? Mark has diagnosed it correctly. Though Jesus kept the essential precepts of the Law, these scribes and others had detected at a very early stage of the

15. Shortly before his departure for Africa as a missionary doctor (1913), Albert Schweitzer published an article on this subject in *The Expositor* (1913), pp. 328–42, 439–54, 554–68.

ministry of Jesus that his teaching, if followed out, would overthrow from the ground up their interpretation of the Law. To say that the sabbath was made for man, and not man for the sabbath (Mark 2:27) was the doctrine of a revolutionary. To say that nothing coming into a man from outside can defile him (Mark 7:15) was to sweep away all the minute rules about clean and unclean kinds of food and ritual purity that made up so large a part of the Jewish Law. Mark presents Jesus as the great liberator; to those on the other side he must have seemed to be the great traitor. It was the accusation that he derived his power from the prince of evil that drew down the severest of all the rebukes that Jesus directed against those who would not accept him. If, seeing what is obviously good and according to the will of God, men can still declare that it is evil, what can even God do to help them out of the mental imprisonment that they have voluntarily chosen? (Mark 3:22–30).

Mark has placed Peter's confession (8:27–30) at the center and at the crucial point of his record.[16] Several points in this narrative require careful attention. In the first place, this is a typical example of the method of Jesus; he asks questions and leaves it to others to declare the conclusions that they have reached through their own observations. Secondly, this messianic confession comes at the most unmessianic moment of the career of Jesus. He has done nothing to fulfill the messianic role as interpreted by the people of his time and even by the disciples themselves; he has taken no advantage of the enthusiasm generated among the people by his miracles; he is not even in the Holy Land, but has gone outside it and is staying in the Hellenistic region of Caesarea Philippi. The significance for Mark of Peter's confession, and this is central in the entire theology of the Gospel, is that it is a confession of faith in Jesus, whatever he may do, and not in any stereotype of what God's Anointed One might be expected to be. Mark's Gospel throughout is a story of the unexpected and the paradoxical. And the very same passage that recounts the triumph of Peter's faith recounts its inadequacy—he was not yet ready to accept the paradox of a suffering Messiah, and in this he was followed by the vast majority of the Jews at the time at which Mark was writing.

Peter's confession took place privately and in a remote place; we are specifically told that a great crowd had gathered when blind Bartimaeus addressed Jesus by the unmistakably messianic title, "Jesus, son of David," and refused to be silenced by others who may

16. For a critical view of what actually happened on that occasion, see **Reginald H. Fuller,** *Foundations of New Testament Christology* (New York: Scribner's, 1965), pp. 109-11

have thought this attribution dangerous both to Jesus and to the one who made it (Mark 10:47–8). Mark has deliberately placed this incident just before the beginning of his passion narrative. Here is a story of the blind man who was able to see, and of those who ought to have been able to see and yet were blind. Once again the parallelism between Mark and John is striking; the story of the blind man in John 9 serves just the same purpose as the story of Bartimaeus, but in John the meaning is made quite explicit: some of the Pharisees ask Jesus, "Are we also blind?" He replies, "Now that you say, We see, your guilt remains" (John 9:40–41).

With notable artistic skill Mark has led his reader through these different answers to the question, Who is Jesus?, and has indicated the inadequacy of them all. What, by the time at which the Gospel was written, had long been recognized by the church as the true answer comes startlingly and unexpectedly, though obscurely, from the lips of a Gentile, when the centurion says of the dead Jesus, "Truly this man was a Son of God" (Mark 15:39).[17] That this was early felt to be surprising and inappropriate is plain from Luke's account, in which the centurion's exclamation is softened down to "Certainly this man was innocent" (Luke 23:47). So Mark has led the reader through those different answers, leaving it to him to work out for himself which of them are wholly unacceptable, which are partly correct, and which alone can be accepted as expressing the true solution of the christological question that the whole Gospel has been written to pose and to answer.

What then is the picture of Jesus Christ that the Gospel of Mark provides? It is a delineation of one who was in every sense a man; yet at three points it goes beyond the ordinary limits of humanity.

The picture is of one who possessed and used unlimited authority. The word recurs with surprising frequency, especially in the early chapters. But this authority is purely intrinsic, and unsupported by external or artificial guarantees. Jesus bids men leave their boats and nets and follow him, and calmly expects that they will obey, though the goal is undefined and the nature of the service demanded is unspecified (Mark 1:16–20). He commands the evil spirits and they obey him; it was this that especially aroused the astonishment of the crowds. But not less astonishing was his manner of teaching "as one that had authority and not as the scribes" (1:22). The Matthean contrast between what had been said to the men of old time and "I say unto you" is not found in express terms in

---

17. Jesus himself had rejected the witness of the evil spirits, since this was not based on the kind of faith that he desired to elicit (1:25; 3:12). The mind of the reader has been prepared by the divine utterance at the baptism; but as Mark records it, this seems at the time to have been limited to Jesus alone.

Mark, yet the idea is everywhere implicit. Here authority depends not on any human authorization or tradition; it is spontaneous and supremely self-confident. Jesus has no hesitation in condemning the tradition of the Jews, and interpreting the Old Testament with a liberality that is peculiar to himself.

What Mark writes must always be read with great care. He is recording the past, but he is all the time thinking in terms of his own day, and of the preaching that is going on in it. The authority that Jesus exercised in his earthly life is the authority he still exercises in the church. It is he who still calls men and women with his voice of sovereign authority and expects that they will follow him. It is his voice that echoes in the proclamations of the preachers, and confirms their word with signs following.[18]

The kingdom that Jesus proclaims is one in which man will be restored to his normal self through being restored to his normal relationship to God; this is what is meant by "believing" the good news (Mark 1:15). It is in the light of this affirmation that we are to understand the miracles of Jesus. Many of these "powers," as Mark usually calls them, are acts of restoration. The paralytic must be enabled to walk (2:11). The withered hand must again become useful (3:1-5). In two notable cases those who had been excluded from society are restored to it—the leper, whose uncleanness made him unfit to enjoy the fellowship of his kind, was made clean (1:40-44); the demoniac, whose story Mark lovingly unfolds in exceptional detail and who had long dwelt in isolation in the tombs, is now found clothed and in his right mind, once again in human society (5:15).

Stress is laid again and again on the fact that Jesus refuses to be regarded as a wonder-worker, a magician. Even those wonders that fall further outside the limits of normal human experience are told, not because they are surprising, but because they are signs of the reality of the kingdom. God is able to feed and care for his people even in the wilderness (6:32-44). Even if they are tempest-tossed and feel themselves forsaken, their Friend and Master is not far away from them (6:48-51).

Once again all these things have to be understood not as mere record but as contemporary challenge and appeal. Mark recorded these stories in order that Christian believers and inquirers might understand the things that they saw going on all around them. Christians belonged largely to the classes that had been despised and rejected of men; in Christ they found themselves accepted and

---

18. This expression is actually drawn from the conclusion of the Gospel that we have judged to be non-Marcan; but it sums up well a genuinely Marcan attitude.

restored to the fellowship of men.   Persecution had happened and
had become a reality; yet experience had shown that the Lord was
not far away, and could uphold and strengthen his threatened
people.

This kingdom, however, is one that will stir up and encounter
opposition.   Restoration must be bought at a price, and the price will
be paid by the One who has come to bring in the kingdom.   Mark
shows few signs of acquaintance with the developed theology of
Paul, and does not put forward anything that could be regarded as a
doctrine of the Atonement; indeed, in view of his evident purpose to
let his theology develop out of his narrative and to keep himself as
strictly as possible to the atmosphere of the period before the Resurrection, it would be strange if he had explicitly developed a theology
of the cross.   But it is not by accident that he included at a turn-
ingpoint in his narrative the saying, "the Son of man did not come to
be served but to serve, and to give up his life as a ransom for many"
(10:45).[19]   This is consistent with the method followed by Mark
throughout the Gospel in the presentation of his theology.   The
declaration that Jesus is a Son of God comes at the moment of his
greatest weakness and apparent defeat.   The Resurrection, when it
comes, will be the proclamation of a victory that has already been
won.

The Christians to whom Mark writes know themselves to be a
ransomed people.   That means that they are under obligation to
accept the law of the kingdom, which is the law of service and
obedience.   They must be willing to follow to the end.   There is no
guarantee for the disciple, any more than there was for the Master,
that he will be delivered from death.   In spite of his strong appeal
the cup did not pass from him (Mark 14:36).   But, for the disciple as
for the Master, there is the assurance that nothing can happen other
than that which is appointed by the will of God; and that, for them as
for him, the victory is won in the patient endurance of suffering.

When we inquire as to the identity of the Christian group for whom
this pioneer work was written, we plunge into a world of uncertainties.   There is no evidence on the basis of which a clear conclusion
can be reached.

Galilee is constantly mentioned in the Gospel.   This has led to the
suggestion, made among others by Willi Marxsen,[20] that the Gospel
was written for Galilean Christians at a time at which eschatological

---

19. We are not at this point discussing the form or the context in which Jesus may have uttered these words, but
only the part that they play in the Marcan presentation of the life of Jesus.
20. Following up suggestions earlier made by Professor Ernst Lohmeyer, *Galiläa und Jerusalem* (Göttingen:
Vandenhoek and Ruprecht, 1936).

expectation was very much in the air. This is not impossible but must be judged extremely unlikely. Proper names in the New Testament often have theological as well as geographical significance; but it is important not to press this principle too far, or we may easily land ourselves in absurdity. Galilee is "Galilee of the Gentiles" (Isa. 9:1), and therefore of special interest to Gentile readers, apart from the undoubted fact that the greater part of the ministry of Jesus did take place in Galilee. When in Mark 16:7 the risen Jesus is represented as saying "he is going before you to Galilee; there you will see him, as he told you," the first readers of the Gospel would be likely to catch an allusion to that extension of the Christian mission that had already taken place and was destined to determine the future of the church. But it is hardly likely that readers in Galilee would need the elaborate explanation of Jewish customs, for which Mark in 7:1–4 has spared so much of his precious space; these things would already have been familiar to such readers.

Ancient tradition associates Mark's Gospel with the church in Rome; it is probable that in this case tradition is correct. Rome was becoming the great center of movement in the Christian world, to which members of many churches streamed in and from which they carried information to every part of the Christian body. If we are right in thinking that this Gospel is closely connected with the evangelistic work of the church and the integrity of its preaching, no center more appropriate than Rome could be found for the production of such a work. If Rome was the place in which it was written, that would go far to explain the rapidity of diffusion implied in the use made of the Gospel by both Matthew and Luke. Rome had better facilities than any other city in the Roman Empire, with the single exception of Alexandria, for the copying and distribution of manuscripts. It is not likely that we shall ever know for certain; the balance of probability supports the view that the first of our Gospels was written in Rome, and at least some years before the fall of Jerusalem in A.D. 70.

The First Epistle General of Peter

The First Epistle of Peter[21] is a kind of waif among the writings of the New Testament. No one quite knows what to do with it, or where to fit it in. This can be illustrated from the great variety of authors, dates, and origins that have been assigned to this letter. In a single year (1946) two outstanding commentaries appeared. That

---

21. For convenience I use the traditional term "Peter" throughout, but without prejudging the question of the actual authorship of the Epistle.

by Dean Edward G. Selwyn,[22] full of classical lore and delicate insights, robustly maintained an early date and Petrine authorship, though recognizing that the unusual expression in 1 Pet. 5:12, "by Silvanus, a faithful brother as I regard him, I have written briefly," implies that Silvanus had had an unusually large share in the actual composition of the letter.   Francis W. Beare comes down with equal confidence on the side of a date in the second century.[23]   No one could doubt either the candor or the competence of these two scholars, who, on the basis of exactly the same evidence, have reached such divergent conclusions.

My own judgment is decisively in favor of an early date.   The writer bids his readers not to be surprised by the phenomenon of persecution, not to regard it as "a strange thing" (1 Pet. 4:12).   It is hard to see how any Christian in the Roman Empire, after the fierce persecution in Rome in A.D. 64–65, could regard persecution as a strange thing, even though he might not himself have been exposed to the fiery trial.   The Roman power had not on the whole been unfavorable to the Christian cause; Luke goes out of his way to stress the general friendliness of Roman officials.   But confidence in Roman justice had been suddenly shattered; the supreme power had become a persecuting power.   The Neronian persecution, indeed, lasted only a short time, and in spite of its ferocity had claimed a comparatively small number of victims.   But the protecting hand of God had been withdrawn from the flock; there could be no certainty as to where next the blow might fall.   The whole Epistle breathes the atmosphere of resolution; the duty of the Christian can be summed up in the words "stedfast in the faith" (1 Pet. 5:9 AV).

Although written in the form of a letter, the little work is in fact a homily, moving, as is the manner of homilies, from point to point without any clear logical structure.   The suggestion has been made that this is in fact a baptismal homily, the address of an overseer to those who have been, or are being, newly admitted to the fellowship.   This cannot be proved with any certainty, but the suggestion is not without its merits; the many practical precepts relating to the life of a dedicated minority in the midst of a potentially hostile and certainly critical majority fit well into such a situation.

Every commentator on the Epistle has drawn attention to the close similarity between the teaching of Peter and that of Paul; there seems to be an underlying unity of *kerygma*, "proclamation," on which Peter, no less than Paul, can draw.   Yet there are a great many

22. *The First Epistle of St. Peter: Greek Text with Introduction, Notes, and Essays*, 2nd ed. (London: Macmillan & Co., 1947).
23. *The First Epistle of Peter: the Greek Text with Introduction and Notes*, 3rd ed. (Oxford, Blackwell, 1970).

differences in detail and surprisingly little correspondence in language. Peter is an original writer with his own way of saying
things. This is the situation that can be observed equally in Mark's
Gospel; the theology is in a broad general sense Pauline, though
there is nowhere any sign of direct dependence on Paul's letters, and
the vocabulary is different. It is the general similarity of situation
that makes it reasonable to place 1 Peter in the same section with
Mark, since both are in all likelihood specimens of Roman theology
and speak to Christians who may at any time be called to face the
reality of persecution.

Attention may be drawn to some special features in the theology of
the Epistle.

It is the expression of particularly warm devotion to the person of
Jesus Christ. There is no exact parallel in the New Testament to the
phrase, "Without having seen him you love him" (1:8). Jesus is to
these Christians neither a character in what is now becoming a
somewhat remote historical past, nor a heavenly man, dwelling in
some distant and exalted sphere, but the well-known friend and
companion of daily life, who can also be appropriately referred to as
the Shepherd and Overseer of souls (2:25).[24]

But there is no doubt at all that this loving Shepherd is also the
Lord—and Lord in all spheres of the universe. The passage in 1 Pet.
3:18-22, in which Christ is spoken of as having preached to the
spirits in prison, has been the bane of expositors from early days until
the present time. But the key to the passage, which in many re-
spects is likely to remain obscure, would seem to lie in the word
"proclaimed"; this is not preaching with a view to conversion,
evangelization, but the declaration of a victory already achieved, by
which the whole universe has been affected.[25]

"Christ also suffered for you, leaving you an example, that you
should follow in his steps" (1 Pet. 2:21) strikes a note rather different
from the Pauline concept of the transformation of human nature from
within through the indwelling of the risen Christ through the Holy
Spirit. But the contrast must not be pressed too far. This single
verse of the Epistle cannot be made the foundation for an extensive
doctrine of the *Imitatio Christi*; such an imitation, if it were possible, would be undesirable. In one point only does the writer urge
his readers to follow the example of Christ—in the willingness to
suffer, as He also has suffered. "He has suffered; you too must be

---

24. The Epistle is fully christocentric. The Spirit is not absent but there are only five clear references to him.
This is one of the points at which the Petrine is distinct from the Pauline theology.
25. Cf. Rev. 5:2. It is not, however, to be thought that the word here translated "proclaimed" is used in the New
Testament exclusively in reference to supernatural proclamation. It is found in other senses also.

willing to suffer; this is the badge of the Christian." Yet the exemplary character of the life and particularly of the death of Christ has been overlooked in many systems of theology; we know what it would mean for us to live as sons of God only because Christ before us has lived as a Son of God, and has made plain to us the meaning of the term.

The ethical teaching of the Epistle is not unlike that set forth in the later Epistles of Paul, though less systematized. This ethical emphasis is unpleasing to some who regard it as a falling away from the freedom and spontaneity of the gospel and a reinstatement of the Law. But this is a misunderstanding. It is true that Paul affirms that "love is the fulfilling of the law" (Rom. 13:10). His great successor St. Augustine expresses it even more tersely: love and do whatever you like. Basing themselves on such utterances the propagators of "situation ethics" put forward the idea that love is enough, and that, if the principle of love is accepted, the right decisions can be made and carried out in each of the infinitely varied experiences of human life. This view suffers from two obvious defects. First, this view tends to isolate the individual or two individuals from the general stream of human life in a way that is practically impossible, and is not admitted by the New Testament—we are all members one of another. Second, this view assumes that the nature of love is already and generally known; this again is not admitted in the New Testament. The *agape* of which the New Testament speaks is the utterly self-giving, unselfregarding love of God as revealed in Jesus Christ; and this can be learned only by those who have accepted Jesus Christ as Lord.

This, essentially, was the objection raised by the Jewish party against Paul's idea that Gentiles could be admitted to the church without undergoing the preliminary discipline of the Law. The Old Testament had taught the love of God and the principle of obligation, though in a manner that must be judged imperfect by New Testament standards. Those who had been influenced by this older revelation had so far been prepared to receive the fuller revelation of love given in Jesus Christ. But the scandals in the church of Corinth and elsewhere had brought it home to Paul that Gentile Christians would not immediately understand the nature of the obligations that they had taken upon themselves in baptism, and that they would hardly be able to work out for themselves practical applications from the splendid abstractions of Paul's hymn to love (1 Corinthians 13). It is this that explains tne increasing ethical emphasis to be found in Paul's later Epistles and in the later books of the New Testament generally. To this rule 1 Peter is no exception.

There is, however, a difference between the Pauline and Petrine applications of the rule of love. Paul's starting point, notably in Colossians, is the idea of the one new man. If the reality of the new man in Christ has been apprehended, certain faults, such as lying and stealing, hardly need to be reproved; they are obviously absurd and self-contradictory (Col. 3:5 ff., esp. 3:9). Such are the fruits in Christian living of a correct analysis of *agape*—and there is no other source or origin for Christian ethical standards. Peter is thinking of the friends to whom he writes as "strangers and pilgrims" (1 Pet. 3:11 AV), a small minority living in a world, the standards and manners of which are contrary to their beliefs. He is, of course, concerned with the community—its unity in love and mutual service ("love the brethren" [2:17])—but even more with the influence of righteous conduct on the reputation of the brotherhood in the world and on the power of witness that it can exercise. "They speak against you as wrongdoers" (2:12); "whereas they speak evil of you, as of evildoers, they may be ashamed that falsely accuse your good conversation in Christ" (3:16 AV). Such utterances are not alien to the thought of Paul, who tells his friends that they are to shine as lights in the world (Phil. 2:15); they do seem, however, to be a specially marked feature of the Petrine presentation of the gospel. "Ethics" and "dogmatics" are nowhere in the New Testament separate disciplines; belief and conduct are always closely related. The writer of this Epistle makes no attempt to separate them; he merely emphasizes certain aspects of the gospel that his friends might be in danger of overlooking.

The organization of the church seems to be rather more fully developed than in the Pauline correspondence. The author writes as a presbyter to presbyters, and the term seems already to have acquired something of the official character that later became regularly attached to it. We see already the dangers of clerical autocracy, and of a grudging exercise of the Christian ministry (1 Pet. 5:1–4). Yet these brief indications must not be pressed too far. Naturally, in any community the older men take the lead; within a very short time what began as a free association of older and wiser men may constitute itself a self-reproducing oligarchy. And the term "presbyter" itself has no official significance; it means simply "an old man"; what other significance it may have is to be read into it in each particular context.

The author feels it right to send this special message to fellow-presbyters; but his ideal is still that of the simple fellowship in which each serves all the rest in the spirit of love, and in which the word of the Lord that he who will be great must become the servant of all has not been forgotten.

A rapid perusal of this little tract, which could so easily have disappeared, leaves on the mind of the reader an astonishing impression of completeness. If all the rest of the New Testament had been lost and we had only this single specimen of early Christian writing, would we lack anything that is essential to Christian belief and to the life of godliness? It is true that the writer does not sound the same depths as Paul or reach the same heights as John; but he does place before us fair and square the picture of one who suffered, "the righteous for the unrighteous that he might bring us to God" (3:18), and lays upon us uncompromisingly the obligation of total surrender and commitment to him.

5

The Tradition of Israel: Matthew, James, Hebrews, Revelation

What in the world is the Christian church to do with the Old Testament? This is a question that has perplexed and embarrassed every generation of Christian expositors; we cannot do with it, and we cannot do without it.

In the second century, Marcion, later rejected by the church as a heretic, solved the problem simply and dramatically by excluding the Old Testament altogether as belonging to a different world of religion from that of Christianity. A neo-Marcionite point of view has recently been put forward by the distinguished Arabist J. Spencer Trimingham in an interesting and provocative book, *Two Worlds are Ours*. According to him Jesus was not and could not be the Messiah of the Jews:

> The retention of a library of Hebrew literature claiming divine sanction
> . . . set up an inner conflict within Christian thought which has never
> been resolved. . . . The Christian church should consider whether it is
> wise to retain the Jewish Bible at all as an authoritative part of its
> canonical writings.[1]

This is not the place to argue out this question in detail. We are here concerned only to note the profound and continuing influence exercised by the traditions of Israel on the development of Christian theology during the New Testament period and far beyond it.

After the fall of Jerusalem in A.D. 70, Jewish Christianity became the faith of a dwindling and eventually separated minority. But within the most orthodox centers of Gentile Christianity the Old Testament continued to play a highly influential role. Four writings stand out as lying particularly within the magnetic field of Jewish influence—the Gospel according to Matthew, the Epistle of James, the Epistle to the Hebrews, and the Revelation (Apocalypse) of

1. (Beirut: Librairie du Liban, 1971), p. 45.

John. It is with the study of these four books that we shall be concerned in this chapter.

The Gospel According to Matthew

Toward the end of our study we shall make some remarks on the origin and place of writing of the Gospel of Matthew. Here it is sufficient to state that this work incorporates almost the whole of Mark's Gospel; that its many correspondences with Luke indicate a common use of what has come to be known as Q material, especially in the reporting of speeches and utterances of the Lord; but that Matthew had access to a source or sources, written or unwritten, of the greatest possible importance, of which no use is made in any other Gospel. The adoption of so much Marcan material is an indication that Matthew is later than Mark;[2] this Gospel appears to have been written late rather than early in what we have agreed to call the Gospel-writing period.

Even on a rapid reading of the Gospel it becomes clear that it is a most carefully constructed work, in this resembling Luke, and thus sharply distinguished from Mark, whose genius as a narrator is not equalled by skill as the architect of a book. The Matthean material is grouped in five large blocks, each marked by a major speech of Jesus: the Sermon on the Mount (5–7); the Woes of the Disciples (10); the Parables of the Kingdom (13); the Nature of the Church (18); and the Days of the Future (23–25). Each is concluded by some such remark as "when Jesus had ended all these sayings" (7:28; 11:1; 13:53; 19:1; 26:1). Although Matthew follows Mark fairly closely when he is making use of him, he is by no means slavish in his methods and makes it plain that he is master of his material; everything will be constrained to serve his purpose, and will be fitted into the development of his theme as he has planned it. Some have attempted to draw a parallel between Matthew's five sections and the five books of the Law in the Pentateuch, but this can hardly be established; it is much more likely that Matthew regarded his book as a work in seven sections (seven being the perfect number according to the Jews), the birth narratives and the passion story together with the five central sections making up the seven.

The generally accepted view is that Matthew is the Gospel for the Jews, and that the Lord is presented in this Gospel as the King of the Jews. Up to a point we shall find this to be true, but not without qualification.

2. It must be borne in mind, however, that some scholars still, following St. Augustine, hold that the borrowing is the other way, that Matthew is the first and original Gospel and that Mark is the abbreviator. Bishop Basil Christopher Butler, among others, is a champion of the priority of Matthew in *The Originality of Matthew: A Critique of the Two-document Hypothesis* (Cambridge, 1951). But quite recently John C. O'Neill has written to "reopen old questions and to question old assumptions" in "The Synoptic Problem," *NTS*, January 1975, pp. 273–85.

The Jewish character of the Gospel is shown unmistakably in the first chapter, where the rather artificially constructed genealogy of Jesus of Nazareth presents him as the Son of Abraham.

The writer thinks throughout in Old Testament categories, and finds Old Testament parallels where we would not be likely to find them. The nature of his view of inspiration needs a little elucidation. It can be summed up in the words of a well-known hymn: "No word from thee can fruitless fall." Every word of the Old Testament has prophetic significance; sooner or later each word must find its fulfillment, and many words find fulfillment in Jesus of Nazareth that will be looked for elsewhere in vain. The suffering servant of Isaiah 53 is the Servant of the Lord in the Gospel, who himself has borne our afflictions and carried our sorrows (Matt. 8:17). When Hosea writes "Out of Egypt have I called my son" (Hos. 11:1), the reference is quite clearly to the Exodus, in which the people of Israel literally came out of Egypt; but by the process that Irenaeus was later to call "recapitulation," Matthew sees the ancient history of Israel renewed and fulfilled in more perfect fashion in the footsteps of the Son of man (2:15). This method of citation would be more readily understood by a Jewish reader than by those whose minds have been trained in the critical methods of Western literary studies.

At one point the Jewish watermark on the Gospel is apparent, even obtrusive. We find here a number of sayings in which it seems to be implied that the Jewish Law is still in force without modification. There can be little doubt that there were Christians of the first and second generations who held exactly this view—that Jesus was no revolutionary, but rather one who guaranteed the eternity of the Jewish covenant by filling it at certain points with a new and more spiritual meaning. There is no reason to doubt that Jesus did actually say, "Think not that I have come to abolish the law and the prophets; I have come not to abolish them but to fulfill them" (Matt. 5:17). It may be thought that the comment that follows, "Whoever then relaxes one of the least of these commandments and teaches men so, shall be called least in the kingdom of heaven" (5:19), is an interpretative clause added to the saying of Jesus by Jewish Christians who did not understand the sense in which Jesus used the words "abolish" and "fulfill," and included by Matthew in his Gospel since this was the form in which the tradition had come down to him. When Matthew adds to the Lord's statement of the two great commandments the explanation "On these two commandments depend all the law and the prophets," he may again be quoting a Judeo-Christian gloss, though taken strictly the words mean no more than what was expressed by Paul when he wrote "love is the fulfilling of the law" (Rom. 13:10).

The Jewish emphasis is everywhere present in the Gospel, but this does not mean that it was written for Jews with a view to making them Christians. This is, in point of fact, the only one of the four Gospels that shows no sign of an evangelistic purpose. It is a church Gospel written for the edification of Christians. Indeed there are reasons for thinking that it was intended to be read aloud in Christian worship[3] and therefore belongs to the beginning of that period in which Christians began to be aware that they had Scriptures of their own and that they need no longer be wholly dependent on the Old Testament.

The Jews are there, but they are there to serve as an awful warning: "It happened to them; it could happen to you. The day of grace came to them and they refused it, so the kingdom was taken away from them; if you in your turn refuse your day of grace, exactly the same judgment can fall upon you." This note of judgment runs all through the Gospel and from time to time is expressed in most menacing terms: "Many will come from east and west and sit at table with Abraham, Isaac, and Jacob in the kingdom of heaven, while the sons of the kingdom will be thrown into the outer darkness; there men will weep and gnash their teeth" (Matt. 8:11–12). It is no accident that, in this carefully constructed Gospel, the first story recorded is that of the wise men from the East. Christian poetic fantasy has so played upon this remarkable narrative that the inner significance of it is hardly ever realized. It is a story of those who knew hardly anything and found everything, and of those who knew everything and found nothing. The chief priests and scribes, when asked where Messiah was to be born, could come up immediately with the right answer from the Book of Micah (5:2); but it never occurred to them to go to Bethlehem and to ascertain what, if anything, had happened. The wise men did not even know where to look; but their following of the ambiguous testimony of a star led them to exceeding great joy (Matt. 2:10).

Matthew's Gospel is written for those who had lost their first love, and were in danger of allowing superficial knowledge to take the place of the depths of faith and of obedience. This does not necessarily imply a very late date for the Gospel. If, as some not unreasonably hold, Matthew was writing for the great church of Antioch and reflects some of the traditions that were current in that church, we need not allow for a period of more than fifty years between the first preaching of the gospel and the descent to a level of spiritual life that made the writing of such a Gospel necessary.

---

3. My friend and teacher Alexander Nairne used to refer to Matthew as the liturgical Gospel. See George D. Kilpatrick, *The Origins of the Gospel According to St. Matthew* (Oxford, 1946), chap. 5, "The Liturgical Character of the Gospel."

Every missionary is familiar with the problem of the "third generation." The late great Bishop Azariah of Dornakal in South India
directed for thirty-two years an extensive movement of simple village people into the church. At the end of that time he found himself
perplexed and frustrated by the attitude of Christians to whom the
faith was no longer a courageous venture into the unknown, but a
rather tepid acceptance of something that had already become part of
the tradition of the fathers. This new generation was more moral but
less religious than that of their grandfathers. They were far better
instructed in the intellectual content of the faith; but this seemed to
lead to acquiescence in what they had been taught rather than to
dynamic spiritual achievement. All this had come about in less than
fifty years from the beginning of the movement.

If such a loss or diminution of the faith has occurred, how is that
which has been lost to be restored? Matthew's answer is a return to
the original sources of the gospel in the life and mission of Jesus of
Nazareth himself. There must be stern denunciations and warnings
of judgment, and these are somewhat liberally supplied in this Gospel. Far more important is a recovery of a sense of who it is that the
Christians are confessing when they make the declaration that Jesus
is Lord, a new awareness of the stringency of his demand for a new
kind of life and of the urgency with which the message was proclaimed to the original hearers. "Not everyone who says to me
'Lord, Lord' shall enter the kingdom of heaven" (Matt. 7:21).

Jesus is Lord. This is the theme of the Gospel. But what does it
mean to confess Jesus as Lord in sincerity and truth? In each of the
five great discourses the lordship of Jesus is presented, in each under
a different aspect.

Chapters 5–7: *Jesus as the Lord of the Covenant*

Moses was the great lawgiver, who combined in himself the functions of prophet, priest, and king. Jesus is here set forth as the new
Moses, who has the boldness, indeed the hardihood, to proclaim,
"You have heard that it was said to the men of old . . . but I say to you"
(5:21, 22). This was an astonishing, in the eyes of Jews a blasphemous, claim to authority. Lawyers and scribes could annotate and
expound the Law of Moses; it was taken for granted that that law,
having come from God himself, could not in any serious way be
modified, let alone rescinded. Here, as in Mark, we encounter One
who speaks with an authority that is intrinsic, requiring no credentials other than the obvious rightness and truth of the declarations
that he makes. Great labor has been expended on finding parallels
in the Rabbinic writings to the sayings of Jesus and not altogether

without sucess.   No parallels, however, can dim the originality of the teaching of Jesus as a whole; he really is talking about God in a new way.   Indeed it is hardly an exaggeration to say that he is talking about a new kind of God.

The Sermon on the Mount is often referred to as though it was a general manual of ethical conduct with a special stress on kindness and tolerance.   It is nothing of the kind.   Apart from belief in the God in whom Jesus believed and whom he proclaimed it has no meaning; apart from implicit obedience to Jesus who proclaimed it, it has no importance.   It is, in fact, a terrifying document.   No other religious leader has ever laid down the rule, "love your enemies" (5:44).   Expositors have often been tempted to evade the stark implications of this commandment.   But this is to treat the text unfairly.   Words are always used by Jesus in the fullness of their meaning.   "Love" means an unlimited and unconditioned willingness to serve; your "enemy" is the man who is out to take away your life.

The originality of Jesus is perhaps shown more clearly in his prescription for happiness in what are commonly called the Beatitudes than in any other context.   Francis Bacon delivered himself of the pregnant judgment that prosperity is the blessing of the Old Testament and adversity of the New.   He was not far from the mark. Deuteronomy, the summing up of the ancient Law, is full of blessings, for the most part of a material kind—on harvest and the fertility of cattle, on the succession of family and children, and so on.   Happiness as seen by Jesus and reported by Matthew involves total self-commitment to the kingdom of God, the renunciation of personal rights, and the willingness to endure suffering and persecution even unto death for the Name.

Chapter 10: *Jesus the Lord of the Disciples*

In chapter 10, as elsewhere, Matthew seems to have gathered into one long and eloquent discourse sayings of Jesus that belonged originally to other contexts and to various periods in the ministry. Once again the emphasis here is on the absolute authority of Jesus, his right to call and to send men as he wills, and to demand of them the utmost in sacrifice and self-giving.   The validation of this claim lies, of course, in the cross of Jesus—the Master will not send the disciple to face anything that he himself is not willing to face.   To this there is no direct allusion in the chapter, except in the phrase, "it is enough for the disciple to be like his teacher, and the servant like his master" (10:25); but the thought of the cross seems to have been constantly present in the mind of Matthew as he compiled the discourse.

Here the expositor is confronted by a problem that runs through the whole of New Testament theology, and indeed through the whole of church history. In all ages the church of Jesus Christ has been persecuted—though there have been periods longer and shorter of the "peace of the church." But why in the world should Christians be persecuted? Their only desire is to live at peace with all men and to serve as they are able. Why then this tragic record of sufferings? The enemies of Jesus seem to have understood him in some ways better than the disciples. They saw, as the disciples did not, that Jesus is the great revolutionary, whose teaching, when taken seriously, undermines all existing social orders and constitutions of society, and almost every form of organized religion. Caste in India and tribalism in Africa inescapably feel themselves threatened by the gospel; persecution is usually justified not on religious grounds but on the basis of the conviction that the Christians have shown themselves to be the enemies of mankind, or at least the enemies of the existing social order. There is no reason to suppose that this situation will be radically modified this side of the Second Coming of Christ; his teaching cannot be reconciled with the many refuges of the spirit that mankind constructs for itself; the more closely Christians set themselves to follow Christ, the more certain it is that Matthew 10 will be found to have set out accurately the fate of the disciples and the destiny of the church in the world.

Chapter 13: *Christ the Lord of the Kingdom*

We have many parables from the lips of Jesus. Why did Matthew select just these seven to serve as a panorama of the kingdom and of the demands that it makes of those who desire to enter into it? The answer may be given in a phrase that is used a number of times in this Gospel: "many are called but few are chosen."

Extensive studies have been made in recent years, notably by C. H. Dodd and Joachim Jeremias,[4] of the original form and meaning of the parables and of their setting in the life and ministry of Jesus. As the church told these stories again and again in worship and in the work of Christian teaching, they tended to undergo modification and to be understood not so much as part of the messianic preaching of Jesus as in relation to the contemporary needs and problems of the church. The interpretations given of the parables of the sower and the tares (13:18–23; 13:36–43) seem to have grown out of the reflections and meditations of the worshipping church. When Matthew selects certain parables and interprets them in the light of his own theology, and of the situation of the church he is addressing, he is

4. Charles H. Dodd, *Parables of the Kingdom* (New York: Scribner's, 1961) and Joachim Jeremias, *The Parables of Jesus* (New York: Scribner's, 1954; rev. eds 1963, 1971).

simply exercising that freedom in the arrangement and organization of material that we have seen to be characteristic of the art of Gospel-writing in the early church.

Two of the parables in chapter 13 express the exclusive nature of the claim that the kingdom makes upon those who would enter into it. The finder of the hidden treasure and the merchant seeking goodly pearls both have to sell all that they possess in order to obtain the object of their desire (13:44–46). "Who chooseth me must give and hazard all he hath."[5]

Three of the parables contain the idea of selection and rejection. Much good seed is sown but much is lost; of the four types of hearers enumerated in the interpretation only one is found acceptable in the end (13:18–23). The field of the farmer will yield a mixed crop. The judgment of God seems to be delayed and must not be anticipated by overzealous servants; but in the end the judgment will be inexorable and irrevocable (13:37–43). Any net cast into the sea is likely to bring up a mixed catch of good and of worthless fish. No sensible fisherman is likely to burden himself with the unprofitable; there is bound to be a process of selection in which only the useful will be retained (13:47–51).

The intensity and severity of the warnings can have one purpose only—to remind those who profess and call themselves Christians that much more is required than mere outward conformity. The kingdom of heaven is the greatest of all possible possessions; but there can be no such thing as cheap salvation; there is no place in that kingdom for divided or conditional loyalties.[6]

Chapter 18: *Jesus the Lord of the Church*

Every student of the Gospels knows that the word *ekklesia*, "church," occurs three times only in the four Gospels, and that these occurrences are all in Matthew (16:18, 18:17). The flexibility of the New Testament vocabulary is so great that this fact need not in itself be considered especially significant. It remains, however, true that Matthew is the ecclesiastical Gospel; the concerns of a developed Christian fellowship are more clearly reflected in it than in the other three.

There has been much argument, not all of it very profitable, on the question of whether Jesus ever intended to found a church at all. In part this is an argument about words. Whereas English has only one

---

5. Shakespeare is not infrequently a good commentator on the New Testament. The quotation is from *The Merchant of Venice*, act 2, sc. 7.

6. For an interesting analysis and exposition of this chapter with special reference to the themes of "rejection" and "acceptance," see Jack D. Kingsbury, *The Parables of Jesus in Matthew 13* (Naperville: Allenson, 1969).

word in common use, "church," German has two—*Kirche*, which nearly always carries some connotation of formal organization, and *Gemeinde*, which suggests fellowship rather than order.   In Matt. 16:18, "on this rock I will build my church," Luther in his German translation rendered *ekklesia* by *Gemeinde*.   The first great English translator of the sixteenth century, William Tyndale, basing his translation to some extent on that of Luther, tried to bring in "congregation" as the regular rendering for *ekklesia*, for exactly the same reason—that the word "church" had come too much to suggest the medieval church with its wealth and its top-heavy organization, and not the simple fellowship of the original disciples.   But he has not been generally followed; whether we like it or not, in English we are churchmen.

If, then, our question means, Did Jesus foresee all the future developments of the community of believers and make provision for them?, the answer must be decisively No.   Jesus shows himself for the most part unconcerned about organization, and, in contrast with that other great religious leader, the prophet Muhammad, left his followers singularly few rules to guide them in their pilgrimage.   If, on the other hand, we are asking whether at a fairly early stage of his ministry Jesus foresaw that a new community would come into being, of which he himself would be the center, the answer must be an equally decisive Yes.   The appointment of the Twelve was more than the selection of an especially intimate group of hearers; these are the representatives of Israel as the people takes on a new shape based on a new allegiance.   And when Jesus says, "It shall not be so among you" (Matt. 20:26; see also Mark 10:43), he is indicating the existence of a fellowship that will be held together by certain principles which will separate it from all the many fellowships also existent upon the earth.[7]

By the time that Matthew's Gospel came to be written, fifty years of the existence of this new community had made it clear that even the fellowship of which Jesus is the head cannot maintain itself in unsullied purity.   "Offences," scandals, will of necessity creep in, and the community, if it is to survive, must take steps to guard itself against the disintegration that follows upon the undue toleration of "offences" (18:7–14).[8]   One of the prerogatives of every community is that of deciding who does and who does not belong to it.   In the last resort the Christian community may have to declare, after due warning, that this or that member is no longer a member—he has

---

7. This is well worked out in Robert N. Flew, *Jesus and His Church*, 2nd ed. (London: Epworth Press, 1951).
8. The RSV translation, "temptation to sin," is not a very happy paraphrase of a word that is difficult to translate.

made himself as a Gentile and a tax collector (18:15–20). But this is not the whole story. The provision for excommunication is immediately followed by the splendid hyperbole of the answer given by Jesus to Peter's question about forgiveness—not seven times but seventy times seven; in this the true nature of the redeemed community is seen (18:21–22). And this lesson is reinforced by the parable of the lord who, faced with the servant who owed him an enormous sum, was moved with compassion (that favorite word of Jesus), and generously forgave him the whole (18:23–30).

Chapters 24-25: *Jesus the Lord of the Future*

As regards eschatological expectation, Matthew is largely dependent on Mark and adds little that can be called original. He does stress the suddenness and unexpectedness of the coming of the end. In the Old Testament the flood came upon a careless people at a moment at which it was wholly unprepared for catastrophe (24:38–9): "so will be the coming of the Son of man." No man knows when that hour will be; the only possible preparation is constant watchfulness and readiness, qualities in which Matthew seems to find the church of his own day deficient.

What Matthew has added to the teaching of chapter 24 is the set of three parables of judgment in chapter 25—the ten virgins; the three servants; the sheep and the goats. The offenses for which the failures are condemned are carelessness, timidity, and insensitiveness. The attendants on the bridegroom knew perfectly well that they would have long to wait; they had had ample time to make provision. The idle servant knew his lord's nature; he should have been willing to take at least the minimum risk to show a profit at the lord's return. The "goats" needed only a little more sensitiveness to the needs of others, and they too would have ministered to the Lord in his brethren, and have shared in the reward accorded to the "sheep." The demands of the Lord are always exacting but they are not unreasonable; they will be recognized as obligations by those who have taken seriously what is involved in the confession of Jesus as Lord.

Matthew lacks, perhaps, the vigor and attention to detail that make the writing of Mark perennially attractive. But his Gospel has an amplitude and a dignity that account for its being placed first in almost every list of the Gospels and its having been through the centuries the favorite Gospel of the church. And of all the Gospels this is the one that leads up to the most splendid conclusion.

I have suggested elsewhere[9] that the concluding verses of the

9. In a little book called *What We Know About Jesus*, World Christian Books no. 60 (London: Lutterworth Press, 1970), pp. 83–84.

Gospel (28:16–20) are to be taken as Matthew's summary of the Resurrection proclamation rather than as actual words of Jesus himself; but that such words could equally well have been written by almost any faithful Christian of the second or the third generation as the expression of his own experience of what it means to be a Christian.

He had seen that all power has been committed to Jesus Christ in heaven and on earth. He had experienced this in observing the transformed lives of men and women drawn out of a world of sin, and in the creation of fellowship where the world had decreed inequality, separation, and division.

The old limitation of the covenant of God to the Jewish people had now been done away with in the exaltation of Jesus as Lord. The church was now faced with a task that would be coextensive with the inhabited world and that, as one generation succeeded to another, would last until the end of time.

The church would go out into a world of suffering and conflict. But there would be no cause for anxiety or despondency. The Resurrection had made permanent and universally available the presence of that Master who had come to the disciples, walking on the turbulent waves, when they were in terror and peril of death. That presence, guaranteed "to the close of the age," was the pledge of victory and of the fulfillment of all the purposes of God.

The Epistle of James

The Epistle of James presents us with a multitude of problems. Its origins are clearly in the Jewish world, so much so that some scholars have thought that it was originally a Jewish work, later rather superficially adapted to Christian use. But it is written in excellent Greek, with a wide vocabulary of words found nowhere else in the New Testament. It does not read like a translation, and seems to be the product of a vigorous and imaginative mind, expressing itself freely in a language in which it is completely at home. The questions of date, authorship, and purpose remain perplexing, and there is as yet no agreement about them.[10]

In one of the most learned commentaries ever written on any book of the New Testament, Professor Joseph B. Mayor assembled every possible argument in favor of James the brother of the Lord and head of the Jerusalem church as author of this Epistle.[11] This accumulation of argument has not proved generally convincing, and those

---

10. The difficulty about language becomes much less if we take the view, which is gaining ground, that the Hellenistic element in early Christianity among the Jews was much stronger than we had earlier supposed. That community may well have included members capable of writing excellent and idiomatic Greek.

11. *The Epistle of St. James: The Greek Text with Introduction, Notes and Comments* (London: Macmillan and Co., 1892; 2d. ed. 1913).

who would defend this traditional ascription of authorship are a minority among scholars.[12]   But another section of Mayor's minute study of the Epistle does seem to have yielded results of permanent value.   It is true that the name of Jesus Christ occurs only rarely in the Epistle.   But too many conclusions should not be drawn from this omission, since the Epistle has the character of a homily and not of a dogmatic treatise.   What is notable is that the teaching of James corresponds at point after point with the teaching of Jesus, especially as that is given in Matthew's Gospel.   The only at all exact verbal correspondence is in the last chapter: "let your yes be yes and your no be no, that you may not fall under condemnation" (James 5:12; cf. Matt. 5:33–7).   But this is only one obvious link and echo, alongside many that are subtle and less obvious.   It is unlikely that the writer had before him a copy of the Gospel; it is possible to say with some confidence that he was familiar with one of the streams of tradition on which Matthew drew for the composition of the Gospel, that the tradition had a specifically Jewish character, and that we are therefore right in studying this Epistle immediately after the Gospel according to Matthew.

Martin Luther, as is well known, had a low opinion of this Epistle on the ground that it did not effectively "put forward the case of Jesus Christ," and so dismissed it as an "epistle of straw."   Great man as he was, Luther was at times at the mercy of his prejudices.   He must at one time have studied the Epistle of James, which he translated into German along with all the other books of the New Testament.   But he seems never to have asked himself what the teaching of the Epistle really is, whether the apparent disagreement with Paul is as profound as he imagined it to be, and whether the teaching of this Epistle on the subject of faith is not an indispensable complement to that of Paul himself.[13]

The Epistle seems to belong to just that stage in the life of a church that we have already identified in Matthew.   There is outward conformity and regular worship.   Christians are no longer only the poor and needy but may even appear in church in fine clothing and wearing a golden ring (James 2:2–3).   But where is the transformation of character without which an assembly cannot be an assembly of the people of Christ?

We may turn at once to the central and contentious subject of the

---

12. But see Bibliography, below.

13. The whole "Preface" is now readily available to students in Werner G. Kümmel, *The New Testament: The History of the Investigation of its Problems* (Nashville: Abingdon, 1972).   This will enable the English reader to form his own estimate of Luther as a New Testament critic, and to consider how far his judgment is acceptable.

meaning of the word "faith" in this Epistle. Faith, as Paul understood it, looks back to the past, to what Jesus Christ has done once for all, and to the promises of God made real and effectual to us in him, though not excluding the consequences of faith as these are to be realized in Christian living. The concern of James is with the immediate present, and with practical obedience to the will of God. Faith is in fact for him immediate obedience to the command of God. This is certainly a different sense from that in which Paul uses the word; but is it for that reason illegitimate? With two forms of pseudo-faith James has no patience. There is the faith that is no more than intellectual assent to a formula. Any intelligent schoolboy can learn the Apostles' Creed by heart in twenty minutes, recite quite correctly "and in Jesus Christ his only Son our Lord," and yet have no intention of following out the demands implied in what he has correctly learned and repeated as the essential content of the faith. On such faith James remarks succinctly that the demons also believe and tremble (2:19). Even worse is the faith that accepts in theory the demands of faith but in practice denies them; that says to the hungry "be warmed and fed" (2:16) but will not lift a finger to ensure that the hungry and needy really receive that of which they stand in need. Both these forms of faith are found in the church in every age; the warnings given in this Epistle will never be out of date.

Paul's teaching on faith was peculiarly open to misunderstanding and abuse. He himself admits that in his own lifetime he was accused of teaching antinomianism: if you believe it does not matter in the least what you do (see Rom. 3:1–8). This was an obvious calumny. More dangerous is the exaltation of faith at the expense of good works to the point at which faith itself may appear as a good work, indeed as the only good work that can be demanded of a Christian. On this can follow a complacent self-satisfaction that disregards the plain demands of Christian charity.

It is unlikely that James had seen any of the Epistles of Paul. It is not even necessary to suppose that he had any direct knowledge of Paul's teaching on justification by faith or that he was deliberately criticizing it. He was aware of the spread of teaching, as far removed as could be imagined from the intense moral earnestness of Paul, which was threatening to paralyze the effective witness of the church. Paradoxically he takes the very text from Genesis (15:6) about the faith of Abraham that Paul had used as one the pillars of his own doctrine, and turns it to serve a very different purpose. He does make use of the term "justify," but once again he uses it in a sense different from that intended by Paul. We may translate it "vindicate," and this is a perfectly legitimate sense of the term: Abraham was vindicated as a true believer in God by his immediate willingness to obey the mysterious command to sacrifice his only son (James 2:21). If Paul had ever encountered the letter of James, he would no doubt have been surprised at the turn that the argument had taken; but he knew Greek well enough to recognize that, in a situation very different from that in which he had written the Epistle to the Galatians, James was right in emphasizing an aspect of faith with which he had not felt himself called to deal.

Apart from a number of difficult verses there are few books in the New Testament that stand so little in need of a commentary as the Epistle of James. If we use the term "theology" in the narrow sense of dogmatic theology, and ask what contribution James has made to the development of the Christian creeds, the answer may be "precious little." If, however, we understand theology in the broader sense of the elucidation of all that the coming of Jesus Christ has meant to the life of the world, we shall accord him a high place among our teachers. He deals with life in the church as it actually is; the reader finds himself forcibly arraigned by his pungent and picturesque accusations. "The tongue is a little member and boasts of great things . . . the tongue is a fire. The tongue is an unrighteous world among our members . . . set on fire by hell" (3:5, 6, 8). Then as now gossip seems to have been one of the great evils in the life of the church. Then as now there was no Christian virtue more important than charity in speech and none more difficult to practice.

In chapter 5 the style of James rises to the eloquence and power of that of an Old Testament prophet. In the society he knows there is a possessing class. It manifests all the characteristics of that class—vanity, self-indulgence, arrogant disregard of the elementary principles of social justice (5:1–6). James does not urge the oppressed, as some Christian leaders of our own day are inclined to do, to fly to arms in defense of their rights. He rests upon the certainty of judgment: these things are not a matter of indifference to the Lord of hosts, and one day in the coming of the Son of man his judgment will be revealed from heaven (5:7–9). In the New Testament there is comparatively little about what a later age has learned to call social justice. If we neglect the message of James, we may fail to realize that this also is an essential aspect of Christian concern.

The Epistle to the Hebrews

The writer of the Epistle to the Hebrews is the great anonymous of the New Testament. Once it had been recognized that, though much of the thought of this great work is Pauline, it is impossible that it could have been written by Paul himself or even under his direction—style and thought decisively rule out the possibility—lists of candidates for the authorship began to be drawn up and to grow.   Luther suggested Apollos, and this is a conjecture that has won favor with a number of later scholars.   All that we know of the earlier history of Apollos is that he was an eloquent man and that he came from Alexandria (Acts 18:24–28).   The writer to the Hebrews was certainly an eloquent man.   His Greek is the best in the New Testament, and he alone among the New Testament writers makes use of acknowledged rhetorical forms and schemes.   Experts have noted parallels between his handling of the Old Testament and that practiced by the learned Philo of Alexandria, an older contemporary of Paul and of the writer to the Hebrews, a Jew who wrote copiously in the attempt to make available the profundity of Hebrew thinking, in Greek dress, to his own people and to others as well.   So Apollos is certainly a suitable candidate for the honor of being accepted as the writer of the Epistle.   But if we are wise we shall be content to answer this question, like so many others that arise in our study of the New Testament, with the simple admission, "We do not know."   We shall be in good company.   The great Origen, as quoted by Eusebius,[14] tells us that "who wrote the Epistle God only knows certainly."

Nor can we say certainly when, where, and in what circumstances the letter came to be written.   It has generally been taken for granted that the name under which it has long passed, "To the Hebrews," corresponds to fact.   But as we have seen, Christians of Gentile origin were hardly less eager in their pursuit of knowledge of the Old Testament than their brethren of Jewish origin, and a group of Gentile Christians may well have been avid listeners to the kind of exposition of the Old Testament our writer provides.   It is, however, almost certain that the writer was a Jew.   This is our great example in the New Testament of prophecy in the Christian sense of that term, not as foretelling the future, but as inspired exegesis of the Old Testament text, showing how Christ is to be found in all the Scriptures.

Bishop Hugh W. A. Montefiore has recently argued that "probably" the Epistle to the Hebrews was written at Ephesus by Apollos to the church at Corinth, and especially to the Jewish Christian members of it, in A.D. 52–54.[15]   This attempt to find a place for the

---

14. *Historia Ecclesiastica*, VI, 25.
15. A *Commentary on the Epistle to the Hebrews* (London: A. & C. Black, 1964).

Epistle within the Corinthian correspondence has not met with wide acceptance. There is a good deal to be said for the older view that the letter was written to a group of Jewish Christians who, as the clouds of war began to lower over Jerusalem, were tempted to wonder whether the old allegiance to the Law and the prophets ought not in such a time of crisis to take precedence over the new allegiance to Jesus Christ. Against this view it must be recalled that the writer's argument is related entirely to the ordinances of the tabernacle, and that there is no clear reference to the temple in Jerusalem.

When we turn from the somewhat speculative question of date and authorship, our way becomes plainer. The writer shows us in considerable detail the spiritual situation in which he finds his readers. They manifested a tendency to settle down and not to go forward in their Christian faith. This Christians are never allowed to do. When the church ceases to be the pilgrim people of God, it ceases to be the people of God. Hence the urgent and reiterated appeals and rebukes, the aim of all of which is to get this too complacent and sedentary group of Christians on the move again, to persuade them to recover their status as pilgrims.

This central aim accounts for the special sense in which this writer uses the word "faith," so different from the usage of both Paul and James. If Paul looks back to the past and to the promises of God, and James to immediate obedience as the criterion of a genuine faith, the writer to the Hebrews looks forward to the future—faith is the response of obedience to the call of God to go out into an unknown and unguaranteed future. Abraham went out not knowing where he was to go (Heb. 11:8). This can be taken as characteristic of all the heroes who are commemorated in chapter 11. Moses could have stayed in Egypt as the son of Pharaoh's daughter; but something forbade him to stay and drove him out to the life of a Bedouin, and later of a leader of Bedouin exiles. Joseph saw in confident faith the return of his people to their own land, and gave a commandment for the disposal of his bones in that distant future (11:22). It is all summed up in the splendid declaration of 11:13 (AV) "These all died in faith, not having received the promises, but having seen them afar off, and were persuaded of them, and embraced them, and confessed that they were strangers and pilgrims in the earth." There it all is: "seen them afar off"; "strangers and pilgrims in the earth." That was faith in A.D. 76; it is faith still in 1976.

The main structure of the argument is simplicity itself. The Jews prided themselves on their many privileges; if Christians really understand what has been given to them in Christ, they will find that in every case their inheritance is very far better than that of the Jews. The Law was given at Sinai by the mediation of angels (cf. Gal. 3:19; Acts 7:53). No Christian would have felt any need to question this Jewish tradition; but how can even the greatest of the ministering spirits (Heb. 1:14) enter into comparison with the One to whom God himself has said, "I will be to him a father, and he shall be to me a son"? (Heb. 1:5). There was hardly a limit to the veneration paid by the Jews to Moses, who had been a king in Jeshurun, among the people of the righteous (Deut. 33:5). Yet what after all was Moses but a servant, whose glory fades with the coming of the Son, the heir, for whom all these things were made? (Heb. 3:1–6).

The old covenant, made with Israel by blood in the wilderness, was valid in its day. Now a new covenant, also sealed with blood, but based on new and better promises, has come; "in speaking of a new covenant he treats the first as obsolete. And what is becoming obsolete and growing old is ready to pass away" (8:13).

The central section of the Epistle deals with priesthood. T. W. Manson once made the brilliant suggestion[16] that the key to the understanding of this part of the Epistle lies in the Epistle to the Galatians. The writer of Hebrews had read and understood that letter. He had grasped Paul's remarkable doctrine of the ceremonial Law as "the interim" between the period of forward-looking promise, which was the period of Abraham, and the period of promise fulfilled, which was the period of Jesus Christ. He said to himself, "How will that work out, if we apply it to the ritual law of sacrifice?" He found that here too the principle of the "interim" applies—the Law made nothing perfect (7:19).

Looking back into that dim and distant past he finds, for the elucidation of his argument, the mysterious figure of Melchizedek, the priest-king who met Abraham after his victory over the kings of the East, brought him forth bread and wine and blessed him (Gen. 14:8–20). There had been much speculation in Jewish circles about this Melchizedek, and our writer was far from being alone in finding him interesting and challenging. He appears suddenly in the narrative of Genesis without explanation and equally suddenly disappears "without father or mother—and has neither beginning of days nor end of life" (Heb. 7:3).

The Old Testament narrative depicts him as being greater even than father Abraham—it is the greater who blesses the lesser and receives tithes from him. This greatness is reiterated in the appar-

16. In conversation with the writer. I have not found in his published writings any detailed exposition of this idea.

ently casual reference in Ps. 110:4: "You are a priest for ever after the order of Melchizedek." Here we encounter the primeval, archetypal figure in whom the true nature of priesthood is set forth, in comparison with which the priesthood of the descendants of Aaron was only a shadow, having a reflection of the good things to come, but not the very reality of those good things (Heb. 10:1).

Why could the Law make nothing perfect? The writer draws attention to a number of defects in that transitory priesthood. Then, at the height of his argument, he points out with unerring precision that defect which made all the carefully prescribed sacrifices under the old Law in the last resort ineffective—the animals lacked that one thing which alone can make sacrifice real, free will. It was of course a requirement in the ancient world that the animal must seem to go willingly to the sacrifice, as in that moment which John Keats has caught and immortalized for us in his "Ode on a Grecian Urn"; but any thoughtful observer even in that rather callous ancient world was well aware that this was mere artifice—bulls and goats cannot offer themselves as willing sacrifices. And so the writer is led on to one of the profoundest statements in the New Testament on "the doctrine of the Atonement." In Ps. 40:8 he has found a clear picture of the One who was to abolish all animal sacrifices in the simple words, "I come to do thy will, O God." In some expositions of that doctrine we almost receive the impression that it would not have mattered very much *who* died, provided that someone died. This writer makes it clear that it was all-important that it was Jesus Christ who died, since his death was only the final expression of a total surrender of his will to God, which began with his birth, was maintained unblemished and uncontaminated through the thirty-five years or so of his earthly life, and was consummated by his death outside the camp. "By that will we have been sanctified through the offering of the body of Jesus Christ once for all" (Heb. 10:10).

In the Jewish world the offering of animal sacrifices ceased many centuries ago, and it is unlikely that it will be reintroduced, even if the authorities of the state of Israel should decide to take possession of the Dome of the Rock, now in the hands of the Muslims. A Jewish theologian might have some difficulty in finding justification for this radical departure from the Law contained in ordinances. The Christian has no such difficulty; why continue with the shadow when the substance, the reality, is already there?

The writer of Hebrews does not leave his argument at this point. In the moving ritual of the Day of Atonement the high priest entered once a year into the holiest place of the earthly sanctuary. Christ in the power of his own sacrifice of himself has entered into the true, the invisible, sanctuary. And here we are given the answer to the question, "If the doctrine of the Ascension is in any sense true, what has Jesus been doing since he ascended into heaven?" "He always lives to make intercession for them" (Heb. 7:25). The term "intercession" must not be taken too narrowly, as though it meant no more than "offering prayers," though this, too, is one meaning of the word. The intercessor is one who enters the lists on another's behalf, "the king's champion"; or, if we like to put it in rather more modern terms, he is the one who represents us in a country to which we are on our way but which he has already reached. Here the Judeo-Christian concept of the exalted Messiah reaches its highest point; this high priest is higher than the heavens (Heb. 4:14). But it would be a mistake to think of Jesus as a now remote object of faith. Because he has entered into the holiest place of all, he has opened for us the way, and we are under obligation to enter as he has entered before us, now, today, in the experience of Christian worship and not in some vague eschatological future (Heb. 10:19–22).

Even now we are not yet at the end of the story. On the Day of Atonement (Leviticus 16) the high priest did not tarry in the sanctuary; he came out to tell the expectant people that all was well, and that for another year their reconciliation with the holy God had been achieved. So Christ also shall appear to those who look for him in a salvation in which sin need no longer be thought or spoken of (Heb. 9:28). "That day of wrath, that dreadful day" has here become the day of exultation, the true note of which has been caught by Frances Ridley Havergal in her simple hymn, "Thou art coming, O my Saviour, Thou art coming, O my King."[17]

But to look for the coming of Christ is not to sit with folded hands as though there was nothing more to be done. There is a way to be followed, a race to be run, looking to him who endured the cross, despising the shame (Heb. 12:1–2). For this writer, as for the others in the group of writings that we are now studying, persecution is a part of the inheritance, an ever-present possibility for all, for some an actual reality, in A.D. 76 as in 1976. Jesus suffered outside the city, just as the bodies of the beasts offered as sin-offerings were burned outside the encampment in the wilderness. We may not suppose that we can take refuge within the city, whether it be the city of law, or of tradition, or of ancient ways. The harsh command of faith runs as follows: "Therefore let us go forth to him outside the camp" (Heb. 13:13).

The challenge is uncomfortable. Yet this in many ways austere

---

17. Those who have been puzzled by the words "Hear we not thy golden bells?" will find the answer to their perplexity in the passage on the Day of Atonement in Leviticus 16, together with Exodus 28:33–35.

and disturbing Epistle ends with one of the most memorable blessings in the series that is scattered through the writings of the New
Testament: "Now the God of peace, that brought again from the dead
our Lord Jesus, that great shepherd of the sheep, through the blood
of the everlasting covenant, make you perfect in every good work to
do his will, working in you that which is well-pleasing in his sight,
through Jesus Christ to whom be glory for ever and ever.   Amen"
(Heb. 13:20–21 AV).

The Revelation of John

Many views have been held as to the date, origin, and authorship
of this, the last book in our printed New Testament.   Some have
associated it with the first great persecution of the Christians, which
took place in Rome through the direct action of the emperor Nero in
A.D. 64–65.   To others this date appears too early, and they find the
historical location of the book thirty years later in the persecution
under Domitian toward the end of the first century.   Yet others think
in terms of a first and a second edition, or of a succession of revisions
and interpolations.

It would be a help to our study of the theology of this perplexing
book if these historical and critical questions could be finally settled.   Yet the loss we suffer through the unsettled state of these
questions is not really very great, since the theology of the book is to
a large extent independent of, and can be studied without reference
to, the answers given to questions of that type.   On four theological
points there is likely to be little difference of opinion: (1) this is a
work that stands in the tradition of Israel, as we have come to
understand that term; (2) the writer of Revelation is addressing
himself to churches, the life of which is marred by complacency and
self-contentment and that are urgently in need of revival; (3) this is
especially urgent, in view of the fact that persecution can be presented not as a probability but as an inescapable certainty; and (4)
the method that the writer follows, in his purpose to reawaken faith
and to strengthen his friends to face the ordeal of suffering, is once
again the presentation of Jesus as Lord, in his own peculiar accents
and in the apocalyptic style he has adopted as appropriate to the
delivery of his message.

No other book of the New Testament is so fully permeated as this
by the language and thought of the Old Testament, so that in this case
as in that of the Epistle of James some scholars have concluded that
we are here dealing with a Jewish document that has undergone
some rather perfunctory Christian revision.   The quotations from

the Hebrew Scriptures are very numerous. The classification of the quotations according to source yields highly interesting results. Naturally the influence of the Book of Daniel is profound. But the concluding chapters in which we are introduced to pictures of the new Jerusalem are full of echoes of the ancient visions of the restored Jerusalem set forth in the closing chapters of the Book of the prophet Ezekiel, a work of which hardly any use is made in other parts of the New Testament (Ezekiel 43–48). Moreover, though the writer can write when he wishes in correct Greek of the first century A.D., at other times he uses a strange jargon that seems to represent the style of a man who thinks in a Semitic language, Hebrew or Aramaic, and writes down his thoughts in Greek with little regard for the requirements of Greek accidence or syntax.

The Book of Revelation does, however, recognize quite clearly the difference between the Old and the New, between continuity and discontinuity. The earthly Jerusalem is no longer the Holy City; it is "the great city which is allegorically called Sodom and Egypt, where their Lord was crucified" (Rev. 11:8).

Here, as in other parts of the New Testament, but perhaps more clearly than anywhere else, we are given vivid pictures of churches that stand in need of spiritual renewal. Guided by the Spirit, the writer sends messages as from the risen Lord to seven churches in Asia (chapters 2 and 3). Among them two are commended without reservation. For four the message is compounded of praise and blame, and the church of Ephesus is especially singled out by the judgment, "you have abandoned the love you had at first" (2:4). Of one church, Laodicea, the picture is wholly unfavorable; here all is tepid, neither hot nor cold, and this is of all states the most dangerous, since it breeds a self-satisfaction out of which it is hard to shake a church. The church of Laodicea is in danger of total rejection by the Lord (3:14–22).

Christians in all ages have been inclined to idealize the early church. The achievement of the men and women of the first generations was certainly remarkable enough. In face of the immense difficulty of believing that a crucified Jew could be the Savior of both Jew and Gentile, they had believed and had maintained their faith before a hostile and incredulous world. They had endured persecution at the hands of Jews and Gentiles alike. They had produced a considerable volume of imperishable literature. It is not hard to imagine that they must have been a race of supermen. Yet the New Testament itself gives no ground for any such supposition. Rather, the New Testament shows groups of men and women characterized by the same imperfections as their successors in all generations; as frail as we are when assailed by temptation, as likely to be attacked by doubt, as liable to descend rapidly from the summit of eager conviction to the valley of conformity, compromise, or ill-founded self-satisfaction.   The composition and transmission of the New Testament by such ordinary people was one miracle.   The survival of the Christian church is another.   It really was through very ordinary people that the church came into existence and held on through manifold possibilities of annihilation.   It was to people very much like ourselves that the writer of the Book of Revelation communicated the awe and the splendor of his visions.

The writer is firmly convinced that the church of his day is about to enter on a period of persecution such as it has never yet had to endure.   He himself had been relegated to the island of Patmos "on account of the word of God and the testimony of Jesus" (1:9); the circumstances are not clear, but the reference can hardly be to anything other than a judicial sentence of exile.[18]   This may be an early warning to the church.   There has already been another; in Pergamos an unknown Antipas has sealed his testimony with his blood (2:13).   And now the writer sees the day of universal desolation approaching; for this the believers in every place must be prepared.

What gives to the visions of the Apocalypse (the Greek term by which the Book of Revelation is also known) their peculiar intensity is the method of the writer, who sees immediate human happenings against the background of the immense and ceaseless conflict between the powers of good and the powers of evil, between God and his adversaries in the spiritual realm.   The action takes place simultaneously on earth and in the heavenly realm.   There is no doubt of the ultimate victory of God.   But equally there is no doubt as to the reality of the conflict in which every single believer is called to be engaged.   To convey the truth of the vision that has been granted to him the seer makes use of the imagery of Jewish apocalyptic.   Old Testament prophecy usually spoke to a particular historical situation and interpreted that situation in the light of the purposes of God.   Apocalyptic looked to the time of the end, and spoke in terms of signs and cataclysms in the physical universe by which the events of the end would be introduced or accompanied.   This unfamiliar imagery makes the Book of Revelation difficult reading for the student in the

---

18. Patmos is neither a barren reef nor a desert. It was a place of some importance in the world of Roman commerce. But the reference to tribulation and patient endurance makes it almost certain that the seer was not in Patmos of his own free choice.

twentieth century. It has also led to many fantastic interpretations by which the minds of believers have been perplexed. There is no counting the interpretations that have been given, from Nero to Hitler, of the mysterious number of the beast, which is also the number of a man, six hundred three score and six (Rev. 13:18).[19] We can leave the study of these fancies to commentaries and specialist studies. Our task is simpler: to consider the essential theology of the book, the way in which one writer understood the being and the dominion of Christ and tried to convey to his readers assurance as to the final triumph of their faith.

This writer, like others whose works we have studied, sets himself to elucidate in his own way and in his own idiom that earliest of Christian affirmations, "Jesus is Lord." In the last chapter of the book, which is also the last chapter of the Bible as we have it, the risen Lord speaks of himself by the simple human appellation: "I Jesus have sent my angel [or, my messenger] to you with this testimony for the churches" (22:16). But to this the answer of the church is "Come, Lord Jesus" (22:20).

The theme of the book is set out in the first chapter, and here we find again that trinity of concepts, resurrection, Spirit, reconciliation, which has become familiar to us in other contexts. The whole book bears witness to Jesus Christ, the faithful witness, who is the firstborn of the dead (1:5). Greetings are sent to the churches in the name of the seven spirits who are before the throne of God (1:4). The number seven implies perfection—the spirits perfectly express and carry out the will of the One who sends them. It is the same Jesus who loved us and freed us from our sins, and has made us a kingdom, priests to his God and Father—a comprehensive statement of the meaning of redemption and reconciliation with God through Christ (1:5–6).

This exordium is followed by a splendid vision of the glory of the risen One, so alarming that the seer falls at his feet as though dead (1:17). The risen One is seen walking in the midst of the candlesticks, which symbolically represent the churches, just as one like a son of the gods was seen walking in the burning fiery furnace with the three young men who refused to deny their faith in face of the flames of persecution (Dan. 3:25). This risen One is still recognized as one "like a son of man." And yet he is also a Son of God "who has eyes like a flame of fire" (Rev. 2:18). He is aware of all that is going on in the churches, can penetrate to the reality below the appear-

---

19. A fascinating discussion of the number and its meaning will be found in Robert H. Charles, *The Revelation of St. John*, reprint (Naperville: Allenson, 1959), 1: 364–68.

ance, can attribute praise or blame with the certainty and assurance that arise from perfect knowledge. He is the Lord of the church, and he speaks with divine authority.

No summary can do justice to the theology of the book. The simplest approach, perhaps, is to study carefully the many names and titles by which the One who is the center of that theology is described.

Some of these titles are unique in this book, and full of significance. He is the Alpha and the Omega, the first and the last, the beginning and the end (1:11; 22:13). He speaks of himself as the root and offspring of David, a reminder of the Jewish strain that runs throughout the book (cf. Isa. 11:1). He is the bright and morning star (Rev. 22:16). We look out on a world of darkness and disarray, still evidently at least in part under the control of evil powers. What greater consolation can man have than the knowledge that our morning star, our light-bringer, has risen, and that as he ascends the sky and shines out over the wild and wasteful ocean, he brings the unshakable certainty that the last word is not with the darkness and that the day is at hand?

Not all these titles bring cheer and consolation. The Lamb that has been slain (Rev. 5:6,12) is also the warrior and the judge. He goes forth riding on a white horse to smite the nations and to rule them with a rod of iron (19:11–15). He has a name inscribed, King of kings and Lord of lords; in that capacity he will "tread the winepress of the fury of the wrath of God the Almighty" (19:15–16). Such doctrine is very disagreeable to modern man, who tends to reject the element of severity that must be present in any love worthy of the name, and to concentrate only on the gentler aspects of love. But must it not in reality be so? Can evil be eternal? Does it not contain within itself the seeds of its own destruction? Must there not be in the end a total discrimination, a final separation, between that which is good and that which is evil? We need not feel ourselves committed to the lurid imagery of *Dies Irae*, "the day of wrath." We shall do well to remember that there is much in the imagery of the Book of Revelation that is not to be interpreted in isolation but seen in the light of all that we have learned elsewhere of the love of God revealed in Jesus Christ. Yet evil is terrible, as we have learned to our cost in this twentieth century. The imagery of Revelation is saying something that we do well not entirely to forget.

Rome is now no longer the friendly power, which on the whole has served as the protector of the Christians; it has become the wicked city, "drunk with the blood of the saints and the blood of the martyrs of Jesus" (Rev. 17:6). The term "Babylon the great," here used as a designation of Rome, is drawn from a much earlier prophecy of judgment, to be found in chapter 13 of the Book of Isaiah. But, as we read, we become dimly aware that the seer in Revelation is concerned not merely with the destiny of a single city but with something that runs right through the history of the human race. Babylon is not simply imperial Rome; it stands for that arrogance of the human spirit that sets out to master its own world in independence of God, that arrogance which was seen long ago in the builders of the tower of Babel (Genesis 11), again in Nineveh and Tyre and Babylon, and is all too manifest among us today. If God is God, all that sets itself up against him must in the end learn to submit to him, or else recognize that the judgment of God is simply the working out to the bitter end of that principle of self-destruction inherent in all that is evil.

In spite of the many disasters that the writer sees coming upon mankind, he never for a moment doubts either the victory of Christ (the words "victor," "victory," "vanquish," occur more often in this book than in the whole of the rest of the New Testament put together), or the final deliverance of those who are faithful to him. The book moves on two levels. Below we are stunned and deafened by the confusions that surround us. At intervals we are lifted up to the tranquility of heaven, where the will of God is already being done. It seems that at certain points the writer is drawing on his experience of Christian worship. The visions of chapters 4 and 5, with their angels and living creatures and twenty-four elders who combine the twelve patriarchs of the old covenant with the twelve apostles of the new, appear to bring before us an idealized representation of the Christian fellowship assembled for worship on the first day of the week, the Lord's Day (1:10). Much of the language of the Book of Revelation has passed into the liturgical tradition of the Christian churches. If for nothing else, the book would have been worth preserving for its seven great songs of praise, and for the repeated Alleluias that are the Christian expression of confidence in God in the face of all that the powers of evil can achieve.

So, at the end, the book leads out into the most detailed picture given to us in the New Testament of the final victory of Christ. Here, once again, we encounter the Alpha and the Omega, the first and the last, the beginning and the end. Genesis 1 was not the first chapter of the Old Testament to be written, nor Revelation 22 the last of the New. But the Bible, as it has been received by the church, begins with, "In the beginning God created the heavens and the earth" (Gen. 1:1), and ends with new heavens and a new earth, no longer exposed to that transitoriness that in Scripture is associated with the heaven and earth which shall pass away (Mark 13:31; Rev. 21:1). It has often been noted that the Bible begins in a garden and ends in a city. But this is a city that retains the characteristic features of a garden. Here is the river that makes glad the city of God (Psalm 46). Here is the "tree of life" (Gen. 3:22), no longer inaccessible to men—the cherub with the flaming sword (Gen. 3:24) has become the guide of the seer to the heavenly Jerusalem (Rev. 21:9).[20]

Amid all these wonders the christocentric character of all New Testament theology comes again to the surface: "Its temple is the Lord God the Almighty and the Lamb . . . its lamp is the Lamb . . . the throne of God and of the Lamb shall be in it" (Rev. 21:22, 23; 22:3). So in the end it is the Lamb that was slain who has triumphed over the beast and the false prophet and all the rest of them. Victory remains with love. After all the frightful menaces of judgment the book comes back to the standing invitation of the Christian imperative: "The Spirit and the Bride say 'Come.' And let him who hears say 'Come.' And let him who is thirsty come, let him who desires take the water of life without price" (22:17). Even in the Book of Revelation we are not so far away from the great "Come unto me" of the Jewish Gospel (Matt. 11:28). And the last word of combined warning and encouragement comes from the Lord himself: "Be assured that I come without warning," to which the church, echoing the "Jesus is Lord" of the primeval creed, has in all ages replied, "Come, Lord Jesus!" (Rev. 22:20).

---

20. "There shall be no more sea" (21:1). The sea here is the deep, Tiamat of the Babylonian myth, the element of chaos and resistance to God's will. George B. Caird, *A Commentary on the Revelation of St. John the Divine*, Black's New Testament Commentaries (London: A. & C. Black, 1966), p. 65, remarks that "the sea, whether on earth or in heaven, belongs essentially to the old order, and within that order it stands for everything that is recalcitrant to the will of God." When that no longer exists, there is no element of disharmony, and therefore none of that threat of impermanence which hangs over this universe as we know it.

6

In the Gentile World

We have now worked through four books, which we have seen reason to believe are closely related to the Jewish tradition as that was maintained, in part reformed, in the fellowship of the believers in Jesus. Even a casual reader is likely to feel as he passes to Luke and Acts that he has left one world and passed into another. The gospel is now taking hold among the Gentiles, and they are finding their own characteristic ways of giving expression to it. The two books, comprising as they do about one quarter of the New Testament, are clearly important. Yet they present us with a great variety of critical questions, and on these there is less agreement among scholars than in almost any other area of New Testament study. Some of these questions are of theological and not merely of historical interest, and we cannot leave them entirely on one side.[1]

It has generally been held that these two books, the Gospel of Luke and the Acts of the Apostles, are from the hand of a single author.[2] Tradition affirms that this author was none other than Luke the beloved physician, the companion of Paul, to whom Paul makes affectionate reference in Col. 4:14 in terms that imply quite clearly that this friend is of Gentile origin. This identification receives strong support if we take the view that in the famous "we-sections" of Acts the writer is actually drawing on his own travel diaries or recollections. It is argued on the other side that it is unlikely that one who had been a companion of Paul would give no indication of ever having seen any of the Pauline Epistles, and at certain points would diverge rather sharply from the Pauline theology.

The Book of Acts ends with Paul in Rome and no mention has been

---

1. It is not necessary quite to accept the pessimistic judgment of Adolf von Harnack that "All faults that have been made in New Testament criticism are gathered as it were into a focus in the criticism of the Acts of the Apostles" (*Luke The Physician*, New Testament Studies I [London: Williams and Norgate, 1909]). But it is disturbing that so little progress has been made to any agreed results.

2. Not all agree. "The Case Against the Tradition" was forcefully stated by Hans Windisch in Frederick J. Foakes Jackson and Kirsopp Lake, eds., *The Beginnings of Christianity*, 5 vols. (London: Macmillan & Co., 1920–1933), 2:298–348. More recent research has added little new material. But the case has been reopened in a cogent article based on very careful linguistic work: A. W. Argyle, "The Greek of Luke and Acts," *NTS* 20 (July 1974): 441–45.

made of his death.   From this some have argued in favor of an early
date for Acts—the death of Paul is not mentioned for the good reason
that it had not yet happened at the time at which the book was
written.[3]   A different explanation is that Luke intended to write a
trilogy, and that the third part, dealing with the later ministry of Paul
and the great persecution under the emperor Nero, either was never
written or has entirely disappeared, leaving no trace in the mind and
in the records of the church.   Finally, it is argued that, in the case of
the Gospel at least, there are evidences that it was written after the
fall of Jerusalem in A.D. 70, and that both books seem to represent a
stage in the life of the church more developed than that which it had
reached at the supposed time of the death of Paul.[4]

When the critical questions retire, theological questions can advance.   In this connection the first and obvious theological question
is, Why did it ever occur to anyone that a history of the church should
be written?   The earliest Christians would have been astonished at
the suggestion; if the interval between the Ascension and *Parousia*
(the "Second Coming" of Christ) is to be as short as Christian faith
then supposed that it would be, why should any record of it be
written down?   If Luke was in fact the first man in whose mind the
idea arose, he had one of the qualities necessary for a great historian.   To this he added the gifts of a great writer and a great theological thinker.   This is a most unusual combination; we shall do well to
bear each part of it in mind.   Whereas others saw the church only as
the "eschatological reality," the fellowship of Christ's people that
has come into existence in and for the last days, Luke saw it in a
longer perspective, as a great and expanding reality; the dimension
in which it operates is that of time.   So Luke settles down to record
the dealings of God in the new age with the people of his choice.
Out of a theological insight a historian is born.

It was not unknown in the ancient world for a historian to sit down
to write the history of his own times.   Thucydides, in his history of
the Peloponnesian War, is actor as well as inquirer and recorder.
Cicero, in his multitudinous letters, clearly written with a view to
publication, has left us what is to all intents and purposes a history of
his own age as seen by one man.   Tacitus seems, like Macaulay, to

---

3. E.g., Richard Belward Rackham, whose *The Acts of the Apostles: an Exposition,* The Westminster Commen-
taries (London: Methuen and Co., 1901; 9th ed., 1922) is still valuable.   Harnack, *The Acts of the Apostles,* New
Testament Studies III (London: Williams and Norgate, 1907), was prepared to reckon with the possibility that "St.
Luke wrote . . . perhaps even so early as the beginning of the seventh decade of the first century" (p. 297).
4. Which was written first, the Gospel or Acts?   I am inclined to think that Acts was written first, and that the
Gospel comes from the hand of one who was already a practiced historian; Theophilus, the "friend of God" to
whom both books are dedicated, representing a type, the friendly Gentile inquirer rather than a specific individual, the two prefaces having been added later by the writer to indicate the substantial connection between the
two works.   It is for this reason that I have dealt in this chapter first with Acts, and then turned to the study of the
Gospel.

have continued his history up to "a time which is within the memory of men still living."[5] . So in this respect Luke is not unique. Nor is it likely that he was unacquainted with the great writers of the Greco-Roman world, whom at certain points he closely resembles. Yet in him there is found something not present in any of his predecessors in the art of writing history. Thucydides believed in destiny, that hidden power to which even the gods are subject, and which will work out the vengeance of the higher powers on those who fall into the sin of *hybris*, arrogance, thinking thoughts higher than mortal men should think. Both Polybius and Livy saw manifest destiny in the rise of Rome to power. But this is far less than the theological insight of Luke. To him history is the field of operation of a living God, who guides the destinies of all the nations of men to one single fulfillment in Christ. History for him would have no meaning unless seen as a story in which God and his people are both active. Here he is a successor of the historians of the Old Testament and not of the Greeks. The best preparation for the study of Acts is a close acquaintance with the Books of Kings, in which a similar view of history can clearly be traced, with which Luke was well acquainted and by which at certain points he was influenced.[6]

Luke has written in Acts the history of a little more than a generation of human life. We can realize the extent of our indebtedness to him if we consider the poverty of our information about the events of the following generation. What would we not give for a narrative as concise and vivid as that of Luke, covering events from A.D. 70 to the end of the first century?

What manner of writer, then, is this, the one great historian in the first three centuries of the life of the church?

The first point to notice is his astonishing accuracy in matters of detail. Long ago Sir William Ramsay drew attention to Luke's minute care in referring to officials of the Roman administration in every case by their correct titles.[7] This is no easy thing to do when titles were so varied and so liable to change. An instance of this accuracy, from a slightly different field, has recently come to my notice. In Acts 28:13 we are told that Paul, on his long journey to Rome, landed at Puteoli in southern Italy, "where we found breth-

---

5. Thomas B. Macaulay, *History of England*, 2 vols. (New York: Harper and Brothers, 1849), chap. 1.

6. The influence on Luke of the Septuagint (the Greek translation of the Old Testament) can hardly be exaggerated. Harnack records that of the Greek words peculiar to Luke in the New Testament, no less than 239 (out of 319) are found also in the Septuagint. But the influence is much deeper than of words alone. See Harnack, *Luke The Physician*, p. 170, n.1.

7. First in his book (originally published in 1895) *St. Paul the Traveller and the Roman Citizen*, reprint (Grand Rapids: Baker Books, n.d.). For instance, the magistrates in Thessalonica are referred to by the correct title "politarchs," a word hardly found in Greek literature, but now confirmed by inscriptions, some from Thessalonica itself.

ren." Why there, and not at Ostia, the port so much nearer Rome? The answer is given by Dr. Russell Meiggs in his massive book on Roman Ostia.[8] Ostia was the port that was open to the west and to the traffic with Spain and Gaul; ships from Alexandria and the east docked at Puteoli, from which passengers proceeded to Rome by land. Dr. Meiggs adds for good measure that identifiably Christian remains of an early date are few and far between at Ostia; it is unlikely that Paul would have found brethren there.

It is important not to imagine that this proves more than it does. A writer may be highly accurate in detail, and at the same time misleading in broader aspects of history. There is, however, reason to imagine that a man who is so minutely careful in detail will not be wholly regardless of truth in matters of greater concern.

Luke is a subtle writer. He never tells the reader what he is going to do, never underlines or emphasizes, and at times puts a really important point almost in a parenthesis. In consequence he reveals his secrets only as a reward for really careful study. He holds that baptism is very important as the means of entry into the Christian life. But when he injects the little note that the Samaritans were baptized, both men and women (Acts 8:12; cf. 16:15), he does not draw attention to the contrast between baptism and circumcision, a rite intended only for the male sex; he leaves the reader to infer that equality of man and woman in Christ which Paul found occasion to express in plain terms (Gal. 3:28). It is unlikely, therefore, that he will explain to us the purpose of his history, and the principles on which he has selected from the mass of materials available to him that which was relevant to his theme, and could be crowded into the narrow compass of a papyrus roll. We shall have to do some exploring for ourselves.

When studying so careful a writer, it is always useful to look at the last sentence, and even the last word, of a book. It is certainly no accident that the last word of Acts is "unhindered" (28:31). Rome is the city in which Paul is able to preach the gospel "no man forbidding him" (AV). We have seen already that in the New Testament, geographical terms can acquire theological significance. We are almost certainly right in thinking that for Luke Jerusalem and Rome are more than just cities. Each name has a deeper meaning. Acts is a tale of two cities, in which Jerusalem stands for rejection and Rome stands for hope. Again and again the Jews have been given the opportunity to see and to accept Jesus Christ; again and again they have rejected him. The point comes at last at which Jerusalem itself

8. *Roman Ostia* (Oxford, 1960) Ostia is one of the most extensive and best preserved of Roman cities.

is rejected. Paul had been given the assurance that he must see Rome (23:11). Everything seemed to combine to make this impossible—the arrest in Jerusalem and the probability that he would be judged and condemned there, averted by Paul's demand that as a Roman citizen he should be tried before the emperor, and that meant, of course, in Rome (25:12); the danger that he would be kidnapped or assassinated by Jewish enemies (23:12–15); the fearful perils of the shipwreck (27:14–44); and the final danger from the adder that fastened on his wrist (28:3). But all these things are overruled by divine Providence: "and so we came to Rome . . . and when we came to Rome" (28:14, 16). Luke may have had it in mind to write further. But for the moment his task is done. The apostle of the Gentiles has come at last to the center of Gentile power, and we leave him preaching the kingdom of God (note the appearance of this expression at this point) in a new world of hope and expectation.

This central structure of his book goes far to account for what Luke records and for what he omits. If he knew so much, why does he tell us nothing of the strifes and controversies in the church of Corinth, which Paul recounts in the Epistles to the Corinthians? Luke's aim is different. He sets out to tell us of the spread of the gospel, as the church takes root in one area after another; he will not depict the further history of the church in each place; such reports would belong to a different kind of history from that which Luke has chosen to write.

Much has been made of the differences between Luke and Paul. Of course, there are differences; Luke is much too independent a writer to follow exactly even one whom he regards as highly as he regards Paul. This should not blind us to the similarities and points of agreement. To one point of agreement special attention may be drawn. Paul never wavered in his conviction that the gospel must be preached "to the Jew first, and also to the Greek" (Rom. 1:16). These words were written probably six years after he had called down a heavy malediction on the unbelieving Jews (1 Thess. 2:16): "But God's wrath has come upon them at last." Similarly, in Acts 18:6, Paul, provoked by the blasphemies of the Jews in Corinth, says to them, "I am innocent; from now on I will go to the Gentiles"; but exactly thirteen verses later (Acts 18:19), we are told "they came to Ephesus . . . he himself [Paul] went into the synagogue, and argued with the Jews." In the same way, when he reached Rome, Paul's first act was to call together the chiefs of the Jews in Rome, and to talk to them courteously about the reason for his being in their city (Acts 28:17–29). By this time it had become more than unlikely that

Paul's earlier expectation would be fulfilled and that all Israel would be saved in his lifetime; nevertheless, the offer of life in Christ must be made to them, whether they will hear or whether they will forbear; there will always be a remnant according to the election of grace, and God has not cast off his people.

If we turn now from the last verse of Acts to the first, we shall be introduced more directly to the theology that determines the form and structure of Luke's book: "All that Jesus began to do and to teach" (1:1).   So this is to be a book about Jesus, and there will be continuity between what he began to do and teach in the days of his flesh and what he continued to do in the days when his visible presence was no longer among men.   Once again we note the significance of the human name "Jesus," which here, as so often, draws our attention back to that life which was lived at an identifiable time and place, and from which alone the gospel takes its origin.   The rulers of the Jews, astonished at the eloquence of Peter and John, recognize that they had been with Jesus (Acts 4:13).   When Philip sets to work to elucidate Isaiah 53 for the Ethiopian nobleman, what he does is to preach to him Jesus (8:35).   In the last encounter of Paul with the Jews, it is concerning Jesus that he attempts to persuade them (28:23).

This constant recurrence to the human name can be understood in the light of Luke's doctrine of the Ascension, which he alone among New Testament writers records in some detail.   The last words of his Gospel are: "and they returned to Jerusalem with great joy, and were continually in the temple blessing God" (Luke 24:52–3).   It has been made plain to the disciples, how exactly we are not told, that the physical manifestations of the risen Jesus have come to an end and will occur no more.   But this, so far from being an occasion of sorrow or depression, such as might be the result of a deprivation that had come upon them unexpectedly, is a cause of joy and exhilaration.   The explanation, as Luke has come to understand the event, is that they have come to realize that the presence of the living Jesus is a permanent reality, which can never be taken away from them.

So this Book of the Acts of the Apostles, which in the opinion of some should rather be called the Acts of the Holy Spirit, may best of all be called the Acts of the risen Jesus.   From now on all the Acts of Jesus will be carried out through the Spirit operating in the hearts and wills of men; but it is always Jesus himself, and none other, who is acting through this Holy Spirit.   The term "the Spirit of Jesus" is used once only in the book (16:7);[9] but these words sum up in brief

---

9. And even here the evidence of the manuscripts is divided; but on balance, it seems probable that "the Spirit of Jesus" is what Luke actually wrote.

compass a complete theology. That Spirit of the Lord, who in the Old Testament seems at times almost like an impersonal force, has now been concentrated in one particular manifestation to such an extent that it is almost possible to speak of the Spirit as having himself been reborn. From now on, the Spirit will always be the Spirit of Jesus, carrying to completion what he had begun to do and teach. The name given to Jesus by the angel, Immanuel (Matt. 1:18–23) means "God with us"; the Spirit, as understood by Luke, is God with us today; and the God who is with us is no other than the One whom Jesus always addressed as Father.

The first outpouring of the Spirit in Acts is accompanied by the phenomenon of "speaking in tongues." Luke seems to take it for granted that the confession of faith in baptism will be accompanied by this manifestation of the Spirit (Cornelius and his friends, who receive the Spirit even before baptism [10:44]; the group of "old disciples" in Ephesus, who had not even heard that there is a Holy Spirit [19:1–6]).[10] But he nowhere discusses the question in detail, and gives no indication that he regarded this charismatic speaking as a regular feature of the life and worship of the church. It is recorded that a second time the apostles were filled with the Spirit and that they spoke the word with boldness (Acts 4:31); but there is nothing to indicate that this involved a repetition of the experience of Pentecost. Luke has clearly been much influenced by the story of the elders of Israel in the wilderness; when a portion of the Spirit that was upon Moses came upon them, they prophesied in the camp, but then prophesied no more.[11] That appears to have been a once-forall experience of commissioning; Luke may have held a similar view as to the gift of the Spirit in answer to faith expressed in baptism. He never refers to the kind of problems that Paul had to deal with in the church of Corinth, troubles that had arisen from excessive stress on one manifestation of the Spirit at the expense of the less sensational but in the end more important gifts.

A long list can be drawn up of the activities of the Spirit in the church. To three points special attention may be directed.

It is the Spirit who constitutes the church. Where the Spirit is not, there is no church; even baptism in the name of the Lord Jesus does not suffice (Acts 8:14–17). The statement sometimes made that the church is constituted by word and sacrament is misleading unless it is clearly realized that word and sacrament are no more than instruments that the Spirit uses for the fulfillment of his purposes.

10. I think that in Acts 8:39 the "Western" reading is to be preferred: "the Spirit of the Lord fell upon the eunuch, and an angel of the Lord caught away Philip," with due respect to Richard P. Hanson, who says roundly in *Acts in the Revised Standard Version* (Oxford, 1967), p. 112, "this cannot be the original reading."
11. There is some doubt as to the translation "but they did so no more" (Num. 11:25). But this is the generally accepted interpretation.

When the Spirit is present within the church, his gifts are given to all without distinction—apostles or laymen, Jews or Gentiles, male or female. On this point Luke and Paul are in exact agreement.

Luke is careful to guard against any suggestion that the Spirit can be regarded as some kind of impersonal force; as the Spirit of the living and personal Jesus, the Spirit can only be personal, taking the natural gifts of human beings and lifting them high above their ordinary level, but never overriding them, or interfering with the natural working of the human mind and spirit. The Spirit never comes under the control of human beings. The error of Simon Magus lay precisely in this—that he thought that the Spirit was some kind of special magic, which he could have at his disposal (Acts 8:14–24).

The idea of the Spirit leads on by a natural process of association to the idea of the church. This is a book about the church and the churches. It may well be that Luke, looking back on the history from the plateau reached at the time at which he is writing, has tended to level out some of the hills and valleys that were actually there in the experiences of the growing church. But it would hardly be true to say that he presents an idealized picture of that church.

He believes firmly that the church stands under the direct guidance and protection of God; it is only through the initiative of God working through the Spirit that men and women are added to the church. Ultimate success is therefore guaranteed. But this is no picture of a facile triumph easily obtained. The church is always the church under the cross; its destiny is concisely expressed in words put into the mouth of Paul: "Through many tribulations we must enter the kingdom of God" (Acts 14:22). One of the purposes that Luke has set before himself is to show all the forms of hostility and opposition that the church must expect to experience on its way to glory. We start with the not unnatural hostility of the rulers of the Jews (Acts 4:1–22), which soon breaks out into open and physical violence (5:40), legal from the Jewish point of view, but later taking the form of mob violence, at least connived at by the Jewish authorities, in which Stephen met his death (7:57–8:4). We encounter the pseudo-Jew Herod, prepared to kill one apostle and to plan the death of another (12:1–17). The apostles face the irrational enthusiasm of a less educated populace, too easily turned into a murderous thirst for blood (14:19); an outbreak of Gentile mob violence, which together with the excitability or pusillanimity of local magistrates leads the messengers of the gospel into distressing and humiliating suffering (16:16–40). And so to the commercial factor in the rabble-rousing of Demetrius at Ephesus (19:24–41), where the silversmiths saw that the successful preaching of the gospel would involve them in financial loss.

This is all human opposition. Luke is no less aware of the eerie and uncanny world of the demons; between that world and Christ's kingdom of light there must be inveterate and unappeasable hostility. The demon world meets us in Simon of Samaria, who had long imposed on simple people by his arts (8:9–24); in Elymas the magician who attempted to turn a prudent proconsul from the faith (13:4–13); in the unfortunate girl in Philippi who was possessed by a spirit called Python (16:16–18); in the strange episode of the sons of Sceva, who attempted to cast out devils in the name of one in whom they had not really believed (19:13–17); in the practitioners of magic who were owners of books of enormous value (19:19). Luke uses his sources as he finds them, in most cases without comment. No one familiar with the popular literature of the time is likely to doubt that he is accurately depicting the world of the first century in the area of the Mediterranean; anxiety concerning the presence and the power of the demons was a constant factor in the life of the world in which the apostles were called to bear witness.

Among the forces of opposition to the gospel we find no mention in the Acts of the Roman Empire and its administration. Here historical fact and one of Luke's purposes come close to one another. He wishes to show the Roman authorities as on the whole just and impartial, and friendly rather than hostile to the Christian cause. It can hardly be doubted that this is a true picture of the state of things up to the time of the persecution under Nero, which because of its sheer unexpectedness seems to have come as a tremendous shock to the Christian communities.

The expressions "Gallio cared for none of these things" (Acts 18:17 AV) and "Paid no attention to this" (RSV) have done much harm to the reputation of the proconsul of Achaia; they suggest cynical indifference to the things of the spirit. But this is certainly not the meaning of Luke. He contrasts with the fanaticism of the Jews the calm, temperate attitude of a Roman judge, who knows the limits of his authority and will not allow himself to be drawn into controversies that must be dealt with by the parties themselves and have no place in a Roman court of law. Luke's attitude is very different from that which we have encountered in the Book of Revelation. He would have found himself quite at home among the Christians for whom the great Augustine wrote his treatise on the *City of God*, and who had been convinced that the stability of the whole world depended on the survival of Rome.

The church can survive and even flourish in days of persecution, when its very existence seems to be threatened by forces it cannot control. Luke is well aware that the dangers from within are in every way more serious than those coming from without. He does indeed see the church as a great and expanding reality, moving majestically forward under the providence of God. At the same time he is unsparing in the picture that he draws of a church perpetually threatened by the weeds that grow in its own garden. He relates at length the first sin that undermines the integrity of the new community; Ananias and Sapphira have fallen into nothing worse than the double-mindedness that affects many modern Christians in their handling of their income tax affairs; yet such shiftiness is held to be intolerable in a fellowship founded on the truth of God (5:1–12). Luke, familiar as he is with every detail of the Old Testament story, is almost certainly thinking of the first sin committed after Israel had entered the promised land, and of the condign vengeance visited on the duplicity of Achan (Joshua 7). He does not spare even the apostles, Saul and Barnabas, and records the "paroxysm" (so in the Greek) that leads to the separation between the two and to temporary disruption of a friendship that had survived earlier strains in Antioch (15:39; cf. Gal. 2:13). Even Christians continue to practice their magical arts (19:18) and need sharp warning to bring them to their senses. Luke is our principal authority for the strife that tended to exclude the Gentiles from the fellowship and so to prevent the church from ever emerging from the narrow confines of a Jewish sect (chapter 15). There is no trace as yet of the divergence that we are later to know as Gnosticism; but it is from within the church itself that the grievous wolves are to arise who will threaten to ravage and destroy the church (20:29).

This presentation of the astonishing variety of outward and inward threats to the church makes of Acts a book for all times. We recognize the world of which Luke writes as the world in which we ourselves live, his church as that church we know all so well, with its curiously complex mixture of good and evil. Here we see the art of the great historian as of the great poet. He takes the individual and particular and raises it to the level of universality. We read lesser historians to learn facts. We read the great historians to learn the meaning of human life. Debate will continue as to the relationship between fact and interpretation in Luke's presentation of the early history of the church. We come to him with many questions he does not answer. For all that, his picture throbs with life, and introduces us to those living forces as a result of which the church in the end survived the Roman Empire and became what it is today, the one religious faith that can claim to be genuinely universal.

It is time to turn to the other half of the Lucan presentation of the Christian gospel. The universal element we have seen in Acts gives the key also to the gospel as Luke sets it forth. He is writing the record of events that are central to the entire history of the human race, and that establish their claim on every single member of that race. The genealogy of Jesus is carried back not to Abraham, the father of the Jewish race, but to Adam who is the father of us all, and who by divine appointment was the first and original son of God (Luke 3:24–38). In a list of potentates and rulers, unlike anything else in the New Testament, we are brought into touch with the secular events of the time of Jesus, with the religious history of the Jews in that period, and with the authority exercised in Palestine by the representative of the Roman emperor (Luke 3:1–2). If we cannot say exactly what is meant by the fifteenth year of the emperor Tiberius, that is the fault not of our historian but of the confused chronological system of the Romans, under which the successor of an emperor was often associated with him in authority before his death. So this Gospel is to be a study in history. In this work, as in Acts, the providential rule of God in history is never forgotten. Though the eschatological perspective of the end of time is not as strongly stressed as in Mark or Matthew, it finds its due place in the picture. But these things concerning the story of Jesus are most firmly believed among us because they actually happened; geography, chronology, history, and theology are all inextricably entwined.

Every historian, other than a mere annalist, works to a scheme that helps him to organize and arrange, and need not distort, the complex material with which he has to deal. Luke sees the whole of history as unrolling itself in three periods—one long, one short, and one as yet undefined.[12] All the prophets prophesied until John the Baptist. John himself belongs to that prophetic past, to the period of preparation. He speaks of the coming of the Spirit as belonging to the future, and not as a present reality in which he himself is a participant (Luke 3:16). Then follows the short period of the ministry of Jesus, in which, from the moment of his baptism onward (3:22; 4:1; 4:14) the Spirit is active in a new and special way. It is, however, to be noted that in the record of this period the Spirit is associated with Jesus only and with no one else; even for his closest followers the Spirit is a promise for the future, and not a present possession (12:12). We are at once aware of the sharp contrast in this respect between the Gospel and the other work of Luke. The Acts of

12. This thesis has been worked out in detail by Hans Conzelmann, *The Theology of St. Luke* (New York: Harper & Row, 1961). But see also the criticisms of Conzelmann's understanding of history in Helmut Flender, *St. Luke: Theologian of Redemptive History* (Philadelphia: Fortress Press, 1967).

the Apostles deals with the third of Luke's periods, the period of the church.   The Spirit has now been made available for all believers, so much so that Paul is unwilling to accept as true believers those who have not received the gift (Acts 19:1–5).

Clearly none of this is fortuitous.   The historian is here also theologian, and is giving expression in both books to his understanding of the Spirit.   The Spirit in Acts is the Spirit of Jesus.   But for this to be so, the concept of Spirit had to undergo a radical modification. He must be seen as the Spirit who was the inspiration of Jesus throughout his ministry, and in whose power all his mighty works were done.   This Spirit is, as everywhere in the New Testament, the Spirit of power; but at the opening of the ministry of Jesus in this Gospel, he is identified as the Spirit of gentleness, of recovery and of healing (Luke 4:18).

The special characteristics of the Third Gospel have frequently and correctly been identified.   Almost all who have treated of this Gospel have expatiated on the brillance of the literary style in which it is set forth.   The art of narrative reaches a level of surpassing excellence, especially in such parables as those of the prodigal son and of the good Samaritan.   Not a word is excessive or out of place. Great skill is shown in the choice of just the most expressive phrase. Each works up to a climax of exuberance in the enumeration of all the things that the father did for the returning son, and that the kind Samaritan did for the unfortunate victim of robbery with violence:

> . . . had compassion,
>   and ran
>   and embraced him and kissed him.
> . . . and said Bring quickly the best robe . . .
>   and put a ring on his hands,
>   and shoes on his feet;
>   and bring the fatted calf and kill it . . .
> (15:20–22)

> . . . he had compassion, and
>   went to him and
>   bound up his wounds . . .
>   set him on his own beast and
>   brought him to an inn and
>   took care of him.
> . . . took out two denarii and gave them to the host . . .
> (10:33–35)

It is possible that the number seven in each case is due only to coincidence; it may be, however, that Luke is reproducing a remembered characteristic of the speech of Jesus himself.

There are signs in Luke of an ascetic tendency. He seems at times to think that riches are an evil in themselves and not only in their consequences: "Woe to you that are rich for you have received your consolation" (6:24; cf. 16:19–31). He has a special interest in women and children and has much to tell of them (e.g., 8:2–3). In accordance with his understanding of the universality of the gospel he manifests a special interest in the Samaritans. He does indeed record the incident of the Samaritan village that rejected the pilgrims whose "face was set toward Jerusalem" (9:51–56); but it is no accident that the hero of one of his greatest parables is a Samaritan from the despised and rejected race (10:25–37), and that the only one of ten lepers who returned to offer thanks was a Samaritan (17:11–19).

We have already noted in our study of Acts that the writer is concerned to show the Roman power as just and basically friendly to the Christian cause. It is consonant with this that in his Gospel more than in the others stress is laid on the unwillingness of Pilate to sentence Jesus to death: "Why, what evil has he done? I have found in him no crime deserving death; I will therefore chastise him and release him" (23:22; see also 23:13–16). There is nothing in the writings of Luke the Gentile that can properly be called anti-Semitism; but it is the judgment of Luke the historian that the Jews were primarily responsible for the death of Jesus.

A long list of such characteristics can be made; but such enumeration does not of itself bring us nearer to the question with which we are primarily concerned: What is the theology of this Gospel; what is its understanding of the message and mission of Jesus?

The answer to this question can be given in a single phrase: God accepts those whom man rejects. This can be worked out in reference to four of the most celebrated passages in the Gospel—the two parables already referred to, the prodigal son (15:11–32) and the good Samaritan (10:25–37); the story of the sinful woman (7:36–50); and the story of Zacchaeus (19:1–10).

The parable of the prodigal son is so well known that many of those who read it fail to note the context in which it is set. The three parables in chapter 15—the lost sheep, the lost coin, and the lost son—are in fact specimens of polemical theology. Jesus has been sharply criticized for the inclusiveness of his message, and for the way in which he seems deliberately to choose the riff-raff of the population to be his friends. Throughout the entire history of the church, self-consciously virtuous people, like the philosopher Celsus and the emperor Julian, have made this a main plank in their attacks on the Christian church. No pharisee has ever been able to believe that there is more joy in heaven over one sinner who returns than over the many fat and prosperous sheep that have never gone astray. Jesus indignantly replies that, if they had known what God is really like, they could not have condemned him (Jesus) and must have recognized that he was doing the will of God.

As in the parable of the prodigal son, the emphasis in the parable of the good Samaritan is on the helplessness of the victim, in the one case of arrant folly, in the other of imprudence. The reader will understand the parable only by identifying not with the good Samaritan but with the wounded man lying desperately in need of help. Whether help is given or not depends entirely on the initiative of those who pass by; two withhold it, one gives it. One of the traditional interpretations of the parable sees in the good Samaritan Jesus himself, coming to the rescue of the helpless. This is perhaps going too far in the direction of allegorization.[13] Yet many readers, like Albert Schweitzer in a moving passage in that best of missionary books, *On the Edge of the Primeval Forest* (1922), may have been reminded of the old German hymn which runs:

> I lay in cruel bondage;
> Thou cam'st and mad'st me free.

The story of the sinful woman hardly needs elucidation, though the moving exposition of it by the great Danish thinker Søren Kierkegaard is less well known than it deserves to be.[14] We find the woman in the very last place that we might have expected—in the house of the Pharisee, where she can expect no kind looks but only obloquy and contempt. But gratitude[15] draws her back to give the best gift she can think of in return for the goodness of God. We do not know when or how contact between Jesus and this unfortunate had been established. We are shown clearly the two types: the humble and penitent seeker, who receives far more than she could have expected, and the arrogant man who draws down upon himself the sorrowful rebuke, "my head with oil thou didst not anoint" (7:46 AV).

In the story of Zacchaeus, again, the initiative is taken by Jesus: "I must stay at your house today" (19:5). Once again the generosity of Jesus is countered by the obtuse malignity of the crowd: "he has gone in to be the guest of a man who is a sinner" (19:7). Those who lived through World War II will not find it difficult to understand the intense hatred felt by the Jews in the days of Jesus for the tax

---

13. Malcolm Muggeridge, *Jesus* (London: Collins, 1975), quotes amusingly from St. Augustine, showing how far allegorization of the parables can be carried.

14. *Christian Discourses, and The Lilies of the Field and the Birds of the Air, and Three Discourses at the Communion on Fridays*, trans. Walter Lowrie (London, New York, Toronto: Oxford University Press, 1939), pp. 379–86.

15. Our Aramaic scholars tell us that "she loved much" (7:47) probably represents the Aramaic original, "she was overwhelmingly grateful."

collector, the quisling who had sold himself into the service of the oppressor, and to appreciate the revolutionary quality of the conviction of Jesus that such people could be saved, in fact were much more likely to find salvation than the virtuous whose very virtues stood in the way of their receiving the free grace of God. In this strange world it is much more dangerous to be good than to be bad.[16]

Surely we have heard something like this before. Where was it? Is not this precisely the burden of the Epistle to the Romans, the point to which Paul ceaselessly turns—that God is interested in the ungodly, that he takes the initiative in seeking them out, and that he is willing to accept them on the basis of faith in Jesus Christ alone? Luke is a historian and presents his theology in the form of narrative rather than of a systematized statement of doctrine. We shall not expect to find in him the array of technical terms that sometimes perplex us in the Epistles of Paul. Yet are not both in essence saying the same thing? Even "justification," one of Paul's favorite words, turns up in Luke in a highly significant context. Two men went up into the temple to pray. We are shown in the sharpest form the difference between the good man and the bad, the danger into which the good man is plunged by the very consciousness of his goodness, and the possible salvation of the bad man who is sadly aware of his badness. The sinner went back to his house justified rather than the other (Luke 18:14). What does the word "justified" mean here? We may translate it approximately in English as "accepted." By recognizing exactly who and what he is, by making no attempt to establish any claim upon God, by casting himself wholly and unconditionally on His mercy, he has put himself into the right relationship with God and has made his own the acceptance that God has already made available to him. No New Testament writer exactly resembles any other; each has his own character, his own way of thinking. But surely at this point Luke comes very near to Paul. The element in the teaching of Jesus that is wholly new is just this—that God loves sinners, loves them just as they are, and goes out to seek them even before they have begun to turn to him.[17] This is what the church has always found it hardest to believe and to declare. It is so much easier to believe that God likes good and respectable people, and so to hide the sovereign grace of God under a veil of what is at best conformity, at worst legalism.

---

16. The concern of Luke for salvation is well worked out in Ian Howard Marshall, *Luke: Historian and Theologian* (Grand Rapids: Zondervan, 1971). The sense of his argument is stated on p. 19: "We shall argue that Luke's concern is with salvation as such rather than with salvation history ... Luke's concern is basically with the salvation established by the work of Jesus as an experience available to man."

17. This was recognized by the Rabbinic scholar Claude Joseph Goldsmid Montefiore, *The Synoptic Gospels*, 2d ed. (London: Macmillan and Co., 1927). To this part of the teaching of Jesus he could find no parallel in the Rabbinic sources, which he knew so well.

Luke the missionary had seen this happening all around him; he had seen the lost sheep coming home, the selfish being delivered from their selfishness, the corrupt beginning to learn the meaning of sincerity. And so, though his Gospel is historical in planning and intent, it is to be read throughout in the light of the end to which it leads. The Resurrection sheds its light backward on the whole narrative. The Jesus whom it depicts is no longer an unknown Son of man; he is the One who is known as the risen One through the presence of his Spirit in the church. What he did in the days of his flesh is understood in the light of what he continues to do every day in the life of the church. That this is so is shown by the titles by which Jesus is referred to in this Gospel in comparison with those commonly used of him in the other three. Here he is frequently referred to as the Lord, without any sense of incongruity; this is what the church knew him to be, and therefore it seemed natural to the writer to carry back to the pre-Resurrection period a title that, as far as our evidences allow us to judge, was hardly if ever used before the Resurrection had shown to the believers the glory of the One in whom they had believed.

Consonant with this anticipation of the Resurrection is the note of joy that runs all through this Gospel. It is recorded that Jesus himself rejoiced in the Holy Spirit (10:21)—the Greek word here is one that denotes intense and exuberant joy, almost exhilaration. We have noted already the joy that there is in heaven over one sinner who repents (15:7). The people rejoice and praise God for all the wonderful things that they have seen (13:17). The Gospel ends in scenes of praise and thanksgiving in the temple (24:52).

This, then, is a picture of the active, friendly Son of man, never too much concerned with himself to notice and care for the needs of others. At the same time he is the victorious Son of man, whose triumph is already assured and visible in his mighty works. This means that this Gospel lacks both the dramatic intensity of Mark and the sense of impending judgment that we have noted in Matthew. Not that either quality is entirely lacking. When Jesus is told of the Galileans whose blood Pilate had mingled with that of their sacrifices, his blunt comment is, "unless you repent, you will all likewise perish" (13:1–4; note also 12:49 ff.; 13:25 ff.). The scene of the conflict in Gethsemane is here delineated in greater detail than elsewhere; only here are we told that the sweat of Jesus was as great drops of blood falling down to the ground (22:44). Yet the general tendency of the Gospel is other than that of Mark or of Matthew. With Luke's three words from the cross, we are far removed from the bleak dereliction of the picture as given by Mark, and the single word that speaks of forsakenness.

"Father, forgive them."[18] This is in line with the picture of Jesus given in every part of the Gospel; he is concerned at all times for the lost sheep, even for those who have done the deepest wrong; and this concern is so deep that he is able to forget, at least for the time being, the intensity of his own sufferings and to think only of others.

"Today you will be with me in paradise." The victory of Jesus did not begin with or after the Resurrection; it had already begun. He had proclaimed the kingdom as a present reality—the kingdom is there, because the king himself is there.[19] Now that the king is reigning from a tree, the doors of the kingdom have been thrown wide open, and the first to enter is a crucified robber.

"Father, into thy hands I commit my spirit." So the end is peace. That other cry of "Why hast thou forsaken me?" comes from Ps. 22:1. So also this final utterance (Ps. 31:5), with the remarkable difference that the word "Father" is added to what is found in the Hebrew text. Jeremias has taught us that the use of the intimate term *Abba*, "Father," in prayer was so rare as to be practically unknown among the Jews;[20] the word that he had himself so constantly used comes naturally to the lips of the dying Jesus, and from him was taken over by the worshipping church (Rom. 8:15).

If only the Third Gospel had survived and the other three had been lost, we would have remained in ignorance of much that is taught us in the other three. Yet we cannot but be glad that chance or Providence has preserved for us this radiant Gospel, in which the transfiguration of Jesus is indeed recorded, but only as an episode in that transfigured life, which stretches from the moment at which Jesus comes back from the wilderness to Galilee in the power of the Spirit to that in which he yields up his Spirit to the Father in quiet and tranquil confidence that the will of the Father has been done and his purpose accomplished. Luke has shown us the gospel as that message which by its sheer beauty wins and controls the hearts of men, and introduces them into that kingdom in which the joy of the Lord reigns supreme.

---

18. This first word from the cross is absent from a number of manuscripts of the Gospels. I believe, however, that it formed part of the passion narrative as written by Luke.

19. The meaning of the notable expression, "The kingdom of God is within you" (Luke 17:21 AV; "in the midst of you" RSV) is disputed. It certainly cannot mean, as Tolstoy understood it in his book with this title, an inner mystical experience. The most likely interpretation is that indicated in the text: "You are looking here and there for the kingdom. But it is now no more a future ideal; because Jesus is here, the kingdom is now a present reality; this truth men will ignore at their peril."

20. Joachim Jeremias, *The Prayers of Jesus* (Naperville: Allenson, 1967), pp. 11–65.

7

New Questions and Strange Answers

"The witness with the honest face and the puzzling evidence."
This was how a scholar of fifty years ago characterized the writer of
the Fourth Gospel.[1] In the intervening half century almost every
outstanding New Testament scholar has written on the Johannine
sector of the New Testament. Some opinions that at one time were
widely held have been abandoned; but it would be hard to say that
we are nearer agreement and certainty than we were at the beginning of this century.

We possess a Gospel and three letters, all similar in style and
outlook. Are they by the same hand or from different authors? The
church was slow to accept the two little letters, 2 and 3 John, as
canonical, but this seems to have been due to doubt as to whether
letters written to private persons could be part of the canon of
Scripture rather than to doubt as to their authorship. They seem to
go so closely with the longer Epistle that, if the first is apostolic, it can
hardly be doubted that so are they. Are the Gospel and the Epistles
from the same hand, or must we think of different writers? The
majority of scholars are in favor of the unity of authorship. A smaller
number, among whom C. H. Dodd should be especially mentioned,[2]
hold that the differences in theology are such that we must think of at
least two writers rather than one. But which comes first—Gospel or
Epistles? The majority would probably come down on the side of
the opinion that the Gospel is the more mature work, in which
questions only hinted at in the Epistles are fully and definitively
worked out. But others give what seem to them to be satisfactory
reasons for thinking that the Epistles should be regarded as a kind of
appendix to a Gospel that was already in circulation. Without pro-
nouncing an opinion on all these complicated questions, the judgment may be ventured that Gospel and Epistles belong to the same
period, and to the same situation in the life of the church.

1. Henry Scott Holland, *The Fourth Gospel* (London: John Murray, 1932).
2. Charles H. Dodd, *The Johannine Epistles*, The Moffat Commentary (London: Hodder and Stoughton, 1946).

Since the beginning of the Gospel-writing period a new factor has entered the situation—the immense movement known by the general title of Gnosticism. During the second century this new doctrine spread very widely and became the principal adversary of orthodox Christian faith. Gnosticism existed in a large variety of forms; but the following points would probably have been accepted by all Gnostics as essential to the faith as they understood it:

There are two realms, the realm of light and the realm of darkness. Matter belongs wholly to the realm of darkness and is therefore in its very nature evil. Some fragments of the kindgom of light have become imprisoned, as human spirits, in the realm of darkness. Such spirits, belonging to the spiritual world of light, can be saved; for no others is salvation possible. The means by which salvation is to be obtained is knowledge (*gnosis*).

It is clear that any such scheme is dualistic—it believes in two separate and permanently hostile realms; unhistorical—it deals with principles understood to be eternal and not with events; predestinarian—only those can be saved who are already spiritual; there can be no transition from the material to the spiritual nature; pessimistic—there can be no deliverance for the material creation such as that to which Paul looks forward in Romans 8; intellectualist—everything depends on knowledge rather than on faith; and exclusive—there is a fellowship of select souls, but no place can be found in the fellowship for those who are not already saved.

As to the origins and development of the movement a great deal of uncertainty still prevails. A Gnostic library of the fourth century, discovered at Nag Hammadi in Egypt, has yielded information of great value, and there is almost certainly more to come. There is always the hope of further archaeological discoveries. Within the limits of existing uncertainties, the most probable account would seem to be more or less as follows:

Various forms of dualism existed in the ancient world. In Greece, from the time of the Pythagoreans in the sixth century B.C., there had existed an ethical dualism, that made a radical distinction between the soul and the body in which it has become imprisoned. The soul in its nature is pure, immortal, and akin to the divine; it must hope to escape as soon as possible from the body, which weighs it down and is generally evil in its tendencies. Such views were widely disseminated by people known as Orphics, and many evidences of them are to be found in the writings of Plato. A rather different and more metaphysical kind of dualism came in from Iran and from the teachings of Zarathustra (also sixth century B.C.). Here the whole universe was seen as the field of conflict between the great god of light, Ahura Mazda, and the dark power of evil, Angro Mainyu. In some forms of Zoroastrian thought there appears to be a hope of some final victory of the powers of light. But the main emphasis lies on the apparently endless conflict between the rival powers.

Where the ethical dualism of the West and the metaphysical dualism of the East encounter one another, Gnosticism is born. The most likely place for this encounter would be the great cosmopolitan city of Alexandria, just at the meeting place of East and West. A considerable part of the population of Alexandria was Jewish. This might account for those Judaistic elements that appear to be present in some forms of Gnosticism.

The problem of time, When?, is even more elusive than the problem of place. When did Gnosticism as a distinctive movement come into being, and at what point did it begin to influence the thinking of the Christian churches? One view, rather widely held and to be found in the writings of Rudolf Bultmann and others of his school, is that Gnosticism in its main outlines is pre-Christian, and that before the New Testament was written it had put forward the idea of a mediator, a redeemer, through whom the imprisoned souls could find their way back from the world of darkness to the world of light. If this were so, it might not have been difficult for the early Christians, in their somewhat fumbling efforts to express their faith in Jesus, to take over the concepts of the Gnostic redeemer and to use them for the expression of a faith that had its origins in a very different world. There has been, however, in recent years an increasing consensus that, though certain elements in Gnosticism go back to very early times, Gnosticism in any systematized form did not come into existence until, at the earliest, the closing years of the first century; and that, if a redeemer is found in Gnosticism, this is due to borrowing in the reverse direction—Gnosticism found the doctrine of the redeemer already well developed in Christianity and took it over, modifying the figure considerably in the process of fitting it into its own mythological understanding of the universe.[3]

When, then, did Gnosticism begin directly to influence Christian thinking? The idea of knowledge, *gnosis*, is of course present in Christian thought from a very early date. A kind of primitive Gnosticism existed in Corinth as early as the days of Paul. There were there Christians who boasted of their esoteric wisdom, regarded themselves as spiritual and perfect, and despised those who did not come up to their level of understanding. Paul finds it necessary to deflate them. He tells them that "As for knowledge, that is something that we know perfectly well that we all possess. Knowledge

3. For details of literature, see Bibliography, below

serves merely to inflate a man's vanity; it is love alone that builds us up into the likeness of Christ" (1 Cor. 8:1, paraphrase). There is a deep difference between this cold intellectual knowledge and that after which Paul strives: "that I may know him and the power of his resurrection, and may share his sufferings" (Phil. 3:10). In Christian knowledge this personal note seems to be always present—knowledge is of a person and not of a theory.

Gnosticism in this less than technical sense could have grown up anywhere and at any time during the first century. The influence of Gnosticism as a system seems to be evident first in the Johannine writings and to take the form to which in the second century the term "Docetism" came to be applied (this term comes from the Greek verb *dokeo*, "to seem, to have the appearance of"). Since to the Gnostic matter is essentially evil, whereas the divine is pure and cannot enter into any contact with evil, the idea of any real incarnation of God in Jesus Christ was unacceptable. God might please to take on the appearance of a body and so manifest himself to us; but such a body could not have any physical reality. And, since God is perfect and no assault can be made on his perfection by anything outside himself, he might choose to appear to suffer, but such sufferings cannot be more than illusion.

The writer of the Johannine Epistles is apparently inveighing against doctrine of this kind when he writes: "Every spirit which confesses that Jesus Christ has come *in the flesh* is of God; and every spirit which does not confess that Jesus Christ is come *in the flesh* is not of God" (1 John 4:2–3). For the same reason he affirms that Jesus is he that came by water and by blood. There are three that bear witness—the Spirit by whose operation Jesus came into the world to show himself to man; the water of his baptism by which he was sealed as the messenger of God; and the blood of his death by which he became the savior of the world (1 John 5:5–8; cf. 4:14).

The writer of these Epistles has three main points to make against the false teachers, or false disciples, by whom the faith of believers is threatened—that they create division where there should be unity; that they fail to show the spirit of love expressed in charitable action such as must be characteristic of the believer; and that they fail to realize that laxity in moral conduct is incompatible with the profession of faith in God who is light and in whom is no darkness at all (1 John 1:5). This last point is shown to have been essential by much that we learn of the Gnostics in the accounts later given by the Fathers of the church. They seem to have swayed between asceticism, the denial of the elementary rights of the body, and antinomianism, the belief that there is no law that the spiritual man is any longer bound to obey. If the body is evil, then it must be denied the gratification of any of its desires (asceticism). If the body has no real connection with the soul, it cannot matter what it does; the gratification of its lusts cannot affect the soul, which belongs by nature to another world and remains incorruptible and uncorrupted (antinomianism). With all this the writer will have nothing to do: "Little children, let no one deceive you; he who does right is righteous as he is righteous. He who commits sin is of the devil; for the devil has sinned from the beginning" (1 John 3:7–8). So intense is his feeling of the dangers to which the fellowship is exposed that at times he seems to transgress his own injunctions regarding charity in the instructions he gives as to the way in which those who are in error are to be treated: "If anyone comes to you and does not bring this doctrine, do not receive him into the house or give him any greeting" (2 John v. 10).

The spread of Gnosticism in the second century had much to do with the formulation of Christian orthodoxy, as we find it set out in, for example, the extensive writings of Irenaeus toward the end of that century. The church rallied around three principles of conservation. The first was the formation of the canon of the New Testament; these are the books that are known and acknowledged by all; other books that claim to convey a secret and esoteric teaching have no authority. Secondly, the church began to accept brief formulations of the faith in the form of creeds, in which the doctrines accepted by all true believers were succinctly set forth. These creeds were exclusive as well as inclusive; the phrase "Maker of heaven and earth" was inserted to exclude the Gnostic view that matter is evil and that its origin is not to be sought in the good God. The third strand is the historic episcopate. The significance of the bishop is that he was a public official of the church; his teaching was open and accessible to all, except insofar as there were reservations as to the amount of truth to be committed to those who were not yet baptized. Any idea, therefore, of a secret tradition from the time of the apostles, such as was claimed by the Gnostics, was unhistorical and lacked any well-founded claim to be received.

This appeal to history is, as we have seen, characteristic of the New Testament church. It deals not in philosophical or mythological speculation, but with events that were known to all, with a recognizable body of believers existing in time and space, and with teachers whose credentials were open to inspection by any interested party. This being so, it is not surprising to find that a teacher of an earlier generation than that of Irenaeus, faced with Gnosticism in an incipient form, turned back to history and believed that the best antidote to false teaching would be a gospel, written throughout in awareness of the new ideas that were beginning to circulate, but without direct confrontation with them.

We have four Gospels and not only three. The traditional view was that the Fourth Gospel was the work of the apostle John, written in old age, probably in Ephesus; that it is just as good a historical source as the other three, but that it supplements their presentations both in history and in theology through the deeper understanding of the truth that long meditation and pondering of the historical events had supplied. Radical criticism in the nineteenth century (Baur and the Tübingen school) regarded the work as having been written well on in the second century, much later than the death of the last among the original believers, and treated it as a Hellenistic meditation on the revelation given in Jesus Christ, of no value as a historical source but of the greatest value as showing what could be made of the gospel in a Hellenistic milieu detached from its original Jewish surroundings.

Both of these views are still held. The majority of scholars, however, would regard both views as too sharply defined. Of course there are Hellenistic elements—it is impossible to write in Greek without using Greek words, and every such word has a history. On the other hand, it is now generally recognized that there are also strong Jewish elements in the Gospel, accompanied by awareness of situations in Jerusalem that seem to have been forgotten even at the time at which the synoptic Gospels were written; the Gospel may at many points be based on recollections independent of the synoptic traditions and no less authentic than they. Some have even gone so far as to say that there is nothing in the Gospel itself to exclude the possibility of an early date, perhaps even before the fall of Jerusalem in A.D. 70. Even those who would retain a good deal of skepticism about such views would agree that even in a Gospel that was committed to writing at a late date there may be found very early and reliable historical traditions.[4]

To some extent our interpretation of the theology of the Gospel will be affected by our view of its origins. It may be well to state clearly the position from which this chapter is written. The Gospel was probably written near the end of the first century, but contains a number of very early traditions and is almost certainly dependent in part on the recollections of a Palestinian disciple who knew

4. The most elaborate treatment of the historical factor in the Gospel so far is Charles H. Dodd, *Historical Tradition in the Fourth Gospel* (Cambridge, 1963). Among supporters of the early date for the Gospel may be named Professor Markus Barth, and also John A. T. Robinson in *Twelve New Testament Studies* (Naperville: Allenson, 1962). Leon Morris contends valiantly for the apostolic authorship: *Studies in the Fourth Gospel* (Grand Rapids: Eerdmans, 1969) and *The Gospel of John*, New International Commentary of the New Testament (Grand Rapids: Eerdmans, 1970). Leander E. Keck argues for the view that early tradition may be found in late documents. J. N. Sanders believes (1968) the author of the Gospel to have been Lazarus.

Jerusalem well and was entirely at home in Jewish customs. The early tradition linking the Gospel with Ephesus may be accepted as having reasonable historical probability. If the disciple whose memories come to us through the Fourth Gospel was in fact John the son of Zebedee, the Gospel as we have it may come to us rather from the hand of one who had often heard him speak than from the apostle himself.

When we pass from these prior questions to what is actually written in the Gospel itself, the first thing that we shall notice is that here the evangelistic purpose of Gospel-writing is more clearly stated than in any other Gospel: "These are written, that you may believe that Jesus is the Christ, the Son of God, and that believing you may have life in his name." (John 20:31). The writer is in the strict sense of the term an evangelist—one who sets forth the good news of the mighty acts of God in Jesus Christ; the aim of his proclamation is to awake conviction, otherwise called faith, in the minds of men who through this conviction will attain to salvation in Christ, otherwise called eternal life. We can only speculate as to the hearers for whom the words were originally written. We may think perhaps of a group of intelligent Hellenistic Jews in one of the great cities of the Roman Empire, together with interested Gentiles who had gathered around them; a group concerned about the new message that had been brought to them by Christian believers, but not yet ready for that decisive step of self-commitment that would separate them finally from the world of Greek philosophy, from the adherents of the old Law of Israel, and from those who were seeking a new wisdom in the speculations of Gnosticism. This evangelistic purpose determines the character of the Gospel as a delineation of the tremendous drama of faith and unbelief.

The Gospel opens with a prologue that, though it differs markedly in style and content from the rest of the Gospel, must be regarded as a program; it is there to tell us what the Gospel is all about.

In recent years the suggestion has been made that the structure of the prologue as we have it is best accounted for as an ancient Christian hymn, into which prose comments and explanations have been inserted by the Evangelist.[5] A tentative reconstruction of such a hymn might be as follows:

> In the beginning was the Word
> and the Word was with God
> and the Word was God

---

5. One argument against this view is that no agreement has been reached as to which parts of the prologue belong to the ancient hymn. Hence the expression "tentative reconstruction."

All things were made by him
and apart from him
was nothing made that was made.

In him was light
and the light was the life of men.
The light shineth in the darkness
and the darkness overcame it not.

That was the true light
that lighteneth every man
by its coming into the world.

It was in the world
and the world was made by it
and the world knew it not.

The Word became flesh
and dwelt among us
full of grace and truth

Of his fullness
have we all received
and grace for grace

No man has seen God at any time
the Word only begotten
he has shown him forth.[6]

Logos, "Word," is thrown out as a challenge. What can it mean?
There is a parallel in the Book of Revelation; when the great warrior,
who is called Faithful, goes forth, "the name by which he is called is
the Word of God" (Rev. 19:13). This makes it clear that the term was
not unknown in Christian circles as a title of Jesus Christ; but this
does not carry us much further in trying to understand what is meant
by it in the Fourth Gospel. R. H. Charles, a great authority, tells us
that "we have here another of the numerous instances of community
of diction between the Apocalypse and the Fourth Gospel, in many
of which there is no community of meaning."[7]
  The word *Logos* had had a long history in the Greek language. It

6. I believe that this is one of the passages in which no Greek manuscript gives us the true reading. The evidence
is divided; RSV reads "the only Son" in the text, and gives "God" in a note. This conceals the difficulty. The
expression "God only begotten" is strange; "only-begotten Son" would be an obvious correction for a scribe to
make. I believe that "Word only begotten" is the true reading; thus the hymn goes full circle and brings us back at
its end to its beginning. It is to be noted that the expression "only-begotten Word" was not unknown to early
Christian writers, and is once used by the great Origen in his Commentary on the Fourth Gospel. See *A Patristic
Greek Lexicon* (1961), s.v. "Logos." For a different view, see Charles K. Barrett, *New Testament Essays*
(Naperville: Allenson, 1972), pp. 27–48. Barrett rejects the idea of an early "hymn." "The Prologue is not a
jig-saw puzzle but one piece of solid theological writing. The evangelist wrote it all."
7. Robert H. Charles, *The Revelation of St. John* (Edinburgh: T. & T. Clark, 1920), 2:134.

was used in many different senses—reason, proportion, and so on—
especially in the Stoic system of philosophy.   Professor W. K. C.
Guthrie in his great *History of Greek Philosophy* lists in fact no less
than eleven different senses in which it can be used, and gives it as
his judgment that none of these bears any relation to its use in the
Fourth Gospel.[8]   The readers are likely to have had some awareness
of this background history of the term; perhaps its very flexibility
did something to commend it to the writer of the Gospel.   Yet it is
doubtful whether Greek philosophy is the direction in which we
should look for enlightenment.   By opening his Gospel with the
words "In the beginning," the writer deliberately points us back to
the first verse of the first chapter of Genesis; it is as though he had put
up a little flag to indicate to us that what follows is to be taken as an
inspired commentary on that first chapter of the Bible.   When the
relevant words are written out in parallel, this becomes quite clear:

Genesis	John
In the beginning	In the beginning
God created	All things were made
And God said	was the Word
Let there be light	the light was the life of men.

The Word of which the prologue speaks is the creative Word of God;
we meet this Word again in Ps. 33:6: "By the word of the Lord the
heavens were made, and all their host by the breath of his mouth."
And this creator God is also the self-revealing God; from the beginning he has been showing himself to the world; the final manifestation of the *Logos* is the end-term of a long process that stretches
throughout the whole of human history.

   The recognition of this Old Testament clue to the interpretation of
the prologue is of the greatest importance, since the principle holds
good for the Gospel as a whole.   The writer seems to hold the whole
of Old Testament Scripture in solution in his mind, and the use he
makes of it is striking and original.   "I said, You are gods" (10:34);
"Not a bone of him shall be broken" (19:36).   These verses are not
quoted elsewhere in the Gospels.   But the debt goes much further
than direct quotation: "As Moses lifted up the serpent in the wilderness" (3:14).   The writer takes it for granted that readers will immediately recognize the allusion to Num. 21:4–9, and will see the
point of the reference   A good deal of attention has of late been
directed to this Old Testament watermark on the Fourth Gospel;
much yet remains to be done before it will be possible to say that the

8. William K. C. Guthrie, *History of Greek Philosophy*, 4 vols. (Cambridge, 1962–1975), 1:420–24.

subject has been fully explored. Three points in the prologue require particular attention.

By stressing the work of the *Logos* in creation, the writer separates
himself decisively from the Gnostic outlook on the world. To the
Gnostics the created world as material was evil; this writer shares the
Old Testament view that, when God created the world, he made all
things very good.

"The Word became flesh" (1:14). It would be impossible in four
words to express more completely a repudiation of the Gnostic view
of salvation. *Sarx*, "flesh," denotes human nature in its weakness,
its limitation, its earthiness, its kinship with the animal and material
world; not necessarily in its sinfulness but at least in its propensity to
sin. "Became" implies a totality of identification, in which nothing
is withheld and beyond which it is impossible to go. This, as
Clement of Alexandria rightly said, is a spiritual Gospel; it sees all
things in the light of the divine eternity; but it can be spiritual only
because it fully accepts also the reality of the earthly and the human,
and shows forth salvation through the entry of the divine eternity
into the world of time, the entry of the spiritual God into the world of
flesh.

"No one has ever seen God . . . he has made him known" (1:18).
The Gnostics asserted the unknowableness of God, and up to a point
all reverent Christians must follow them; the gap between man
who is finite and God who is infinite is one of the realities that will
persist both in time and in eternity. But at this point Christians and
Gnostics part company. Gnosticism spoke of God as *Bythos*, the
"abyss" that no human thought can penetrate; and as *Sige*, "silence,"
that unknown world from which no voice can reach our world until
there has been a descent through endless aeons, manifestations, by
which at last some kind of communication between God and man
becomes possible. Christian faith will have none of this. God may
be inscrutable; but if he is really God, there can be nothing to
prevent him from making known everything of himself that can be
known by man. And this is exactly what God has done. He is not
silence, he is utterance. As Paul taught the Colossians, we have no
need of principalities and powers to fill the gap that separates us from
God; he has direct access to us and we have direct access to him, and
this access is in One whose name at last is given, "Grace and truth
came through Jesus Christ" (John 1:17).[9] The Law had only a
shadow of good things to come; the reality (and that is what the word

9. Note that the word "grace" occurs in this Gospel in the prologue and nowhere else. It is not found in either
Mark or Matthew.

"truth" means here as so often in the Johannine writings) came with Jesus Christ.   The Law could effect none of those good things it showed forth; in Jesus Christ law for the first time became effective through the gift of grace.[10]

Each of the other Gospels anchors itself in history by recording the ministry of John the Baptist.   The Fourth Gospel follows suit: "There was a man sent from God, whose name was John" (1:6).   It is unlikely that this writer was acquainted with any of the other Gospels in the form in which we have them.[11]   He shared with them access to a wide range of traditions; but when he does cover the same ground as the synoptic writers, he seems to have it in mind to correct rather than to confirm the traditions of which they have made use. So in his references to John the Baptist there is a highly individual tone.   There may be a special reason for this.   We have a hint in Acts 19 of the existence of a sect of believers who had received only the baptism of John.   At a considerably later date we find something of the same tradition in the writings of the strange sect of the Mandaeans, which still exists in very much reduced numbers in Iraq.[12] If at the time at which the Gospel was written there was still in existence a somewhat strong movement for the adherents of which John rather than Jesus was the true Messiah, the writer might well feel impelled to put the two in their proper relationship; there is a wide difference between the true light and the witness to the light (1:8); the friend of the bridegroom who stands and hears his voice plays a very different part from that of the bridegroom himself (3:30).   Jesus is throughout at the center of the picture as this writer paints it.   From the second chapter onward the Gospel depicts the development of faith and unbelief, and of the life-and-death confrontation in which faith is finally vindicated.

The writer's method is peculiar to himself and is liable to cause perplexity if it is not understood.   He starts, in chapter after chapter, with a narrative, clear, vivid, and vigorous; but, as he allows his mind to dwell on what he is recording, we are given as it were a series of dissolving views in which the figure of the original speaker becomes steadily less distinct, and we find ourselves listening to the voice of the Evangelist alone.   It is hardly possible to determine exactly at what point the Lord ceases to speak and the thread is taken up by the

10. See note 9 above.

11. Naturally, on this subject opinions differ.   But I do not think that the argument set out by Percival Gardner-Smith, *Saint John and the Synoptic Gospels* (Cambridge, 1938), has been substantially shaken.

12. There are certain affinities between the Fourth Gospel and the Mandaean writings; any influence of these writings on the Gospel seems to be ruled out by the difficulty of dating any of them earlier than the second century.   This is one of the points at which British and German scholarship tend to divide; almost all British scholars have accepted the verdict of Francis C. Burkitt, *Church and Gnosis* (Cambridge, 1932), that the Mandaean documents are dependent on Christian sources rather than the other way around.

Evangelist. Chapter 3 starts with a dialogue between Jesus and Nicodemus, a leader among the Jews; the theme is the difference between the adaptations of human conduct that the Law requires, and the radical new beginning that Jesus both demands and makes possible for men: "You must be born anew" (3:7). As far as verse 12, we feel some confidence in the view that Jesus is speaking. But when we have reached verses 20 and 21, "every one who does evil hates the light . . . he who does what is true comes to the light," we are aware that it is the voice of the Evangelist himself to which we are listening. But at what point does the transition take place? The faith of myriads of Christians has taken John 3:16 with its five verbs—God so *loved* that he *gave* . . . that whosoever *believeth* should not *perish*, but *have* everlasting life—as containing the whole Gospel; but are we here listening to the words of Jesus himself, or is it the Evangelist who is interpreting for us what he has come to know as the truth of the gospel?

What this amounts to is that the element of interpretation is greater in this Gospel than in the other three. Not that it is anywhere absent. We have seen that each of the Evangelists is a theologian, selecting and arranging his material often down to the last detail to convey to us his understanding of the meaning of salvation. Hardly anywhere shall we find bare historic fact with no indication of its place in the story of salvation. This writer, like the other three, has his feet firmly planted on the ground; he too is relating the story of a man who actually lived and breathed; at moments he is at pains to emphasize the reality of that humanity (e.g., 4:6). But when it comes to interpretation, it is not always easy to see the link between the historic fact and the heights to which it is the intention of the writer to guide us.

This is what is meant when we say that the Gospel is written throughout in the perspective of the eternity of God. For this writer, history is never mere recording; it involves always the apprehension of a purpose of God who is always at work; only when that purpose has been grasped can the significance of the history be rightly understood. This is nowhere more evident than in the treatment by this writer of what are commonly called the miracles of Jesus. In Mark these are powers, irruptions of the mighty God to put right that in his creation which has gone astray, and so to show that the kingdom of God is already here. In the Fourth Gospel the mighty acts are signs. The veil that ordinarily hides the mystery of God is for the moment rendered transparent and we are enabled to see what God is in reality doing all the time. In the Old Testament the manna in the wilderness was the great indication of God's ability and willingness to care for his people even under the most unpropitious circumstances. But those who ate of the manna in due course died (John 6:49, 56). The new sign of the feeding of the five thousand can be understood on three levels (and this, too, is characteristic of the method of this Evangelist). Some thought only of a welfare state in which there would be provision for the physical needs of all (6:26). Others understood the loaves and fishes in terms of the messianic banquet, which it was believed that God would provide for his people at the end of time. Only those with the insight needed to read the sign aright are able to realize that what Jesus has come to bring is the bread of life. This is something infinitely greater than the manna; he who eats the flesh of the Son of man and drinks his blood has eternal life, and will be raised up at the last day (6:48–54).

The story of the raising of Lazarus is the greatest of all the signs, leading up as it does directly to the story of the Resurrection of Christ. Yet here too what the sign shows is something far greater than the sign itself. The raising of the dead man shows that Jesus has the power over life and death; but Lazarus will in due course die again and die conclusively as far as this world is concerned. The sign is interpreted for us. Jesus himself is the resurrection and the life (11:25); he who believes in him can never die. The death of the body is reduced to a purely physical event, interesting but of no great significance. What is of importance is that continuity which is secured in the relatedness of the human spirit to the living God through faith in Jesus Christ. The one who believes "has passed from death to life" (5:24).

This relationship of sign to reality determines the picture given in this Gospel of the One whom in one context only it calls the Savior of the world (4:42). It does indeed offer a picture of one who was truly man, as is witnessed by the frequent use in this Gospel of the term "the Son of man."[13] But the great sign is Jesus himself. He points all the time beyond himself to a greater reality; and that reality is the unchanging will and purpose of God. This gives to the presentation a certain tone of inevitability—this is the way in which things had to happen. And so the story unrolls itself, not mechanically, but with the majestic progress of a drama in which the end is seen from the beginning. This Gospel alone does not include any account of the temptation of Jesus. There is an account of Gethsemane (though that name is not here used; John speaks of a garden, but the New

13. In John 9:35 the manuscript evidence is interestingly divided between "Son of God" (AV) and "Son of man" (RSV text; "Son of God" [margin]). It can hardly be doubted that "Son of man" is what the Evangelist wrote. In this Gospel Jesus nowhere directly claims for himself the title "Son of God," though he comes nearer to it than in the other three (e.g., 10:36).

Testament nowhere puts the two together). But this is not a story of agony and uncertainty; Jesus is throughout in charge of the affair, "knowing all that was to befall him" (18:4). The scene of the Crucifixion is not one of dereliction and dismay, but of quiet fulfillment and triumph, summed up in the single word, "It is finished [accomplished]" (19:30). The end of the purpose as long foreseen has now been reached, and now there is nothing more that needs to be done.

Signs are not easily read, and their meaning can be penetrated only by the eye of faith. In this Gospel, as in that of Mark, the central question is simply this: Who is this Jesus of Nazareth? This question is as relevant to the readers as it was to the actors in the Gospel story. Time and again we are given lively extracts from the debates that the presence of Jesus occasions among the Jews: "Many of them said, He has a demon and he is mad... others said, These are not the sayings of one who has a demon. Can a demon open the eyes of the blind?" (10:19–21). We are introduced to the irritation and frustration produced by the method of Jesus, which, as we have seen before, leaves it to the questioner to find his own answer: "How long will you keep us in suspense? If you are the Christ, tell us plainly" (10:24). "Who is this Son of man?" (12:34). But to the direct question "Who are you?" they are not granted the plain and simple answer that they desire; that answer can be given only to faith, and where there is no faith there can be neither answer nor understanding: "I told you that you would die in your sins; for you will die in your sins unless you believe that I am he" (8:24).

We may think that, in recording these discussions, the Evangelist has been influenced by memories of the embittered disputes that arose between Jews and Christians as the differences between church and synagogue hardened into permanent alienation. One of the grounds on which a late rather than early date is assigned to this Gospel is precisely the extent to which this alienation is already evident. "The Jews" are now the enemy, those who have rejected belief; the term no longer signifies the chosen people of God.

The appeal of Jesus is constantly to those works through which the discerning eye can become aware of the immediate presence of God, and of the intimate relationship in which the One who does the work stands to the One in whose name they are done. "If I am not doing the works of my Father, then do not believe me. But if I do them, even though you do not believe me, believe the works, that you may know and understand, that the Father is in me and I am in the Father" (10:37–8). But the works are important only because they point both to the Father and to the Son. Jesus in this Gospel does set out his own claims more plainly than the other three: "I and my Father are one" (10:30). This is the experience to which the believers in Jesus had come; they could not think of Jesus without thinking of the Father, and they could not think of God without thinking also of the Son. It would be a mistake to read into this saying all the later metaphysical discussions of Christian theologians as to the relationship between the eternal Father and the Son; the reference is rather to the perfect oneness of will and purpose in which the Son is united to the Father. Yet the answer put into the mouths of the Jews does succinctly express the objection that through the centuries Jews and Muslims have raised against the Christian gospel as the church has come to believe it: "We stone you for no good work but for blasphemy; because you, being a man, make yourself God" (10:33). They were right; the claim is either true or blasphemous.

Just as unbelief hardens into the hostility that in the end leads to murder, so faith is led onward from step to step into an understanding of the peculiar intimacy of the believer with his Lord, which is itself the reward of faith. This intimacy is far deeper than any human friendship; it can be expressed only in terms of mutual indwelling: "He who eats my flesh and drinks my blood abides in me and I in him" (6:56). Human friendship and love constitute a protest against the apparent separateness of selves walled in by the barriers of the body, and to an astonishing degree break down those barriers. "My true love hath my heart, and I have his" expresses perfectly the feeling of those who have experienced the depths of human relatedness. Awareness of the love of God in Christ adds a dimension that is not present in any purely human love; yet this deeper relationship is not wholly inexpressible, since the analogy is a true analogy; man's love for man is an overflow from the love of God and genuinely indicates that which it cannot fully express. It is Jesus himself who says to his disciples, "I have called you friends" (15:15).

This experience of the indwelling Christ, in John as in Paul, is closely associated with the doctrine of the Spirit. The Spirit who will come is the Spirit of the risen Lord, the Advocate whom the Father will send in the name of the Son (14:26); therefore during the period of the ministry of Jesus the Spirit must be a promise for the future and not an experience of present reality. Jesus had already received the Spirit without measure (3:34), but the Spirit is not yet given to believers. The difference between the two epochs is set forth in a phrase so stark and startling that few among translators have felt able to take it literally: "The holy Spirit was not yet, because Jesus was not yet glorified" (7:39). Almost all versions render "the

Spirit was not yet given," and this is in fact the reading of some manuscripts. But this is not what the Evangelist wrote. If the Spirit is the Spirit of the risen and glorified Jesus, then before the Resurrection that Spirit in a very real sense does not exist and cannot be given to men. Naturally John with his deep roots in the Old Testament knew well that the Spirit was in existence and was at work long before the coming of Jesus Christ into the world. But for him "the Word became flesh" marks a radically new beginning, even though set in the context of "in the beginning was the Word." His doctrine of the Spirit may have been influenced by similar ideas.

The closing discourse of Jesus to his disciples as given in this Gospel (chapters 13–17) gives us, more than any other section of the New Testament, clear and basic teaching on the meaning and nature of the Holy Spirit, the Advocate who will be with the disciples as friend, guide, and helper when the visible presence of Jesus is withdrawn from them.

How did this discourse come to be written? Light may be thrown on the problem by the brief section, 12:44–50. This comes at the close of the long section in which we have been following the growth of faith and unbelief, and leads out into that confrontation in which faith is almost submerged, to emerge again triumphant in the concluding section that deals with the Resurrection. Though the passage opens with the words, "Jesus cried out and said . . .," what follows is to be taken not so much as an actual discourse of Jesus as a careful summing up of much that had gone before. Here are many of the motifs that run through the previous chapters: light and darkness, seeing and believing, judgment, life everlasting, the oneness between the Father and the Son. So in chapters 13–17 we have a mingling of diverse elements: actual remembered words of Jesus (a surprising number of parallels to the synoptic tradition; the Jesus who says, "Let not your hearts be troubled" [14:1] is clearly the same as the Jesus who had said earlier to his perplexed disciples, "Take heart; it is I; have no fear" [Mark 6:50]); theological interpretation; and profound meditation on the presence of the living Christ through the Spirit in the experience of the believing community. It is not possible to separate the three strands; this writer of genius has used his subtle art to weave together all the separate threads into a single whole.

The keynote of the whole discourse is to be found in the words, "I will not leave you like orphan children; I am coming to you" (14:18 as in the Greek).[14] The reference here is not to that final coming at

---

14. There is a touching parallel in Plato's *Phaedo* of the feelings of the disciples of Socrates when they realize that the death of their master can be no longer postponed.

the end of the world, of which we have read so much in the synoptic
Gospels.   The eschatological perspective is by no means absent
from this Gospel.   Such recurrent phrases as "I will raise him up at
the last day" (6:39, 40) make it plain that there is to be a final
consummation as well as a present fulfillment of the will of God.
But there has been a change of perspective and of emphasis since the
days of earlier eschatological expectation.   Eternal life is now not
only a promise but a present possession: "he who hears my word and
believes him who sent me has eternal life; he does not come into
condemnation" (5:24; note the flexible changes in tense throughout
the discourse from 5:17 onwards).   So here also "I am coming to
you" speaks of the coming of Jesus in the Spirit, which is to take
place as soon as the Resurrection has vindicated the wisdom of God
in the death of his Son.   The real absence that had filled the grim
hours in which they did not "as yet know the scripture, that he must
rise from the dead" (20:9) is now to be replaced by that real presence
which can never again be taken away from the church.

The task of the Spirit will be to complete that which Jesus has
begun.   "He will teach you all things" (14:26).   He, the Spirit of
truth, "will guide you into all the truth" (16:13).   But this he can do
only because he will remain faithful to that which has already been
spoken.   The unity between Father and Son, so often stressed in this
Gospel ("what I say, therefore, I say as the Father has bidden me"
[12:50]) is to be reflected in the unity of the Spirit with the Son in
whose name he is sent forth; "whatever he hears he will speak"
(16:13).   His work in relation to the world can be summed up in
three words: sin, righteousness, and judgment (16:8).   These may be
interpreted as challenge—men must believe or accept the penalty of
unbelief; vindication, in that the central proclamation of the Christian faith is always the witness to the Resurrection of Jesus; and
triumph, in that the decisive victory in God's war with evil has been
already won, though the skirmishes may continue through a future
the duration of which no man can even guess.   Persecution and
suffering are not part of the foreground of this Gospel, but they are
never very far away.   The church is always the church of the crucified Son of man.   So this section of the great discourse ends with
the warning, "In the world you have tribulation"; but this warning is
at once swallowed up in the triumphant declaration, "I have overcome the world" (16:33).

So in chapter 17, in the prayer that since the sixteenth century has
been known as the High Priestly Prayer of Jesus, the mind of the
reader is lifted up from the immediate crisis to the worldwide sig-

nificance of these events: "I do not pray for these only, but also for those who are to believe in me through their word" (17:20). We may feel that here the Evangelist is looking back on the years during which he has been watching the progress of the gospel, as it has spread in province after province of the Roman Empire. But also he seems rightly to have interpreted the mind of Jesus as he faced the certainty of death—this death is something that will affect the destinies of men far beyond the narrow limits of the Jewish world. There is nothing in this chapter that is local or temporal; perhaps it is for this reason that it has become favorite reading in ecumenical gatherings. The prayer ends with a splendid summary of the purpose of the ministry of Jesus: "that the love with which thou hast loved me may be in them, and I in them" (17:26 AV). "The Father loveth the Son." Even the careful reader of the Gospel may be forgiven if he cannot immediately complete this clause; with slight variations it occurs three times: the Father loves the Son, and has given all things into his hand (3:35); the Father loves the Son, and shows him all that he himself is doing (5:20); for this reason the Father loves me, because I lay down my life, that I may take it again (10:17).

One of the recurring themes of the Gospel is "lifting up." "As Moses lifted up the serpent in the wilderness, so must the Son of man be lifted up" (3:14). "I, when I am lifted up from the earth, will draw all men to myself" (12:32). The second of these quotations is interpreted by the Evangelist as referring to the manner in which Jesus met his death (12:33). But this writer is accustomed so to hide meaning within meaning that it is impossible for the reader ever to be sure that he has grasped all that is intended. Beyond the physical lifting up we are to see the lifting up in glory that is the central theme of the Gospel: "We beheld his glory, glory as of the only Son from the Father" (1:14); "to behold my glory, which thou hast given me in thy love for me before the foundation of the world" (17:24). Jesus has come from the Father; he goes back to the Father. From chapter 13 onward, and perhaps even earlier in the Gospel, we are reading the story of the return of the Son to the Father, and this means the manifestation of that glory which has for the most part been hidden, but which by a kind of anticipation the disciples have seen at one point or another during the ministry (e.g., 2:11). In this upward movement the cross plays a central role; the moment of deepest humiliation is also the opening of the period of the triumphant glory.

This being so, there is no need in this Gospel for any narrative of what is commonly called the Ascension. It is true that the risen

Jesus says to Mary, "I have not yet ascended to the Father. I am ascending to my Father and your Father, to my God and to your God" (20:17). Yet in a sense all that is to happen has happened. There are no forty days between Resurrection and Ascension, no further period of waiting for the coming of the Spirit. On the very day of the Resurrection, the risen Lord meets the disciples and conveys to them consolation, commission, power, and authority for the work that they are to do:

> Peace be with you.
> As the Father has sent me, even so I send you.
> Receive the Holy Spirit.
> If you forgive the sins of any, they are forgiven; if
>   you retain the sins of any, they are retained.
>   (20:21–23)

When he has done this, there is no more that the Lord need do. Yet one more word is added, not for the sake of the disciples but for the sake of the readers of the Gospel to the end of time. When Mark's Gospel was written, many were still living who had seen Jesus in the days of his flesh. If the Fourth Gospel does in fact draw largely on the memories of one who belonged to the generation that had known Jesus intimately in the days of his flesh, the old man (as he calls himself in 2 and 3 John) must have known himself to be almost the last survivor of a steadily diminishing band. (Chapter 21, which is an appendix to the Gospel as originally written, suggests that he is the very last of all [21:20–24]). Years have passed. The Fourth Gospel is a vivid narrative, with countless small touches that spring either from actual memory or from extraordinarily skillful construction. But even to the first readers the record of Jesus must have come as a story of long ago, of things that had happened before they were born, and were now mediated to them at a great distance. They may have been inclined to say, as we of so much later a generation are also inclined to say, "If only I could have been there." To them is given the final consoling word: "Blessed are those who have not seen and yet believe" (20:29).

If we think only of Jesus of Nazareth, these things do indeed belong to a very remote historical past. But in the coming of the Spirit, Jesus, as Søren Kierkegaard so often and so finely said, is our contemporary. The One to whom we have been introduced in the spiritual gospel is "Jesus Christ, the same yesterday, and today, and for ever" (Heb. 13:8).

8

Response to Response

Of the twenty-seven books that make up the New Testament canon, we have now considered in some detail twenty-two. Five remain —2 Peter, Jude, 1 and 2 Timothy, and Titus. This is a miscellaneous collection of small works, which cannot easily be fitted in with any other section of the New Testament. They form a kind of appendix. If they had been excluded from the canon and so allowed to disappear, our theological loss would not have been very great; there is little in these works that is not to be found elsewhere in one form or another in the New Testament. Yet here they are in the canon, and a study of New Testament theology that failed to take note of them would be incomplete.

A useful clue to the classification of the New Testament documents is a consideration of the response to the gospel expressed in each document, and of the circumstances in which such a response is likely to have been made. There is first the response of those who themselves heard the preaching of Jesus, and who were the eyewitnesses of whom Luke speaks in the prologue to his Gospel. Then follows the response to this response—the response of those who heard the message from the apostles or from those who had heard and answered the call they proclaimed. This response falls into two sections—more spontaneous in the period of the Epistles, when churches were coming rapidly into existence and experiencing their first difficulties and problems; more reflective in the period of Gospel-making, as great theological minds turned back to the story of Jesus from John the Baptist to the Ascension, and strove to extract from it the last drop of its meaning. Both these periods were brilliantly creative. At the end we come to a time in which much of that spontaneity and creativity had been lost, and we are faced with what looks like a response at third-hand to the message of Jesus. In spite of sporadic brilliance of phrase and of theological insight, we are moving here on a more conventional plane; the church, still faced with inward and outward perils, is now to find its strength in clearer definitions of doctrine, better organization, and a more rigid exercise of discipline. All these can be understood as forms of return to the living Lord, as a response to his claims; but the response is muted; it belongs to a period of consolidation rather than of gallant and perilous adventure. Let us start by looking at the little tract known as the Second Epistle of Peter.

Few scholars today defend this as a genuine work of the Galilean apostle. Those who do so find it difficult to hold that Peter can have been in any direct sense the writer of the first Epistle that bears his name. Vocabulary, style, and atmosphere are so different that it is hardly possible that both letters can have been from the hand of the same author, even if we suppose him to have been helped by amanuenses. It is a fact that in the ancient world many authors did write under names other than their own. An example can be found not very much later than the period with which we are now dealing in that strange work called the Epistle of Barnabas, which can hardly be later than A.D. 140, but cannot possibly have been written by Barnabas the companion of Paul. Once this habit of early Christians has been understood, there can be little difficulty in accepting 2 Peter as a pseudonymous work, belonging to the latest stages in the development of the New Testament.

If this is so, there are no certain indications as to the date or authorship of the Epistle. But the reference to Paul's letters, "There are some things in them hard to understand, which the ignorant and unstable twist to their own destruction, as they do the other scriptures" (2 Pet. 3:16), unlike anything else in the New Testament, may provide us with a clue. If the letters of Paul, almost unknown for a generation except in those churches that had actually received them, had suddenly appeared, as there is reason to suppose, in a collection published about the year A.D. 90, and if those letters were being used, as they may have been used in the lifetime of Paul himself, as an argument in favor of antinomianism ("let us do evil that good may come" [Rom. 3:8]), this would provide exactly the situation in which such a letter as 2 Peter might be profitably sent out to the churches. Incipient or developing Gnosticism, as we have seen it in the First Epistle of John, soon began to show signs of moral indifference; the appearance of such antinomian tendencies in the church is one subject dealt with in the Epistle of Jude and in 2 Peter.

This short letter is an impressive document. Its style is vivid and picturesque and reaches a high level of denunciatory declamation. All this is combined with a deep sense of pastoral responsibility for

the welfare of the flock. 2 Peter cannot be regarded as a witness of
the first importance to the truth of the gospel; yet it would certainly
have been a pity if it had been allowed to disappear. In each of its
three chapters the Epistle deals with a theme of capital importance
in the life of the church.

First, the writer stresses the need for progress in the apprehension
of what it means that we are partakers in the divine nature ([1:4] a
Hellenistic phrase this, not used elsewhere in the New Testament).
It was a characteristic of the Stoic tradition to draw up lists of virtues
and the contrasting vices, and it may well be that our author was
aware that he was following Greek examples. But there are qualities in his list that mark it out as specifically Christian. "Brotherly
love" we might perhaps find in a Stoic list; but love, *agape*, though
the word itself was not unfamiliar in the Greco-Roman world, has
obtained a new significance through the revelation of the love of God
in Jesus Christ.   The writer validates his teaching by linking it
directly to the historical manifestation of God in Christ; the resemblances between his account of the transfiguration of Jesus
(1:16–19) and those to be found in the Gospels are so close as to
suggest that he had at least one written Gospel before him. And,
though his reference to the inspiration of Scripture is directed in the
first place to the Old Testament Scriptures, it is at least possible that
he was aware of the growth of a collection of Christian Scriptures,
which are also liable to be wrested from their true sense by the
private interpretation put upon them by Gnostic teachers (1:20–21).

In the second chapter the writer turns to his main theme, disregard
by Christians of the most elementary moral precepts, so as to "in-
dulge in the lust of defiling passion and despise authority" (2:10).
Here he has absorbed into his text almost the whole of the little
flysheet that passes under the title the Epistle of Jude.[1] This writing
deals with one single point, the peril arising to the church from
"ungodly persons who pervert the grace of our God into licentious-
ness, and deny our only Master and Lord, Jesus Christ" (v. 4). One
picturesque illustration is piled upon another to make plain the
worthlessness of such professing believers and the certainty of the
judgment that will fall upon them.

An interesting touch in Jude is the reference to the Book of Enoch
("the seventh from Adam," [v. 14 AV]), an apocalyptic work unknown
in the Christian world except in fragmentary quotations until the
Scottish traveler James Bruce brought back from Ethiopia in 1773

1. Did Jude use 2 Peter, or did 2 Peter use Jude? It is impossible to establish priority with complete certainty, and
both views have been held by good scholars. On balance it seems more probable that the longer work has
absorbed the shorter.

three manuscripts in the Ethiopic language. Enoch must come before us again in the concluding section of our study. Here it is to be noted that this is the only direct reference in the New Testament to those many Jewish apocalyptic works that were circulating in a limited number of copies in certain Jewish and Hellenistic circles.

The sustained denunciation that makes up the main body of the leaflet falls rather disagreeably on ears sensitive to a measure of anger that appears to be alien to the spirit of the gospel. The writer must have felt the danger to be extremely grave. Yet even this harsh little book includes a noble exhortation to progress in the Christian life: "But you, beloved, building up yourselves on your most holy faith; pray in the Holy Spirit; keep yourselves in the love of God; wait for the mercy of our Lord Jesus Christ unto eternal life" (vv. 20, 21); and one of the finest blessings or commendations in the New Testament: "Now to him who is able to keep you from falling and to present you without blemish before the presence of his glory with rejoicing, to the only God, our Savior through Jesus Christ our Lord, be glory, majesty, dominion, and authority, before all time and now and for ever. Amen" (vv. 24, 25).

And so back to 2 Peter. In his third chapter the writer deals with that false sense of permanence, the disappearance of the apocalyptic element in the faith, which is a recurrent temptation to the church, especially in times of outward peace and prosperity: "all things have continued as they were from the beginning of the creation" (3:4).[2] To this the writer's answer is a vivid picture of the destiny that awaits the physical universe, when "the heavens will be kindled and dissolved, and the elements will melt with fire" (3:12). This passage may well be derived from a Stoic description of one of those periodical cataclysms in which it was believed that a whole universe would disappear, to be replaced in due course by another similar universe. It could serve equally well as a description of what might happen if some wandering body were to come too near to our little planet, and draw it out of its regular orbit into too close proximity to the sun.

The lesson that the writer derives from this doctrine of the transiency of all earthly things is neither a strained expectancy of future blessings nor an ascetic withdrawal from the ordinary life of the transitory world. It is a plain and simple exhortation to recognize the obligations to which we are committed by the faith: "Since all these things are thus to be dissolved, what sort of persons ought you to be in lives of holiness and godliness?" (3:11). The only certain

2. Ernst Käsemann has discussed the problem in an essay, "An Apologia for Primitive Christian Eschatology," in *Essays on New Testament Themes* (London: SCM Press, 1964), pp. 169–95. He has few good words to say for the Second Epistle of Peter.

sign of life is growth; therefore we are to grow in grace and knowledge of our Lord and Savior Jesus Christ (3:18). It is not for us to count the times and seasons; "with the Lord one day is as a thousand years, and a thousand years as one day" (3:8). We have better things to do than to lose ourselves in anxious calculations as to late or soon.

The so-called pastoral Epistles, 1 and 2 Timothy and Titus, present us with a variety of problems, which served historically as the starting point for serious critical study of the New Testament.[3] Four distinct views are held as to the date, authorship, and character of these three letters to individuals.

The traditional view is that these are letters of Paul, related to the period of liberation he enjoyed after his first trial and to a second period of imprisonment that led up to his final condemnation and death.

Some hold that the letters are essentially Pauline, and that the differences from his usual style and vocabulary are to be accounted for by a larger participation than usual on the part of a secretary or assistant.

A third view, widely held, is that the Epistles, especially 2 Timothy, include genuine fragments of Pauline writings, but that these have been embedded by an editor in blocks of material of considerably later date.

Some deny any connection of these letters with Paul, and would assign to them a second-century date. The Pauline flavor in that case would be due to the skill of a writer who knows how to echo the authentic Paul, while all the time giving expression to the views and situations of his own time.

Even if it were possible to establish firmly the view that there is no Pauline element at all in these Epistles, it is hardly possible to place them later than A.D. 80. There is in them hardly a trace of that Gnostic dualism we have found elsewhere in the later books of the New Testament. What the recipients are warned against is "myths and endless genealogies, which promote speculations rather than the divine training that is in faith" (1 Tim. 1:4); "wrangling among men who are depraved in mind and bereft of the truth . . . a morbid craving for controversy and disputes about words" (1 Tim. 6:5–4); "stupid, senseless controversies . . . that . . . breed quarrels" (2 Tim. 2:23). The writer is less specific than we could wish as to the precise nature of these disturbances and false teachings; what he tells us does, however, suggest Jewish rather than Hellenistic influence.

3. In the work of Ferdinand Christian Baur, *Untersuchungen über die sogenannten Pastoralbriefe des Apostels Paulus* (Stuttgart: 1835).

We have seen that in certain areas of the church Jewish influence continued to be strong right up to the time of the final break between church and synagogue. If this understanding of the situation is correct, it suggests that the pastoral Epistles are earlier than the Johannine writings, in which the Jews are clearly identified as the enemy, and Hellenistic Gnosticism is already beginning to assail the purity of the church.

More important than date is the question of theology. What is the theology with which the writer desires to meet and to confound these other teachers, who, if not false teachers in the ordinary sense of the term, are garrulous and so occupied with trivialities as to obscure both the challenge and the glory of the gospel?

These letters are a recall to faith. Yet the moment this word is pronounced, we become aware of a shift in meaning. We have already noted three shades of meaning in the word, as used by, respectively, Paul, James, and the author of the Epistle to the Hebrews. The pastoral Epistles seem to represent a fourth tradition, in which the meaning of the word "faith" has become formalized and has taken on the sense of a recognized and authoritative body of doctrine. We trace something of this development in Jude, verse 3, where the faithful are urged to "contend for the faith which was once for all delivered to the saints." In 1 Tim. 4:1, "some will depart from the faith" suggests a departure from the standards of orthodoxy approved by the writer. Those who have erred from the faith in 1 Tim. 6:10 have wandered away from the approved tenets of Christian morality. When Paul, as represented by the writer, says "I have kept the faith" (2 Tim. 4:7), the meaning may be, "I have kept unsullied my loyalty to my Lord"; it seems, however, that here also he is referring to inflexible loyalty to that form of doctrine which had been committed to him, and from which in a long life of missionary service he had never departed.

There seems to be, in all religious systems, an irresistible tendency toward dogmatic formulation. This tendency is to be found not only in Christianity but also in Buddhism and in Islam. The Society of Friends maintains, more than most other Christian bodies, the liberty of the Spirit; yet it is possible to recognize in the history of the Quakers the development of something that can only be called a Quaker orthodoxy. There has never been a less systematic Christian thinker than Martin Luther; yet within forty years of his death the great movement he had called into being was in danger of being smothered under the mountainous weight of Lutheran orthodoxy. It is not surprising that the same tendency is to be observed in the early story of the Christian movement.   This is, perhaps, something that we should not too much regret.   Not everyone can remain always on the heights of individual spiritual discovery; a large part of the religious life depends on the support of a community, and will be expressed in the following of a routine; this becomes dangerous only if the human spirit becomes so sunk in routine as to be no longer sensitive to the movement of the divine Spirit when it calls to new discovery and adventure.   A religious movement that depends too much on emotion is likely to discover that, when the first emotion has died away, as in time it certainly will, nothing at all is left.   Something more than emotion is needed.   "The faith" may be less exciting than "faith."   Yet it may be a necessary element in conserving, if not creating, the continuing image of Jesus Christ among men, and holding the fort until the time for new creative discovery has come. The pastoral Epistles do not make the same contribution as the Epistle to the Romans; yet it may be recognized that they too serve a legitimate and Christian purpose.

It is in line with this purpose of conservation that these Epistles concentrate so much attention on the organization of the churches.   We are still some way from the strict episcopal organization we encounter in the letters of Ignatius (about A.D. 110).   But we have traveled a considerable distance from the flexible organization of the earliest Christian communities.   We do, indeed, find the same terms as are used, for example, in the Epistle to the Philippians; here as there we find "overseers" and "servants" (deacons).   But elders also play their part in the scene, and appear to have been introduced into their office by a special act of ordination (Titus 1:5); the reference to an overseer two verses later suggests that "elder" and "overseer" may be in fact alternative terms for the same office.   Timothy, too, had been admitted to office by the laying on of hands (2 Tim. 1:6), and by this means a special gift of God had been conveyed to him.   In another context the gift is associated both with prophecy and the laying on of hands by a corporate body, the company of the older men (1 Tim. 4:14, paraphrase).[4]   Nowhere are we told the nature of the office into which Timothy had been solemnly inducted.   Neither Timothy nor Titus is to be a bishop in the later sense of that term—the chief pastor of a single city, and of the congregations meeting in that city or in its immediate environs.   The task assigned to each is much more that of a deputy apostle, with the oversight of a number of churches and the exercise of much the kind

4. The term "presbytery" is used only here in the New Testament of a body within the Christian church (earlier, of the authorities of the Jewish people).   It is common (no less than twelve occurrences) in the letters of Ignatius, about A.D. 110.

of superintendence that Paul himself had exercised during the period before his imprisonment. In all this there is an element of conjecture—we just do not know in detail how the early churches were organized. But the movement is away from flexibility in the direction of rigidity; away from the spontaneity of immediate response to the Holy Spirit and in the direction of codes and rules.

There is nothing wrong with codes and rules in themselves. No society has ever managed to exist entirely without them. Studies of what are generally thought to be simpler societies, such as those of the Australian aborigines, have shown the extreme complexity of the traditions, all unwritten, by which the fabric of the tribal life is kept together. The problem for every society is to find the right balance between spontaneity and order. Uncontrolled spontaneity may lead simply to the dissipation of energy. The maintenance of too strict an order may result in the disappearance of originality and the substitution of conformity for experiment. In its long history the church has erred more often on the side of order than on that of freedom; the disciplinarian who produced these letters may be regarded as one of those whose works have in a measure contributed to this result.

A large part of these letters is given up to controversy with those who are obscuring the purity of the Christian message, and to rather tedious rules on such subjects as widows and how they are to be looked after in the church. But this is very far from being the whole story. In these letters we find gems of insight and expression, bearing witness to a level of inspiration that we find only rarely in Christian writings of a later date. "Christ Jesus came into the world to save sinners. And I am the foremost of sinners" (1 Tim. 1:15). Here is a fragment of an ancient Christian hymn:

> Great indeed is the mystery of godliness:
>   manifest in the flesh
>   justified in the Spirit
>   seen of angels,
>   preached unto the Gentiles,
>   believed on in the world,
>   received up into glory. (1 Tim. 3:16 AV)

"God did not give us the spirit of timidity but a spirit of power and love and self-control" (2 Tim. 1:7). "The goodness and loving kindness of God our Savior appeared" (Titus 3:4).

The pastoral Epistles have been the source and parents of an extensive progeny in the church orders, which over the centuries have tried to capture and to codify the church's life. But that life cannot be reduced to codes and rules; it will always escape from every attempt to tie it down to its past, since it always looks toward a future in which the one continuing element is "Jesus Christ, the same, yesterday, and today, and for ever" (Heb. 13:8). The pastoral Epistles deserve their place in the canon of the New Testament because they are not yet far from the source of that life, and from the flexibility of response that it engenders. The relationship of the apostle Paul to the writing of these letters raises questions that may never be finally answered. But the writer, whoever he may have been, who wrote the words, "Henceforth there is laid up for me the crown of righteousness, which the Lord, the righteous judge, will award to me on that Day, and not only to me but also to all who have loved his appearing" (2 Tim. 4:8) was perhaps as near in thought to the great apostle as Paul himself had been in his own day to the Founder and Lord of the church.

9

What Lies Behind It All?

In what we call the first century A.D. a tremendous force entered into the life of men and changed the whole course of human history since that date. What was that force?

Through chapter after chapter we have been studying the consequences of that impact. We have been able to identify at least five streams of tradition, which came into existence as groups of believers in Jesus set themselves to preserve the memories of the past and to interpret that which they were experiencing as present reality Each of these traditions is a reflection, or a shadow, of the Christ Can we pass beyond the differences in the various accounts to find an underlying unity of event that has given rise to them all? How far can we advance toward identification and definition of that solid body, "my tree," which has cast all these various shadows? How near can we come to seeing him not just through the eyes of many beholders but as he was in the simple majesty of his historical existence?

This is the question that, sooner or later, every theology of the New Testament must face. If the task is pronounced impossible of accomplishment, we are left with a history of Christian opinions; but the central theological issue is left as an impenetrable mystery. The shadows remain, but as to the nature of the tree nothing can be said. Even if so pessimistic a conclusion is not arrived at, it has to be admitted that the task of penetrating beyond the minds and thoughts of the early believers is no easy one.

Jesus of Nazareth, like those other great religious teachers, Gautama Buddha, Socrates, and the prophet Muhammad, left nothing in writing. In the records we encounter him reading aloud in the synagogue from the prophet Isaiah (Luke 4:16–20). He could read; it must be taken as probable that he could also write. But the only occasion on which he is represented in the act of writing is found in that detached story of the woman taken in adultery, which in our

Bibles has found its way into John's Gospel, 8:1–11.[1] He seems to have felt it sufficient to commit himself to the minds and memories of the believers, and to the enlightening power of the Holy Spirit whom he would leave with them.

Throughout his ministry Jesus seems to have spoken northern Aramaic, that form of Semitic speech akin both to the Hebrew and to the Syriac, which became a lingua franca over large areas of the Middle East. He must have known well the Hebrew of the Old Testament.[2] Living as he did in the neighborhood of such Greek-speaking cities as Tiberias, he can hardly have been wholly ignorant of Greek; but he seems never to have used that language for the purposes of his ministry. This means that every saying attributed to him (with the exception of one or two Aramaic phrases) has come to us through the mediation of a translation. Translation always involves an element of distortion; this is especially the case when the transition is from one language-group, in this case the Semitic, to another language-group, in this case the Indo-European.

For twenty years or more the tradition concerning Jesus was passed on orally, and little, if anything, was written down. Inevitably the tradition came to be modified in the process of constant repetition, and reinterpreted as the believers came to see the relevance of his words and works to their own historical situations. We have seen this process at work in the development of the various traditions that have found a final form in the Gospels.

When account is taken of all these factors, it is not surprising that many scholars have returned a negative answer to the question of whether we can know Jesus as he was and can reach definitive conclusions as to what it was that he actually taught.

The most pessimistic conclusion of all is that Jesus of Nazareth never really existed; or that, if he did exist, the original figure has been so lost behind mythological accretions that we cannot know anything with certainty about him. This view was especially associated with the German scholar Arthur Drews[3] and was popular half a century ago. Not much is heard of it today. Better methods of historical investigation and a certain sobriety of temper have led to the conclusion that what we have on our hands is a problem primarily of history and not of mythology.

And yet Albert Schweitzer, at the end of his tremendous survey of

---

1. Note that in some Greek manuscripts these verses are found in other contexts in the Gospels. See the fine discussion in John Henry Bernard, *A Critical and Exegetical Commentary on the Gospel According to St. John*, The International Critical Commentary, 2 vols. (Edinburgh: T. and T. Clark, 1928), 2:715–21.

2. The evidence is complicated. A fresh survey has been made by J. A. Emerton in "Did Jesus Speak Hebrew?" *JTS*, n.s. 12 (1961): 189–212 and "The Problem of Vernacular Hebrew in the First Century A.D. and the Language of Jesus," *JTS*, n.s. 24 (1973): 1–23.

3. *Die Christusmythe*, 2 vols. (1909–1911).

attempts to write the life of Jesus Christ,[4] reaches the conclusion that this is something that cannot be done. The materials available to us are inadequate. In consequence, what all these scholars of the nineteenth century had in the end achieved was to present Jesus as though he had been a man of the modern world and not of the first century. Representation has become misrepresentation and the reality has been lost in the process of interpretation. So what we are left with is a distressing vacuum. Schweitzer's book closes with words that have deservedly become famous:

> He comes to us as One unknown, without a name, as of old by the lake side, he came to those who knew him not. He speaks to us the same word: "Follow me!" and sets us to the tasks which he has to fulfil for our time. He commands. And to those who obey him, He will reveal himself in the toils, the conflicts, the suffering which they shall pass through in his fellowship, and, as an ineffable mystery, they shall learn in their own experience who He is.

Schweitzer has had his day. By a very different route Rudolf Bultmann and his school have reached an almost equally negative conclusion. Bultmann is extremely skeptical as to the extent to which the sources, as we have them, will carry us back to Jesus as a historical person. But, he would maintain, we may be confusing ourselves by asking the wrong questions. Historical research is always subject to the relativities of history. Even if every fact could be firmly established, this could lead us no further than to an encounter with the man Jesus, and this has little to do with the question of salvation. The central question is not Who was Jesus? but What is Jesus for me? The historical question is replaced by the existential, historical research by a challenge, a proclamation, a contemporary encounter; it is in the preaching of the church that the *Kyrios Christos*, "the Christ the Lord," becomes alive for faith.

Once again we are left with a vacuum. It is quite true that mere historical chronicle can never establish truth. It is equally true that historical research could destroy faith—if, for instance, it could be shown that Christian faith rests in the last resort on idle tales or mere imagination. The faith of the earliest Christians was, in point of fact, indissolubly linked to history, to a person who had lived and died in a historical situation, and whom the earliest messengers declared themselves personally to have known. Is a complete dissociation of

4. In German, *Von Reimarus zu Wrede* (1906). The English translation, *The Quest of the Historical Jesus*, appeared in 1910 and was reprinted in 1968 by Macmillan Co., New York. The preface, by F. C. Burkitt, closes with the notable words: "Books which teach us boldly to trust the evidence of our documents ... help us at the same time to retain a real meaning and use for the ancient phrases of the *Te Deum*, and for the medieval strains of 'Jerusalem the Golden.'"

proclamation from history really possible? Is it enough to know of
the great acts of God without knowing also the one through whom
these great acts were accomplished?

Our conclusion need not be as pessimistic as this brief summary
might suggest. In Bultmann's deservedly famous *Theology of the
New Testament* only thirty pages are devoted to the message of
Jesus, as one of the historical presuppositions for the *kerygma*, the
proclamation of the church, against one hundred and sixty pages
dealing with the theology of Paul. But over the last quarter of a
century there has been an extensive reaction, and a rediscovery of
the centrality of Jesus himself—his person, his message, what he was
and did, his direct challenge to the men of his own time—as the
foundation of all that the church is and believes and proclaims.

It is possible to date with accuracy one of the turning points in
theological thinking in this century. On October 20, 1953 Ernst
Käsemann, at that time of Göttingen, delivered a lecture on "The
Problem of the Historical Jesus."[5] Käsemann, a student and in
earlier years a follower of Bultmann, had come to realize the significance of the refusal of the early church to abandon its roots in
history, or to make any radical distinction between the risen and
glorified Christ whom it proclaimed and the humiliated Messiah as
he was in the days of his flesh. How is this to be accounted for? If
the fact is accepted, in what directions may we expect New Testament scholarship to move? "The heart of our problem lies here: the
exalted Lord has almost swallowed up the image of the earthly Lord,
and yet the community maintains the identity of the exalted Lord
with the earthly."[6] "For to his particularity corresponds the particularity of faith, for which the real history of Jesus is always happening
afresh; it is now the history of the exalted Lord, but it does not cease
to be the earthly history it once was, in which the call and the claim of
the Gospel are encountered."[7]

The lecture called out an immediate and extensive reaction—of
dismay among those who regarded this revaluation of history as a
betrayal, of encouragement for those who had always affirmed the
continuity of the Jesus of history with the Christ of faith. The result
has been *A New Quest of the Historical Jesus*,[8] which has occupied
the attention of a whole generation of New Testament scholars.
There has been no attempt, at least on the part of scholars, to go back

5. Now available in English in *Essays on New Testament Themes* (London: SCM Press, 1964), pp. 15–47.
6. Ibid., p. 46.
7. Ibid., p. 47.
8. This is the title of a book by James M. Robinson, Studies in Biblical Theology (London: SCM Press, 1959) expounding the new historical approach.

to the method condemned by Schweitzer and to present the Jesus of history as though he were a man of the twentieth century. Nor is there any tendency to imagine that "mere history"[9] can lead on to Christian faith. But there has been an increasing recognition of the fact that in the Gospels, and especially in the synoptic Gospels, there is a great deal of material that can be accepted as authentic, as genuinely historical, and as going back to Jesus himself. If we eliminate all that can be explained as derived from contemporary Jewish sources, or from the Hellenistic religious traditions of the time, or from the "kerygmatic" proclamation of the growing church, we shall be left, as a remainder, with that which belongs to the tradition as it emanates from Jesus himself. This is the method followed by Norman Perrin in his work, *Rediscovering the Teaching of Jesus*.[10] Some might feel it possible to rediscover more than Professor Perrin has done; the method commends itself as related to the scientific study of history.

One of the notable products of this new movement of scholarship was Günther Bornkamm's book, *Jesus of Nazareth*.[11] What Bornkamm has to say on the subject of *kerygma* and history is of particular importance at this point in our study:

> These Gospels voice the confession: Jesus the Christ, the unity of the earthly Jesus and the Christ of faith. By this the Gospels proclaim that faith does not begin with itself but lives from past history. Of this history we must speak, as do all the Gospels, only in the past tense; and this precisely because of the present in which faith has its being. . . . What the Gospel reports concerning the message, the deeds and the history of Jesus is still distinguished by an authenticity, a freshness, and a distinctiveness not in any way effaced by the Church's Easter faith. These features point us directly to the earthly figure of Jesus.[12]

We shall certainly expect to find a difference between the proclamation *of* Jesus and the proclamation *about* Jesus. There could not be total identity between what he said and what others said about him. At times the difference has seemed so profound that some have been led even to suggest that the real founder of Christianity was not Jesus but the apostle Paul. It is a great gain that today even those who would regard themselves as radical critics are prepared to

9. "Mere history" was my own translation of *Historie*, which Bultmann distinguished from *Geschichte*, "significant history," in my translation of Giovanni Miegge, *Gospel and Myth in the Thought of Rudolf Bultmann* (London: Lutterworth Press, 1960). But it seems to have caught on as a satisfactory rendering of a term for which it was difficult to find an appropriate equivalent in English.
10. (New York: Harper & Row, 1967).
11. (New York: Harper & Row, 1960).
12. Ibid., pp. 23, 24.

admit a real measure of continuity between the "before" and the "after." The task of the student today is frankly to recognize the differences within the unity, but also to consider how far we can recover the unity out of which all the differences have sprung.

It may be possible today to go a little further than the scholars who have so far been mentioned. In what may prove to be the most important book written about the New Testament in the last fifty years[13] Joachim Jeremias has indicated, on the basis of minute study of every verse in the Gospels, a number of areas in which we may feel reasonably confident that the tradition goes back directly to Jesus and to the good news as he proclaimed it.

There are a number of idioms that were unusual in the Aramaic of the time of Jesus and seem to reflect the style in which he himself spoke. It was customary among the Jews to avoid, when possible, the use of the divine name. We find in the Gospels that this is frequently achieved by the use of "the passive of divine action." "Knock and it will be opened to you" (Matt. 7:7) means precisely "God will open to you." This way of speaking in addition served as a means of describing God's mysterious action in the time of the end.

Much of the teaching of Jesus is given in poetical form; retranslation into Aramaic reveals many of the characteristic forms of Hebrew poetry, as found in the Psalms and elsewhere in the Old Testament. It is just the fact that, in the days of Jesus, no one else either among the Jews or in the Greco-Roman world was creating poetry on the level of sublimity that he so often attained:

> Consider the lilies of the field
>   how they grow;
> They neither toil nor spin;
>   yet I tell you
> even Solomon in all his glory
> was not arrayed like one of these.
>   (Matt. 6:25-9)

The earliest form of many of the traditions seems to have been a brief narrative delineating a situation and leading up to a single pungent saying of the Lord. A considerable number of these can be identified. Why does he eat with publicans and sinners? The answer is, "Those who are well have no need of a physician, but those who are sick" (Mark 2:16-17). It seems that even at this early stage interpretation has been at work; the second half of the saying, "I came not to call the righteous but sinners to repentance," may well

13. *Theology of the New Testament*, vol. 1, *The Proclamation of Jesus* (London: SCM Press, 1971).

be an explanatory note added for the benefit of those who might not immediately understand the significance of the Lord's reply.

The scribes were in the habit of adding illustrative material to their teaching, often in the form of fables. But there is nothing like the parables of Jesus in the entire corpus of Jewish writings. Jeremias has no hesitation in writing, "His parables take us, rather, into the midst of throbbing, everyday life. Their nearness to life, their simplicity and clarity, the masterly brevity with which they are told, the seriousness of their appeal to the conscience, their loving understanding of the outcastes of religion—all this is without analogy."[14] When Paul tries his hand at parabolic utterance, as in the picture of the wild-olive branches that had been grafted into the true olive tree (Rom. 11:17–24), he is not notably successful.[15] Jesus stands alone in his mastery of this art.

There are passages of what may be called theological reflection, in which the poetic imagination still plays a memorable part. An obvious example is the story of the temptation. At his baptism Jesus becomes aware that the moment has come at which he is to stand forth as the messenger of God. He cannot but be aware that he is in possession of exceptional powers: what use is he to make of these powers? In eleven verses Jesus sets out in vividly pictorial language the three main areas in which a single false step could have led to betrayal of the cause of God. Theological tomes have been written on the meaning of the temptations. It is not clear that they have added much to what is already present in the words the Lord himself is reported to have used.

It is generally agreed that the passion narrative is the first connected account of any part of the ministry of Jesus to have come into existence. Details as to the trials of Jesus, and as to the degree of responsibility for his death to be attributed respectively to the Jews and to Pilate, have been extensively debated. But in general the narrative puts content into the phrase "crucified under Pontius Pilate," which was later to find its way into the Creeds of the Christian church.

We have thus a very considerable body of material on which we can work in the attempt to ascertain what Jesus actually taught and what he thought about himself. This is not to say that there is no reliable evidence to be found in other parts of the Gospels; but it is always prudent to start with a minimum rather than a maximum claim.

14. Ibid., pp. 29–30.
15. Sir William Ramsay, with his detailed knowledge of Bible lands, has tried to show that Paul may not have been as ignorant of the art of grafting as many of his critics have supposed: "The Olive-Tree and the Wild-Olive" in *Pauline and Other Studies* (London: Hodder and Stoughton, 1908), pp. 219–52.

Students of history will not be unduly disturbed by the various forms in which sayings and parables of Jesus have come down to us. It is a fact that very few human beings can report a conversation or even a phrase quite accurately or can repeat it a number of times without modifying what they have previously said. An amusing illustration of this well-known fact has recently come to hand. All English schoolboys and schoolgirls know that when Oliver Cromwell expelled the Rump of the Long Parliament from the House of Commons, on April 20, 1643, he looked at the Mace and said, "Take away that bauble." We now learn from Lady Antonia Fraser[16] that, though we have three eyewitness accounts of the event, those exact words do not occur in any of the three and that there is no reference in any of them to baubles. For all that, historians agree that the event took place much as it has been described, and that the general sense of what Cromwell said has been preserved.

Furthermore, it must be borne in mind that the early believers understood themselves to be conserving a tradition and not to be creating one. They certainly believed that the living Jesus was still in their midst and was speaking to them. They held that, through ministers inspired by the Spirit, he was making his will known to the faithful, and that this gift of the Spirit might be received and used by any member of the assembly. As they repeated the words of the Lord they modified and adapted them to their own needs and in the light of their own experiences. But there was never any confusion between the contemporary utterances of the Lord through the Spirit and the words they believed him to have spoken in the time of his earthly ministry. Words spoken to the church, as recorded for instance in Revelation, chapters 2 and 3, relate to immediate concerns and to problems faced by the church at the time at which the message is delivered. One of the evidences for the reliability of the Gospels is that they so evidently relate to the time of the ministry, and show hardly a sign of having been influenced by urgent problems of a later date, such as the burning problem of circumcision and of the terms on which Gentiles could be admitted to the Christian fellowship.[17]

We have then, a considerable body of material at our disposal. What use shall we make of it in trying to answer the question, Who was Jesus, and what did he understand himself as having come to do?

The central theme of the preaching of Jesus is the kingdom of God. This theme is not new. Already in the Old Testament we find

16 *Cromwell our Chief of Men* (London: Weidenfeld and Nicolson, 1973), pp. 420–1.

17. It was in this sense that the church accepted from the start the doctrine of the Ascension, though this is rarely referred to directly in the New Testament. The one who is to come is the same as the one who has come; but the difference in tense represents accurately the church's sense of the distinction between the ministry of the human Jesus and that of the invisible Lord.

such phrases as that, for instance, with which the little prophecy of Obadiah ends: "The kingdom ["dominion" NEB] shall be the Lord's" (v. 21). But almost everywhere in the Old Testament there is a measure of association between the idea of the kingdom and the related idea of the deliverance of Israel as the people of God and the reestablishment of the rule of the house of David in Jerusalem. Jesus is at pains to divest his teaching of every shred of this former understanding of the nature of the kingdom. What he is proclaiming is the immediate sovereignty of God, who will take control of all the destinies of men, restore man to what he was intended to be, and overthrow the powers by whom the life of man has been destroyed, maimed, and turned aside from its proper destiny. In New Testament teaching the coming of the kingdom is always dependent on a divine initiative, never on human achievement or on ordered progress. Men may enter into the kingdom; they may proclaim it; they may inherit it (e.g., Matt. 25:34; 7:21). But they can neither earn it nor bring it into being.

All this is set forth by Jesus in terms of the will of an unchanging God for the welfare of his human children. But at the same time all his teaching is colored by a sense of intense urgency. God has now taken the initiative; men are challenged to recognize the realities of the situation and to make such decisions as will qualify them to become sons of the kingdom. The signs of the presence of the kingdom are already there. When John the Baptist asks for his doubts as to the mission of Jesus to be cleared up, he is pointed to these clear evidences: "the blind receive their sight, and the lame walk, lepers are cleansed and the deaf hear, and the dead are raised up," and most important of all, "the poor have good news preached to them" (Matt. 11:4, 5). All these are signs that the power of the kingdom is already at work. Men will neglect these evidences at their peril. Some have refused to recognize them for what they are, and have denied that the power evident in Jesus is a power from God. His reply is stern: "If it is by the finger of God that I cast out demons, then the kingdom of God has come upon you" (Luke 11:20). The Greek word is unusual and striking: "has caught you unaware, has come upon you when you least expected it."

There is a future element in the New Testament concept of the kingdom. "Thy kingdom come" is eschatological; it looks forward to the last time, the time when the last enemy will have been overthrown, and the absolute sovereignty of God will have been established beyond all doubt or questioning. But this future reference does not exhaust the whole significance of the message. When a man puts his whole trust in God, and yields himself up to live in obedience to his will, then there is an anticipation of the reality of the kingdom. If one man, for a period of some thirty-five years, lives in total dependence upon God, with a unique understanding of his will and in unconditional surrender to it, the kingdom is already there. It may well be that the kingdom is present only as a mystery, as a secret revealed only to the eyes of faith—weak, vulnerable, exposed to apparent defeat—as the divine incognito, to use a favorite expression of Søren Kierkegaard. Yet the reality of the kingdom is here among men, and, because it is God's kingdom, it has within it the promise of the final manifestation, the fulfillment of the promise contained in the words "Thou art my beloved Son; with thee I am well pleased" (Matt. 3:22; Luke 3:17).

The outstanding liberal theologian Harnack held the view that Jesus came proclaiming the kingdom of God but that what emerged was the Catholic church.[18] Why did that which played so central a role in the teaching of Jesus disappear almost completely from the proclamation of the early church? Does this mean, as some have supposed, that the preaching *about* Jesus is radically different from the preaching *of* Jesus and that there is hardly any connection between the two? Naturally there are differences. We may find reason, however, to think that the threads of connection are also there.

It is not the case that the term "kingdom" plays no part in the apostolic preaching. The word occurs thirty times outside the Gospels. It is found in all the various strands of the tradition. It is introduced in a number of different contexts quite naturally, and as though it formed part of the ordinary vocabulary of Christian communication.

There is, however, a shift in the direction of that eschatological emphasis that we have noted as already present in the Gospels. God has intervened once; he will intervene again in "the coming of our Lord Jesus Christ and our assembling to meet him" (2 Thess. 2:1). As is to be expected, emphasis on the kingdom reappears in the Book of Revelation. The fulfillment is close at hand, when the expectant church is able to affirm, "The kingdom of the world has become the kingdom of our Lord and of his Christ, and he shall reign for ever and ever" (Rev. 11:15).

The church is aware of living in an interim, "between the epochs." It cannot bring in the kingdom; it can only wait and testify

18. Adolf von Harnack, *What Is Christianity?* (New York: Harper & Row, 1957). The first English translation of Harnack's *Das Wesen des Christenthums* appeared in 1901 (London: Williams and Norgate). See especially Lectures 9 and 10.

and set up signs of the kingdom, to a large extent the same signs as were seen in the ministry of Jesus himself. The church is never to be identified with the kingdom; it is the visible witness to the great invisible reality that for the time being is veiled from the eyes of men. But the end will come, when Christ himself "delivers the kingdom to God the Father after destroying every rule and every authority and power" (1 Cor. 15:24).

In discussions of the kingdom of God, emphasis is usually laid on the first term, "kingdom." But the operative word is really "God." Who is God? It is often supposed that the word is univocal, that it has the same meaning for all those who use it. But this is not the case. When Christians use the word "God," they mean the Father of our Lord Jesus Christ and nothing else. There is a real continuity with the Old Testament. But Jesus is a teacher of superb originality, and what he adds to the idea is more significant than that which he inherits. His God is one who cares for all his creatures without discrimination, and causes his rain to fall on the just and on the unjust (Matt. 5:45). He is kind to the unthankful and the selfish (Luke 6:35). He is intimately concerned about the smallest of living things—not a sparrow falls to the ground without the Father's will (Matt. 10:29). He is like the good shepherd who goes out into the desert to seek his lost sheep until he finds it (Luke 15:4). We may think that when the Fourth Evangelist writes, "I do not say that I shall pray the Father for you; for the Father himself loves you" (John 16:26-7), he is drawing in part on the later experiences of faith; but the words are not inappropriate on the lips of the One in whom the love of the Father was first fully manifest.

A king is not a king unless he has subjects. Jesus bids men enter into the kingdom; but before they can do so there is a condition that must be fulfilled—they must repent. It has been pointed out by many that the English word "repent" hardly does justice to the Greek, which would better be rendered by some word that would imply change of mind or outlook. But even this is hardly adequate. What Jesus is demanding is that men should become wholly other than they are, repudiating the standards by which they have lived so long and accepting an entirely new relationship to God. He did indeed take a serious view of such sins as extortion, oppression, contempt for others, and sexual irregularity. But in his eyes such things are serious only because they are signs of something deeper—the alienation of man from God and therefore from his own true self.[19] Man alienates himself from God by desiring to be the

---

19. Students of Karl Marx will recognize here one of Marx's favorite words, *Entfremdung,* "alienation." It is to be regretted that in his later works Marx seems to have abandoned this illuminating term and the ideas that go with it.

center of his own world, by trying to exercise an autonomy that he was never intended to have. Any attempt on the part of man to establish his independence of God, still more to set up any claim upon God by reason of his virtues or the exactitude of his performance of religious duties, is idolatry; it displaces God from his true position, from his sole and supreme authority in relation to men. Repentance involves acceptance of the realities of the situation—of what God is and of what man is, and of the true relationship between the two. This does not result in servitude but in freedom, man's freedom to be his own true self. "The truth [acceptance of reality] shall make you free" (John 8:32). It does not mean regression to infantile dependence; on the contrary, it opens the way to the attainment of that perfection of manhood seen in Jesus himself.

So the theology of Jesus is one that does not admit of compromise. There must be a complete break with the past, and with everything that merely conventional morality or piety would approve. The sovereignty of God will not brook any rival. When Jesus says, "You cannot serve God and mammon" (Matt. 6:24), he is neither giving good advice nor announcing a commandment; he is simply stating a fact—that is the way things are. Here are two mutually exclusive worlds; a man who has chosen to live in one of them has automatically excluded himself from the other. Mammon stands for the everyday world of use and wont, of getting and spending, in which men speak of legitimate ambition and "plenty of room at the top," in which they diligently try to make the best of both worlds. If a man has set his heart on such things as these, God can never become to him the great reality by which he lives. Jesus will have none of this; the man who has set his hand to the plough and turned back is not found suitable to be a citizen of the kingdom of God (Luke 9:62).

The sharpness of the challenge has led some to suppose that these are rules applicable only in a time of crisis but should not be extended to cover the circumstances of ordinary life.[20] There is truth in this reservation. A rich young man is told to sell all that he has and give to the poor (Mark 10:17–22). This is a moment of crisis. Jesus is on his way to Jerusalem, and the final conflict in which he is to be engaged is already casting its shadow upon his way. At such a time there can be no hesitation; it must be all or nothing. Now it is quite plain that if everyone gave away everything that he possessed to the poor, the only result would be that the rich of today would become the poor of tomorrow and vice versa; the social situation would be neither changed nor improved. Not every command is of equal

---

20. A valuable study of this problem is Harvey K. McArthur, *Understanding the Sermon on the Mount* (New York: Harper & Row, 1960), especially chap. 4, "The Sermon and Ethics," in which the interim ethic, among others, is discussed (pp. 122–23).

application to every situation; there must be a measure of adaptation and flexibility.

But we all too easily allow adaptation to become dilution. We suppose that to deny oneself means a modest amount of asceticism in Lent, and forget the radical demand that self must not be allowed to count for anything in the reckoning of a man's duty toward God. Denial of self does not mean a pathological hatred of self. It is once again simply the realism which recognizes that in all things God must come first, and that, if a man wishes to find himself, he must first be prepared to lose himself for the sake of the gospel. The system of Christian ethics is derived from Christian theology. The central point of that theology is the example of Jesus Christ, and his demand that man should recognize unconditionally the sovereignty of God.

The early preachers of the gospel never lost sight of this aspect of the teaching of Jesus. The place of Mammon is taken by the world, which in many contexts is the society of men as organized in independence of God and without regard for his laws. So the believer is warned that "friendship with the world is enmity with God" (James 4:4). "Do not love the world or the things in the world. For all that is in the world, the lust of the flesh and the lust of the eyes and the pride of life, is not of the Father but is of the world" (1 John 2:15). Demas, who was in love with this present world, is condemned (2 Tim. 4:10). Already in the New Testament there are signs of that unhealthy asceticism which springs from the view that material things are evil in themselves. But for the most part the apostolic teachers are faithful to the words of the Lord and to that necessary distinction he had drawn between the one thing which is essential (Luke 10:42) and all else.

Jesus bade men repent if they would enter into the kingdom of heaven. Did he himself stand in need of similar repentance? One New Testament writer gives a confidently negative answer: "He committed no sin, no guile was found on his lips" (1 Pet. 2:22). This has been the general Christian consensus ever since.

The sinlessness of Jesus, to use a rather unsatisfactory and negative expression, is not something that can be proved by the accumulation of details. It can be inferred from a number of indications that all seem to point in the same direction.

His power over men and over situations is derived from the steady concentration of his will on a single object, the glory of God. Here he stands in marked contrast to other men who are so constantly perplexed and weakened by the division and the distraction of the will.[21] The stories of the temptation and of the conflict in Gethsemane are evidence that this was not an automatic reflex. Jesus was a man, and like other men he had to find his way amid the perplexities of life and the many things that could deflect him from his purpose. His will was as a compass that has to be guarded against everything that could deflect it in order that it may point unerringly to the north. Jesus stands before us in the Gospels as the one in whom this unerring dedication of the will was achieved.

He left on the minds of his disciples the impression of one who lived in unbroken communion with the heavenly Father. He spoke of him with perfect assurance and never in terms of derivative knowledge. He used the Old Testament, but always with penetration and originality; when occasion demanded he had no hesitation in setting aside the Old Testament in the light of his own superior knowledge. He could say, "Father, I thank thee that thou hast heard me. I knew thou hearest me always" (John 11:41-2).

Jesus taught his disciples to pray, "Forgive us our debts, As we also have forgiven our debtors" (Matt. 6:12). There is no suggestion in the Gospels that he ever felt the need to use this or a similar prayer himself. Experience shows that it is not the great sinners but the great saints who manifest the deepest sense of sinfulness, and at times irritate lesser men by affirming that they are the chief of sinners. Advance in holiness seems always to be accompanied by a deepened sense of unworthiness, and consequently by a deeper spirit of penitence. If Jesus had experienced such depths of self-abasement in the presence of God, it is unlikely that these would have left no trace in documents that make no attempt to conceal the cruel things said about Jesus by his foes, or the moments of weakness and uncertainty through which he had to pass.

If Jesus did in fact live in fellowship with the Father unbroken by self-will, ignorance, or disobedience, he could not be unaware of the difference in this respect between himself and other men. This would account at least in part for the element of strangeness, even remoteness, that accompanies him through all the gospel narratives. He is the friend of his followers (John 15:15); he goes as far as it is possible to go in the direction of self-identification with them. Yet there is never for a moment any doubt that he is the leader and they are the followers. None of them aspires to put himself on the

---

21. Note the remarkable variant reading in Heb. 12:3: "who endured such contradiction of sinners *against themselves*," which was accepted as the original reading by Brooke Foss Westcott, *The Epistle to the Hebrews: The Greek Text with Notes and Essays* (London and New York: Macmillan and Co., 1889). He quotes in support Num. 16:38, "sinners against their own selves."

same level as the one who has called them. This attitude is maintained through the two or three generations that are represented in the New Testament writings. There is no familiarity in the approach of the believer to Jesus Christ; he is to be approached with love, but also with veneration amounting almost to fear. The type of the Christian believer is the woman who ventured to touch only the hem of his garment (Mark 5:27). He is, as the Epistle to the Hebrews expresses it, "a high priest, holy, blameless, unstained, separated from sinners, exalted above the heavens" (Heb. 7:26). When the seer of the Book of Revelation sees his risen glory, "I fell at his feet as though dead" (Rev. 1:17).

Jesus, sending his disciples out into the world, warned them that they would have to face hostility, suffering, and even death for his sake. He could draw the lesson from his own experience, from the hostility he had had to face.

Nothing in the story of the ministry of Jesus is historically more certain that the record of his controversy with the Jews and especially with the Pharisees. The controversy had its origins, to some extent, in the relentless hostility of Jesus to the traditions of men through which the law of liberty was used to bring men into slavery to endless rules and regulations. In the extreme case casuistic interpretations of a biblical text could lead to a complete denial of the law of love, and thus enable a son to evade all those obligations toward parents that are the privilege of sonship (the Corban saying, Mark 7:6-8). The Sabbath was intended to be a day of rest and relief for man and beast; it had been turned into a heavy yoke by the prohibition of almost everything that a man might wish to do, unless he was delivered from the obligation by immediate danger to his life. Jesus sweeps all this tangle away, himself healing on the Sabbath day, defending the disciples when they rubbed ears of corn together on the Sabbath day and ate them (Mark 2:23 ff.). The traditions of men could not be allowed to stand if at any point they infringed the good will of God toward men.

Jesus does not protest only against the traditional interpretations of the Law. He regards the Law itself as imperfect and standing in need of correction. If self-giving love is to be the law of life, then such sayings as "An eye for an eye and a tooth for a tooth" cannot be allowed to stand (Matt. 5:38; see Exod. 21:24; Lev. 24:20; Deut. 19:21). No doubt this *lex talionis*, strictly limited penalties instead of the unrestricted vengeance permitted in less civilized societies, was a great advance. But Jesus will go further. Paul has exactly caught the spirit of the Master when he writes, "Love is the fulfilling of the law" (Rom. 13:14).

The independence of Jesus in relation to rules, and his claim to authority to correct the very Torah itself, must have been profoundly shocking to those brought up to regard the Law of Moses as the final word of God to man.   But there was yet deeper cause for the unrelenting hostility of certain groups among the Jews.   The ultimate aim of one kind of religion is that a man should be able to commend himself to God and win salvation at least in part by his own merits. The important thing is that, when the day of judgment comes, the merit in a man's account should be found to outweigh his demerits. The terrible danger in this situation is that it is piety itself that creates the densest barrier between man and God.   "It was Jesus' view that repentance was hardest for the pious man, because he was separated from God not by crude sins but by his piety.   Jesus had such painful experience in this sphere that he was ultimately convinced that this call would be in vain.   'But ye would not' (Matt. 23:37; Luke 13:34)."[22]

If merit is rejected as the basis of true religion, what is the alternative?   The answer of the gospel springs directly from Jesus' understanding of the nature of God.   Though the word "grace" is rarely used in the Gospels, it is not out of place to use it here.   Grace means love, of its own lovingkindness going out from itself toward the undeserving to give them help in time of need.   Jesus sets no limit to this generous grace; thereby he differentiated himself wholly from the religion of merit, and inevitably drew down upon himself the obloquy of the pious.

The term "grace" is of common occurrence in the rest of the New Testament and especially in the writings of Paul.   Technical language about justification by faith and so on has obscured the essential simplicity of the message, which is that God cares for sinners not after they have turned to him, but before.   At this point more than at any other the religion of Jesus is identical with the religion of those who proclaimed him.   "The chief characteristic of the new people of God gathered together by Jesus is their awareness of the boundlessness of God's grace."[23]   This is an exact description of the people of God in the post-Resurrection period, if it is understood that it was in Jesus Christ alone, in what he did and what he said, that they had come to recognize the boundlessness of God's grace.

Much of the original proclamation of Jesus can be recovered from the sources.   Allowing for the inevitable difference between pre-Resurrection and post-Resurrection utterance, it is possible to see that the earliest witnesses had retained much of this original procla-

---

22. Jeremias, *New Testament Theology*, 1:150–1.
23. Ibid., p. 178.

mation.   There is a real continuity between the words of Jesus and
the words about Jesus.   This is the first and easier part of our inquiry.   We have to go on to ask whether it is possible to ascertain
what Jesus thought about himself and about his ministry, and
whether it is possible to trace the same continuity between his mind
and the understanding that the early believers had of him.   This is a
more difficult inquiry.

It may be taken for granted that Jesus regarded himself as the
chosen messenger of God.   This is implied in all the narratives of the
baptism, and in many other passages as well.   But as we have seen,
he could find no easy answer to the question as to how he was to
speak of himself to others.   All the words derived from the Old
Testament, heavily weighted as they were by the Jewish tradition,
were liable to cause misunderstanding rather than illumination.   To
a large extent he avoids the dilemma by using none of these terms in
relation to himself.   Their place, however, is taken by the emphatic
use of the pronoun "I."   It is difficult to render this idiom in English,
where so much depends on the tone of voice.   "I send you forth" in
Matt. 10:16 could be taken as no more than a statement of fact; "it is I
who send you forth," clumsy as the expression is in English, represents rather better the tone of absolute authority for which the emphatic pronoun stands.   This usage is found in all the sources,
including the Johannine, and appears to be without parallel in other
documents of the period.[24]   When Jesus does find it necessary to
speak directly of himself, he tends to use the ambiguous and perplexing term, the Son of man.

What is the origin of this title and what does it mean?   On this
question controversy has raged for generations, and there is as yet no
sign of general agreement.

The facts are startling.   The title occurs eighty-two times in the
Gospels, being found in all of them and in all strata of the traditions.[25]   It is heard from the lips of Jesus alone.   No one else
addresses him or refers to him by this title.   In the whole of the rest
of the New Testament it occurs only once, in the utterance of
Stephen just before his martyrdom: "I see the heavens opened, and
the Son of man standing at the right hand of God" (Acts 7:56).
Otherwise the title disappears from the vocabulary and from the
theology of the early church.   On the basis of this strange silence

24. The seven "I ams" of the Fourth Gospel fall into a rather different category.   Each is a metaphorical saying—I
am the light of the world; I am the resurrection and the life (8:12; 11:25; etc.).   But in each of these the same note of
authority is heard.

25. The number is considerably reduced if we recall the number of parallel passages in the synoptic Gospels.
Jeremias lists twelve he regards as undoubtedly authentic: Mark 13:26; 14:62; Matt. 24:27, 37b; Luke 17:24, 26;
Matt. 10:23; 25:31; Luke 17:22, 30; 18:18; 21:36.

some scholars have argued that Jesus himself never used the title, and that it has its origin in the thoughts and theological ideas of the believers.[26] This view has been carefully argued and plausibly presented; but on the whole the arguments have failed to convince. To have invented such a title would argue an originality in the thoughts of the early church for which there is little evidence in the sources; it is much more likely that the traditions are here correct and that the origin of the term is to be sought in the mind of Jesus himself. This becomes all the more probable if the tradition is correct also in suggesting that the title was used more often in intimate personal converse with the disciples than in public proclamation.

The term is, by all accounts, perplexing, and was probably used to produce if not perplexity at least that questioning spirit which, as we have seen, it was the purpose of Jesus to call into being in the minds of his hearers. Four main views are held as to the sources on which Jesus drew, and as to the use he made of these sources.

In Aramaic, "son of man" can mean no more than "man," a generic name for the human race, or possibly for the typical man. In some of the "Son of man" sayings this meaning may be found. "The Son of man is lord even of the sabbath" (Mark 2:28).[27] The Sabbath was made for man's benefit, and therefore man may use the Sabbath as he judges best for himself and his kind. "The Son of man has nowhere to lay his head" (Matt. 8:20; Luke 9:58). This is usually read as a reference to Jesus; but may it not equally point up a contrast between restless man and the tranquil existence of the animals?

In the Book of Ezekiel the prophet is addressed by the Lord no less than eighty-seven times as "son of man," an address highly appropriate to one who is in some ways the most human of the prophets.[28] Jesus certainly knew the Book of Ezekiel as he knew the whole of the rest of the Old Testament. It is possible that this use of the term "son of man" may have contributed to the development of the idea for his own purposes. It is unlikely that this source was of more than secondary importance.

In the apocryphal Book of Enoch, or rather in that part of the book known as the Similitudes, the son of man plays a prominent part as a mysterious figure long hidden with God, who at the end of time will

---

26. This view was apparently first put forward by Hans Lietzmann in 1896; it has been supported by, among others, Bornkamm, *Jesus of Nazareth*, pp. 226–31.

27. RSV prints with the capital, "Son," thus implying one interpretation rather than another. Cf. Matt. 12:8 and Luke 6:5.

28. George A. Cooke, in *The Book of Ezekiel*, The International Critical Commentary (Edinburgh: T. and T. Clark, 1937), p. 31, well comments: "The title answers to Ezekiel's habit of thought; as a creature he receives from his Creator a designation which is all that a mere man can claim; as a prophet he is the mouthpiece, and nothing more, of the divine will."

come to proclaim judgment and to usher in the kingdom of righteousness:

> And the son of man whom thou hast seen
> shall loosen the reins of the strong
> And break the backs of the sinners
> And he shall put down the countenance of the strong
> and shall fill them with shame.
>
> (Enoch 46:4–6; cf. many other passages)

Can this be the source of the Son of man passages in the New Testament? To many it has seemed that here we have the answer to the conundrum. Robert H. Charles, writing in 1913, states this conclusion quite dogmatically: "This definite title is found in 1 Enoch for the first time in Jewish literature, and is, historically the source of the New Testament designation, and contributes to it some of its most characteristic contents."[29] For sixty years this has been the view most generally held; it certainly fits well with the fact that, of the passages we have identified as authentic, all, with one exception, refer to the Son of man who will come in an as yet undisclosed future.

Nevertheless, there are grave objections to this view. There is evidence that certain parts of the Book of Enoch were known to the Qumran community; it does not necessarily follow that this knowledge was shared in the circles in which Jesus of Nazareth moved. The Similitudes, to which all the son of man passages belong, has not been found among the Qumran sources, and is generally recognized to be later than other parts of the book. The date is still uncertain; but an increasing number of scholars hold the view that these sections are post-Christian, and therefore cannot have exercised any influence on the gospel tradition. The son of man of Enoch is certainly Enoch himself, that mysterious figure of ancient times (Gen. 5:21–24), who according to Jewish tradition had never died, and would come again at the end of time. It is hardly likely that Jesus would identify himself with so obscure a person of ancient times; much more likely he would look back to that passage in Jewish literature from which in all probability the son of man sections in Enoch are themselves derived.

In the vision recorded in Daniel 7 a number of great kingdoms, likened to wild beasts, pass before the eyes of the seer; and then:

---

29. *Apocrypha and Pseudepigrapha of the Old Testament in English, with Introduction and Critical and Explanatory Notes to the Several Books*, (Oxford: Clarendon Press, 1913), 2:155. I must confess to a good deal of sympathy with the petulant remark of the Jewish writer D. A. Chwolson (*Das letzte Passahmahl Christi* [1892]): "It is impossible to ascertain the reality of the Christian faith from the Apocalypse of John or the apocryphal Gospels. In just the same way it is impossible to investigate Judaism as it was in the time of Jesus on the basis of the Book of Enoch or the Book of Jubilees, and similar writings." Quoted by Morton S. Enslin in the reprint of Israel Abrahams, *Studies in Pharisaism and the Gospel*, First and Second Series, 2 vols. in one rev. ed., Library of Biblical Studies (New York: Ktav, 1968), p. ix.

> behold, with the clouds of heaven
>   there came one like a son of man,
> and he came to the Ancient of Days
>   and was presented before him.
> And to him was given dominion
>   and glory and kingdom
> that all peoples, nations, and languages
>   should serve him;
> his dominion is an everlasting dominion,
>   which shall not pass away,
> and his kingdom one
>   that shall not be destroyed.
>
> (Dan. 7:3–14)

An interpretation of the vision is communicated to the seer. When the great savage kingdoms of the earth have passed away "the saints of the Most High shall receive the kingdom, and possess the kingdom for ever, for ever and ever" (Dan. 7:18).[30]

The son of man is here a collective rather than an individual title; it points to the people of Israel and not to one single Israelite. The saints of the Most High have often been identified with the people of Israel as a whole. But this interpretation overlooks the historical setting of the vision. It seems that the vision was recorded for the encouragement of those who were enduring bitter persecution at the hands of the Greek king Antiochus Epiphanes (176–164 B.C.). If this is so, the saints must rather be identified with those who had stood boldly to face suffering rather than compromise their faith as so many of their fellow-countrymen had done. The passage was written, then, at a time at which the saints were in a situation of uttermost weakness and humiliation; yet it promises them power and dominion almost beyond the wit of man to conceive.[31]

Humiliation and glory—these are precisely the elements that we find in the Son of man sayings in the Gospels: "When the Son of man comes in his glory, and all his angels with him, then he will sit on his glorious throne" (Matt. 25:31). "The Son of man goes as it is written of him, but woe to that man by whom the Son of man is betrayed: It would have been better for that man if he had not been born" (Mark 14:21; Matt. 26:21; Luke 22:22). Most of the clearly authentic Son of man sayings point to future glory. An analysis of the gospel tradition shows that the writers, or the sources from which they drew, have

---

30. A readily accessible discussion of the Old Testament passage is to be found in Norman W. Porteous, *Daniel, a Commentary* (London: SCM Press, 1965), pp. 113–17.

31. Ragnar Leivestad, in an article entitled "Exit the Apocalyptic Son of Man" (*NTS* 18, no. 3: 243–68), argues against any connection between Daniel and the Son of man title as used by Jesus. This goes too far. Charles F. D. Moule ("Neglected Features in the Problem of the Son of Man," *Neues Testament und Kirche*, ed. J. Grilka [Freiburg: Herder, 1974], pp. 413 ff.) accepts the connection but works out carefully the inferences that may be drawn from it. The debate will continue; see, e.g., Barnabas Lindars, "Re-enter the Apocalyptic Son of Man," *NTS* 22, no. 3: 52–72.

introduced the term in contexts in which it did not originally occur, and that many of these insertions relate the idea of the Son of man to those of humiliation and suffering. This does not mean that the idea of suffering was not present in the mind of Jesus; indeed it is much more probable that he himself had understood the prophecy of Daniel 7 in the way in which we have interpreted it, and that the term Son of man has been rightly inserted to bring comfort and encouragement to the believers in the face of the suffering they will certainly have to undergo.

Once the corporate character of the Son of man has been grasped, many of the difficulties disappear. The mission of Jesus is to call Israel back to what Israel was intended to be—the people of God. As the majority of the people have rejected the challenge to repentance and to the new life, and as even the disciples have shown themselves sadly slow to understand all that is implied, a change takes place in the mission of Jesus. He identifies himself more and more with Israel—he is the one in whom the true destiny of the people is to find its fulfillment. As opposition hardens into total rejection, it becomes clear to him that that destiny can be accomplished only through suffering and death. For this insight Daniel 7 supplied no basis and no explanation. We must look elsewhere for the source of the inspiration of Jesus. Though Isaiah 53, the Song of the Suffering Servant, is hardly ever directly quoted by him, the hints and allusions are sufficiently frequent to make it probable that this prophecy[32] was constantly in his mind during the closing period of his mission.

Why did the title "Son of man" entirely die out of the vocabulary of the church after the Resurrection? The combination of suffering and humiliation with glory was self-evident to the church in its own daily experience. Paul puts them together in, for instance, Rom. 8:18: "I consider that the sufferings of this present time are not to be compared with the glory that shall be revealed." But the title itself has disappeared. We may gain some light on this remarkable fact if we consider the fate of another title used of Jesus by the early church. In four passages of the Acts of the Apostles (3:13, 26; 4:27, 30) Jesus is referred to as *Pais*; this almost certainly is drawn from the Servant Songs in Isaiah 40–66, and is to be translated "Servant," though the alternative translation "child" or "son" is not altogether impossible. This title is not found in any other context in the New Testament, and, though it does survive elsewhere, especially in

---

32. With this Porteous agrees: "In spite of all that has been written to the contrary, it was probably Jesus himself who, when he appropriated the title 'Son of man' as that best suited to indicate who he was, fused it with the thought of the *Suffering* Servant, and claimed no other Messiahship. See William Manson, *Jesus the Messiah* ([London: Hodder and Stoughton] 1943), chap. VI" (*Daniel, a Commentary*, p. 111).

liturgical texts, it disappears from ordinary Christian usage. The church seems to have felt that a Greek term which could constantly be used of slaves was no longer appropriate to one who was now known as the Lord of glory. The same feeling may have checked the use in relation to the Lord of a title that, in the days of his ministry among the people, he had made peculiarly his own.

When we turn to the title by which Jesus was regularly known in the church, Son of God, we are again faced with difficulties, but not the same as those that confronted us in the attempt to interpret "Son of man."

Part of the difficulty arises from the flexibility with which the term is used in the Old Testament. A certain definiteness, however, is attained when the king of Israel is recognized as standing to God in a special relationship that is best expressed by the term "Son": "I will be his father and he shall be my son" is the word spoken to the ideal king David of the one who should succeed him (2 Sam. 7:14; cf. Ps. 89:26). "You are my son" he said; "this day I became your father" (Ps. 2:7). Jesus constantly addressed God as his Father; in what sense is he likely to have used the term?

In the Western world the first connotation of the term is physical generation—that sense in which Muslims understand and repudiate the Christian use of the word. Moreover, there is often implicit in it an idea of the permanent subjection of the son to the father. To the first point no further answer is needed than the wide range of usages in the Old Testament to which we have already drawn attention. On the second, we may observe that the relationship takes on a rather different appearance in simpler societies in which it is still customary for a son to follow the profession of his father. In a workshop perhaps not very different from that in which Jesus passed the greater part of his working life ("Is not this the carpenter?" [Mark 6:3]), the carpenter's son as he grows up passes through three stages. At first he is simply an observer of the scene, though from quite an early age he will begin to carry out little tasks to help his father, and these will grow in complexity as his skill increases. Gradually the father becomes more dependent on the son, as tasks begin to grow beyond his individual strength. And finally, when the time comes for the father to give up work, the son, having fully learned the "mystery," is ready to take over the whole enterprise. The three stages may be designated "obedience," "understanding," and "intelligent cooperation." These ideas can be traced in detail in the Fourth Gospel, in which the sonship is dealt with in greater depth than in the other three.

Of the three stages, perhaps the most important is "understanding." "No one knows the Son except the Father, and no one knows the Father except the Son and anyone to whom he chooses to reveal him" (Matt. 11:28). This utterance, a kind of Johannine fragment in the synoptic Gospels, is usually interpreted as the relationship between Jesus and the heavenly Father, but it can be understood in a more general way. Who can really understand a father except a son? When the two have worked together through long years at the same bench, there grows up between them an instinctive and intuitive understanding that needs no words for its expression. The son knows all the father's secrets; why should a father withhold anything from the son of his love? So when the Johannine Jesus says, "I know him. If I said, I do not know him, I should be a liar like you; but I do know him and I keep his word" (John 8:55), he is summing up that which had been evident to those who followed him, the confident certainty with which he spoke and went about his business, so different from the hesitancy and unsureness of themselves by which so many of the sons of men are marked.

We shall not expect to find in the New Testament the abstruse metaphysical discussions of the Greek fathers as to the nature of the oneness of Christ with the Father. But they were honest men, not desiring to perplex the faithful, but to give expression to the depth of meaning contained in such Johannine expressions as, "I and the Father are one" (John 10:30).

Did Jesus foresee his own death, and in what sense did he understand it? If we were dependent only on the three predictions of the passion put in the mouth of Jesus by the Evangelists (Mark 8:31, Matt. 16:21, Luke 9:22, Mark 9:31, Matt. 17:23, Luke 9:44, Mark 10:33, Matt. 20:17–19, Luke 9:49), some doubt might be felt as to the answer, since these could be interpreted as "prophecies after the event," read back into the gospel story by the Evangelists in the light of what they knew to have happened. But we are not dependent only on these sayings. Jesus knew well that by his repeated transgressions of the Law as understood by the Jewish authorities of his time, he had rendered himself liable to the death penalty. Recognizing that he stood in many ways in the prophetic tradition, he seems at one time to have thought that he would be called on to endure death by stoning: "It cannot be that a prophet should perish away from Jerusalem. O Jerusalem, Jerusalem, killing the prophets and stoning those who are sent you" (Luke 13:33–34). From Abel to Zechariah the end of the prophetic career was death by violence (Luke 11:51). But apart from the illegality of a death sentence carried out by the Jewish authorities, he may well have come to understand the stratagem planned by Caiaphas; a prophet stoned might come to be regarded as a hero and a martyr; a prophet condemned and crucified by the Romans as a criminal, and therefore subject to a curse (see Gal. 3:13–14, referring to Deut. 21:23), could hardly be honored in recollection by the people of God.

Jesus regarded himself as playing a central role in the purpose of God for Israel, and so for the whole world.[33] Israel as a whole has rejected the challenge to repentance; in consequence the destiny of Israel can be fulfilled only in that one Israelite who will be found faithful to the demands of God, even though, as becomes increasingly clear to him, obedience to those demands will lead to his death. It is not to be thought that he willfully brought death upon himself, in a last attempt to force the hand of God.[34] He knew that he was going to Jerusalem to die, but this was in fulfillment of his vocation as witness, and not through any willful and voluntary self-immolation. The only clear statement of the purpose of his death to be found in the Gospels is in Mark 10:45 (also Matt. 20:28): "the Son of man came not to be served but to serve, and to give his life as a ransom for many." Our Aramaic scholars tell us that "for many" is to be understood as "for all"—there is no hint of any limit to the extent and scope of the ransom (as in 1 Tim. 2:6, "Who gave himself as a ransom for all"). No further explanation is here given of the nature of the ransom or of the meaning of this mysterious word. Yet the repeated "for many" of Isaiah 53 strongly suggests that Jesus is here identified with the Suffering Servant, who is to "vindicate many, himself bearing the penalty of their guilt . . . he bore the sin of many and interceded for their transgression" (Isa. 53:11, 12 NEB).

Did Jesus foresee his own Resurrection? In this context also we shall not allow too much weight to the predictions of the passion and Resurrection. We shall note, however, that the references to rising again are close in phrasing to the prophetic utterance of Hosea: "and the third day we shall rise up and live before him" (Hos. 6:2). This seems to be an expression of confidence in the power of God, who will not suffer his purpose to fail, rather than a definite expectation of the rising again of dead persons and their entrance on a new period of life. Jesus shared the confidence of the Old Testament writers in the power of God to bring his purposes to their rightful end; insofar as we can penetrate his inmost thoughts, it is probably in this direc-

33. One of the best attested of all the words of Jesus is "Many shall come from the east and west and sit at table with Abraham, Isaac and Jacob in the kingdom of heaven" (Matt. 8:11). Each Gospel in its own way looks forward to the mission to the Gentiles, though the time for it has not yet come.

34. This was the view put forward by Albert Schweitzer, *Quest of the Historical Jesus*, pp. 370–71. On this see also Stephen Neill, *Interpretation of the New Testament* (Oxford, 1966), pp. 199–200. Schweitzer has had few followers in this interpretation.

tion that we should look for the source of his confidence as he faces a dark and threatening future. We should never underestimate the depth of his wisdom and understanding; it is not necessary to credit him with an exact foreknowledge of what resurrection from the dead might be.

The cry of dereliction from the cross, faithfully recorded by Mark (15:33) and Matthew (27:46), implies that Jesus was not exempt from human weakness, and that on the cross he had to face the last and most grievous temptation of feeling that his work had indeed been a failure and that his death would be an end without a new beginning. But the words are a quotation from Psalm 22, a Psalm that begins in desolation and ends in triumph. It is unlikely that Jesus would have separated one from the other. He cried out a second time with a "great voice" (Mark 15:37). The contents of the second cry are not given; but the expression "with a *great* voice" in the Greek (cf. Acts 16:28) does suggest a shout of triumph rather than a bitter cry of despair.[35] Jesus had lived in the closest fellowship with the God whom he addressed as Father. He believed himself to stand at a focal point in the development of the purpose of God for the world. He was convinced that God, who had brought his people out of Egypt in the great event of the Exodus, and had led the blind by a way that they knew not to bring them back out of exile to their own land (Isa. 42:16), would not allow his purpose in this new stage of its development to fail, even though the plan might involve the death of the one chosen to bring it to its fulfillment. He had pondered the words of the prophet: "Yet the Lord took thought for his tortured servant, and healed him who had made himself a sacrifice for sin; so shall he enjoy long life and see his children's children."[36]

To some it may seem that this is a minimum interpretation of the mind of Jesus as he faced the approach of death. If so, this approach has been deliberately chosen. The Resurrection was so central in the experience and proclamation of the early church that we have to reckon with the possibility that some of the experience of faith has been read back into the records of the event. It seems wise at this point to draw only on what seem to be the earliest of the traditions, and to recognize that later interpretation may have amplified the original record. If Jesus was mistaken in thinking that he stood in a

35. This is the interpretation given by both Luke and John. Jürgen Moltmann in his recent book *The Crucified God* (New York: Harper & Row, 1974) bases his central argument on the cry of desolation as expressing "the fatherlessness of the Son and the sonlessness of the Father." His exposition is moving, but takes no account of the second cry, and the possibility that it might involve considerable modification of his argument. On this see further Otto Betz in Gerhard Kittel and Gerhard Friedrich, eds., *TDNT*, trans. Geoffrey W. Bromiley (Grand Rapids: Eerdmans, 1974), 9:294.

36. Isa. 53:10 NEB. Note that this translation involves a correction of the Hebrew text, which at one point is unintelligible as it stands.

unique relationship to God, then of course his expectation of resurrection was an illusion.   If he was right, then the New Testament may be right in assuring us that his confidence in his heavenly Father was not misplaced.

One question remains.   What were the "eschatological" views of Jesus as he looked beyond his immediate concerns to a more distant future and to the "end of the age"?   Here the twentieth-century reader finds himself faced by exceptional difficulties.   Much of the language is derived from the Jewish apocalyptic tradition; where so much is symbolic, it is hard to determine how much, if anything, can be taken literally.   Of that which is recorded, how much goes back to Jesus himself, and how much is due to interpretations given by the disciples, in language that was familiar to them, of what they believed themselves to have heard from the lips of the Lord himself?   There is no simple answer to any of these questions.

We may well suppose that Jesus was gifted not only with remarkable *insight*, "he himself knew what was in man" (John 2:25), but also with unusual *foresight*, such as would enable him to discern the signs of the times; and yet this is not to suppose that he saw spread out before him such a map of human history as would enable him to settle chronologies and to define movements that in his day were not yet conceived in the womb of time.   Within these limitations, certain affirmations can be made with a measure of confidence.

With the Old Testament writers, Jesus held that the universe is at all times directly dependent on the will and the actions of God.   God is no "deistic" deity, who, having created the world, then leaves it to run itself on inner principles that will work themselves out in predictable events.   History is full of surprises.   It moves from crisis to crisis, *kairoi* the Greeks would have called them, in which retrospectively the action of God can be unmistakably seen.[37]

The first of these eschatological crises is the coming of Jesus himself "in these last days" (Heb. 1:1).   This is a crisis in the literal sense of the word—judgment and discrimination.   All men who hear are challenged to stand and deliver.   On the believer the judgment will be the judgment of life; far otherwise for those who with hardened and impenitent hearts refuse the proffered gift: "O Jerusalem, Jerusalem . . . would that even today you knew the things that make for peace!   But now they are hid from your eyes" (Matt. 23:37; Luke 19:42).

---

37. To the prophetic writers the great *kairos* was the Exodus from Egypt, in which Israel was constituted a covenant people of God.   Christians were not slow to see in the Resurrection of Jesus Christ the greater Exodus. Note the use of the word *exodos* in Luke 9:31 (RSV renders "departure"), and the early use in Christian worship of Psalm 114, *In exitu Israel*, as the Easter Psalm.

Second, there is the crisis of the war between the Jews and the Romans. Nearly forty years were to pass before the war actually broke out, the period from the green to the dry (Luke 23:31). But so sensitive an observer as Jesus could hardly spend time in Jerusalem in the period of his ministry without realizing what was bound to happen if the Jews moved steadily forward in the grooves that they were engaged in hollowing out for themselves. The fall of Jerusalem was indeed an apocalyptic event, and left traces on the entire history of the world. But the end was not yet.

Each crisis marks the end of one age and the beginning of another. The age of the church follows upon the age of Jesus. But there will be a time of the end, unlike any other; when that last age ends, there will be no other to follow it. That final crisis is to be preceded by signs and wonders, by great tribulations and the proclamation of the gospel to all nations.[38] Then the sign of the Son of man will be seen, and he will gather his elect from the four winds of heaven, from the ends of the earth to the ends of heaven. But no detailed description of the end is given. It will come as and when God wills; a stringent warning is given against any attempt to fix the times and seasons and to pry into secrets which God has hidden within his own power; to these not even the Son has access (Mark 13:32).

On these eschatological symbols the minds of the early Christians eagerly fastened. Much of what they wrote has clearly been influenced by the Old Testament and by some of the apocryphal writings. But their prophecies are distinguished from those of the Jews by the central place given to the Son of man, or as they now know him, the Lord Jesus, the one who is to come again. In one of the most strikingly apocalyptic passages in the Epistles, Paul sees "the Lord Jesus . . . revealed from heaven in flaming fire, inflicting vengeance upon those who do not know God, and upon those who do not obey the Gospel of our Lord Jesus" (2 Thess. 1:7–8). Here we are not far from the great white throne of the Revelation, and from him who sat upon it: "from his presence earth and sky fled away, and no place was found for them" (Rev. 20:11).

The language of the eschatological passages in the New Testament, vivid as it is, is sober in comparison with that of the Jewish apocalypses from which in a measure they have been derived. And the lesson they convey is sober enough. The obligation laid on the believer, in the words of Jesus and in the interpretations of them, is

---

38. I take this to refer to a final angelic proclamation and to the summons to all nations to appear before the judgment seat, rather than to the slow, steady proclamation of the gospel by the church, for which the term "evangelize" is more commonly used.

simply that of constant readiness and alertness, since the end will come without warning and they must guard against the danger of being caught unaware. And those who wait are to recognize that their watch is neither endless nor hopeless. The Master whom they await is one whom they know well, and who will certainly return (Mark 13:32–6). The central message of eschatology can be expressed in the exquisite words the poet Coleridge wrote about the stars: "And everywhere the blue sky belongs to them, and is their appointed rest and their native country and their own natural homes, which they enter unannounced, as lords that are certainly expected, and yet there is a silent joy at their arrival."

As far as we have been able to follow, the witnesses to Jesus after the Resurrection picked up at point after point elements that had been present in the message as Jesus himself communicated it, amplified them, expressed them in their own way in the light of fuller knowledge, but in all essentials remained faithful to the original proclamation. The Master who is invisibly present with them is the same as the Master who once walked the lanes and roads of Galilee. At certain points, three in particular, the Gospels go beyond the limits of ordinary human speech. They have to handle events, or ideas, that fall outside the limits of historical recording, and are related to mysteries of which the Evangelists are aware but that surpass the powers of human understanding and utterance.

Not long after the Resurrection, believers began naturally to inquire concerning the Lord—Where has he gone, where is he now? After a rather longer period had elapsed they began to ask, equally naturally, Where did he come from, and what was the manner of his coming into the world?

The Gospel of Matthew and that of Luke give accounts of the birth of Jesus that, though they differ in many details, agree on the essential point—that the birth of Jesus was other than that of ordinary men, since it took place without the intervention of a human father. There is no corresponding account in the Gospel of Mark as we now have it, and hardly any sign in the rest of the New Testament of any interest on the part of Christians in the subject.[39]

This is, surely, what was to be expected. The first Christian preaching took as its themes the passion and Resurrection of Jesus Christ. As Gentiles began to pour into the church, it became necessary to answer their questions as to the ministry and teaching of Jesus. Inquiry as to his origins was likely to come at the end rather than at the beginning of the development of Christian faith.

39. Allusions may be present in John 8:41 and Gal. 4:4; but in any case these are no more than allusions.

In the days of Jesus there were current in the Mediterranean world a number of highly unedifying stories relating to the physical impregnation of mortal women through visits from the immortal gods.[40] There are no close parallels to the stories given in the Gospels. And attempts to derive these accounts from the Hellenistic world are bound to fail, because of the purely Jewish character of the Gospel narratives as we have them. The account in Matthew has to do with Jewish ideas of betrothal, marriage, and possible separation. The name given to Jesus by the angel, Immanuel, is Hebrew and looks back to Isa. 7:14, "God with us." The Lucan narrative seems to represent the experience of those sometimes called the "quiet in the land," the devout souls who, steeped in the knowledge of the Old Testament, possessed their souls in patience waiting for the day when the Lord would visit his people. Here, as in Matthew, there is no trace of Hellenistic influence; the story moves in a world of faith that is familiar to us from the Old Testament. The beautiful canticles with which the narrative is adorned breathe the spirit of Old Testament piety; the *Magnificat* recalls the Song of Hannah in 1 Samuel 2, the *Nunc Dimittis*, the language of Second Isaiah (especially chapter 49).

The two different accounts of Jesus' birth that had come into existence within fifty years after his death may have sprung from a single original tradition that was considerably earlier than either. In that case, the birth stories, far from being a late addition to the Gospel material, belong to an early period in the growth of the traditions, though it is probable that each was known only to a limited circle of believers.

What is the theological import of the stories? Christian thinkers from the beginning have been perplexed by the combination of the old and the new in Jesus of Nazareth. The disciples were overwhelmed by the sense of newness, by the revolutionary character of the doctrine that he brought and the life that was made available in him. And yet all this took place within the framework of that which was already very old. Unless the prophets had prophesied, Jesus could not have come as the fulfillment of the promises spoken through them. The church as the Israel of God stands in direct continuity with the Israel of God. It would be impossible to find a symbol, or an act of God, that could more perfectly express both newness and continuity than the virgin birth of Jesus.

---

40. I would not myself have selected but can only approve the remarkable expression of Dale Moody: "This and other (Gentile) stories constitute nothing more than mythological fornication" (*IDB* 4 [1962]: 791). There are many special studies of the virgin birth of Jesus; everything relevant is to be found in the work of J. Gresham Machen, *The Virgin Birth of Christ* (New York: Harper & Row, 1932), though not all will agree with all his conclusions.

In the earliest proclamation there is as yet no idea of the preexistence of Christ. Paul seems clearly to express such an idea, when he speaks of the grace of the Lord Jesus Christ, "that though he was rich, yet for your sake he became poor" (2 Cor. 8:9). But for any full expression of the idea we have to wait for the Johannine writings. There the Word which became flesh is the same as the Word which was in the beginning. The words attributed to the Johannine Christ, "Before Abraham was I am" (John 8:58) are a clear expression of the belief that the birth in Bethlehem was not the beginning but the coming into the world of that which had been "from the beginning." "Whereas Abraham (like the Baptist, 1:6) came into existence at a definite moment, He, the Lord, the Word of God, is above and beyond time."[41] From this declaration to that of the Nicene Creed, "begotten of his Father before all worlds," is no long step.

In the narrative of the Transfiguration what some would call the mythological and others would prefer to call the poetical element in the Gospels is at its most evident. The emphasis in the stories, as they are presented to us, is placed on the experience of the disciples at a crucial movement in their development. Peter's confession of faith in Jesus as the Christ has been made; they need now to be strengthened to realize that from this time on the road will be downhill all the way, and to accept the strange new thought that Jesus is a Messiah whose vocation is to be fulfilled through suffering. Previously none of them had been called to share the lonely vigils of Jesus on the hills. When Peter and others had tracked down Jesus to his place of prayer (Mark 1:35–39), the prayer was immediately broken off, and Jesus returned to his public ministry. Now the time has come at which they can be admitted to an even closer fellowship.

Much of the symbolism is intelligible to us in the light of Old Testament usage. The cloud indicates an overwhelming sense of the presence of the divine; to this the response of the disciples is the intense awe that falls on men in such a situation (Mark 9:6), and either stuns them into silence or causes them to utter such foolish words as those of Peter, who imagines that that which can last only for a moment can be made permanent. It was only after the Resurrection that they came to understand that the *Shekinah*, the "overshadowing presence of God," there shown for a brief space, was to become the abiding experience of the new life in Christ. "Behold the dwelling of God is with men. He will dwell with them, and they shall be his people, and God himself will be with them" (Rev. 21:3).

This impression of men moving about in worlds not realized is

41. Robert H. Lightfoot, *St. John's Gospel: A Commentary* (Oxford: Clarendon Press, 1956), p. 195.

naturally at its most powerful in the records of the Resurrection. "It is a matter of constant surprise to me that the revelation of the risen Lord to his disciples seems often to be treated as if it were barely more than a remarkable event, whereas we have every reason to believe that at first the solid earth must have seemed to reel beneath their feet, and the stars to be about to fall."[42]   That was the atmosphere of the day of Resurrection, hardly one on which accurate and coordinated reports were to be expected.   Indeed, one of the evidences for the basic authenticity of the narratives is that the Evangelists and editors of the testimony of the witnesses have made hardly any attempt to tidy them up and to remove inconsistencies that must have been evident to any careful reader.

What is more striking than the inconsistencies is the wide range of agreements.   All accounts agree in showing that the Resurrection was regarded as something wholly unlike anything that had ever happened before.   No parallel is to be found in the theophanies, the appearances of the angel of the Lord, in the Old Testament. Lazarus, whom according to John 11 Jesus had raised from the dead, had returned to the ordinary conditions of human life and was found shortly afterward sitting with other guests in the house of his sisters (John 12:3).   All the Resurrection narratives indicate that Jesus has now passed beyond the limitations of human life and is living a life of a very different kind.   And yet there is unfailing emphasis on the continuity within discontinuity, the same paradox we have encountered in the stories of the birth of Jesus:

> It was regarded as of vital importance to the truth of the Gospels that their risen Lord was no disembodied spirit, Luke 24:37, but identical in every way with Him whose company they had shared in the days of His flesh. . . . The doctrine of the immortality of the soul, widely held among the Greeks, or that of the survival of the spirit in some non-material sphere, would have seemed both disappointing and unsatisfying to Hebrew thought.   Whatever changes may have taken place, resurrection must involve restoration to nation, family and friends, recognition by them, and resumption, in some way, of the old activities.[43]

Discontinuity within continuity—this seems to be the relationship between the new covenant and the old.   It seems also to be the relationship between the good news as preached by Jesus and the good news as preached concerning Jesus.   In both he is the center around which everything revolves.

Every book of the New Testament is written from faith to faith

42. Robert H. Lightfoot, *The Gospel Message of St. Mark* (Oxford, 1950), p. 96.
43. Lightfoot, ibid., pp. 88, 107, 108.

(Rom. 1:17), by believers for the edification of other believers, or for those who are not yet believers that they may be brought to the faith. But this faith is not to be confused with mere acquiescence or intellectual assent; it involves death and life, confrontation and commitment, as almost every book in the New Testament makes plain, to a way that is inseparable from danger and suffering. It is, to borrow again a phrase from Shakespeare,

> a wild dedication of yourselves
> to unpath'd waters, undreamed shores.[44]

The true meaning of faith can be learned only on pilgrimage, and to the end of time the people of God will be the pilgrim people. But this is not an unaccompanied journey. The experience of the believing company is always that of the two disciples who walked to Emmaus on the evening of the first Easter Day: "Jesus himself drew near and went with them" (Luke 24:15).[45] He expounds to them the things in the Scriptures concerning himself. The result is a complete transformation of all human concepts of the divine, of all human ideals and ambitions, of all the rules of conduct and practice by which men have striven to give form and expression to their ideals. Now there are no more rules, only one abiding presence, one recognition that "one died for all, that those who live might live no longer for themselves, but for him who for their sake died and was raised" (2 Cor. 5:15). So, "whether we live or whether we die, we are the Lord's" (Rom. 14:8).

So theology has its place. There is a place also for what is properly called the study of Christian evidences. But in the end the only valid evidence for the truth of the proclamation is the transformed life of the individual and of the community. So, says Paul, "we all with unveiled faces reflecting as in a mirror the glory of the Lord are being transfigured from one degree of glory to another, by the operation of the Lord, who is the Spirit" (2 Cor. 3:15, paraphrase).

---

44. *The Winter's Tale* act 4, sc. 4.

45. For a moving evocation of the scene, see Malcolm Muggeridge, *Jesus* (London: Collins, 1975), p. 13: "The road to Emmaus, walking along which with a friend I found myself living unforgettably through the experiences of the two travellers who took the same road shortly after the Crucifixion, as described in the New Testament. So much so that thenceforth I have never doubted that, wherever the walk and whoever the wayfarers, there is always, as on that other occasion on the road to Emmaus, a third presence ready to emerge from the shadows and fall in step along the dusty, stony way."

Selected Bibliography

Only books available in English have been listed. The great majority of these books have extensive bibliographies that will make it possible for a student to follow up without difficulty any subject in which he is especially interested.

Works of Reference

Black, Matthew, and Rowley, Harold H., eds. *Peake's Commentary on the Bible.* 2nd ed. Thomas Nelson and Sons: New York, 1962.
    Many of the introductory chapters are excellent.
Buttrick, George Arthur; Kepler, Thomas Samuel; Knox, John; May, Herbert Gordon; Terrien, Samuel; and Bucke, Emory Stevens, eds. *Interpreter's Dictionary of the Bible.* 4 vols. Nashville: Abingdon, 1962.
    Shorter articles, but in most cases with carefully prepared bibliographies.
Kittel, Gerhard, and Friedrich, Gerhard, eds. *Theological Dictionary of the New Testament.* 9 vols. Translated by Geoffrey W. Bromiley. Grand Rapids: Eerdmans, 1965–74.
    Contains an article on every single theological term used in the New Testament. Indispensable for detailed study but to be used with caution, as articles are not in every case free from tendentiousness.

Chapter 1. Studies of New Testament Theology

Bultmann, Rudolf. *Theology of the New Testament.* 2 vols. London: SCM Press, 1952, 1955.
    Deals mainly with Paul and John. Based on critical principles that are not wholly acceptable today.
Hunter, Archibald M. *Introducing New Testament Theology.* London: SCM Press, 1963.
    Still excellent as a brief introduction to the subject.
Jeremias, Joachim. *New Testament Theology.* Vol. 1. *The Proclamation of Jesus.* London: SCM Press, 1971.
    Indispensable; but so far only deals with the proclamation *by* Jesus.
Kümmel, Werner G. *The Theology of the New Testament According to Its Major Witnesses—Jesus, Paul, John.* Nashville: Abingdon, 1974.
    As the title shows, the book does not deal with the subject as a whole, but it provides much good, rather conservative exposition.
Ladd, George E. *A Theology of the New Testament.* Grand Rapids: Eerdmans, 1974.
    Conservative, thoroughly documented, very long—661 pages.
Richardson, Alan. *Introduction to the Theology of the New Testament.* London: SCM Press, 1958.
    Scholarly and thorough, but difficult for those who do not know Greek.
Stevens, G. B. *Theology of the New Testament.* Edinburgh: T. and T. Clark, 1899.
    An older book that deals thoroughly with every book of the New Testament but naturally is at certain points out of date.

Introductions to the New Testament

Davies, William D. *Invitation to the New Testament.* London: Darton, 1967.
    Rather popular, but excellent as a first book for those newly approaching the subject.

196

Fuller, Reginald H. *A Critical Introduction to the New Testament.* London: Duckworth, 1966.
Concise and full of meat; as the title indicates, somewhat radical in its approach.
Guthrie, Donald. *New Testament Introduction.* London: Tyndale Press, 1970.
Conservative, but solidly documented.
Kümmel, Werner G. *Introduction to the New Testament.* 2nd ed. London: SCM Press, 1966.
Well-based on a comprehensive knowledge of continental scholarship.
Metzger, Bruce M. *The New Testament, Its Background, Growth and Content.* Nashville: Abingdon, 1965.
Conservative. Reliable, but covers so much ground that the treatment is at times a bit uneven.

The Background in History

Barrett, Charles K. *The New Testament Background: Selected Documents.* London: SPCK, 1956.
A good selection of documents from many sources.
Bruce, Frederick F. *New Testament History.* Edinburgh: Nelson, 1969.
Contains all the information that a student is likely to need.
Filson, Floyd V. *A New Testament History.* London: SCM Press, 1965.
Kee, Howard C., and Young, F. W. *The Living World of the New Testament.* London: Darton, 1960.
Vivid; more popular than the books listed above.
Reicke, B. *The New Testament Era.* Philadelphia: Fortress Press, 1968.
An excellent survey, with an especially good bibliography of continental books.

The Jewish Background

Cross, Frank M. *The Ancient Library of Qumran and Modern Biblical Studies.* London: Duckworth, 1958.
Davies, William D. *Christian Origins and Judaism.* London: Darton, 1962.
Dupont-Sommer, A. *The Essene Writings from Qumran.* Oxford, 1961.
Moore, George Foote. *Judaism in the First Centuries of the Christian Era.* 2 vols. Cambridge, Mass.: Harvard University Press, 1962.
A book that does not go out of date and is still authoritative.
Ringgren, Helmer. *The Faith of Qumran.* Philadelphia: Fortress Press, 1963.
Schürer, Emil. *The Jewish People in the Time of Christ, 175 B.C.–A.D. 135.* New ed., 1 vol. to date. Edinburgh: T. and T. Clark, 1973.
A new Schürer, thoroughly revised, will be an immense boon to the more advanced student.
Vermés, Gezá. *The Dead Sea Scrolls in English.* Reprint. Harmondsworth, England: Pelican Books, 1962.
Cross, Dupont-Sommer, Ringgren, and Vermés will serve as an introduction to the immense literature on Qumran. The documents connected with Qumran have proved to be of limited importance for the study of New Testament theology.

Hellenism

Bultmann, Rudolf. *Primitive Christianity in Its Contemporary Setting.* London: Thames and Hudson, 1956.
Bultmann at his best. The book deals with more than the Hellenistic background.
Foerster, Werner. *Gnosis: A Selection of Gnostic Texts.* Oxford: Clarendon Press, 1972.
Gnosticism cannot be understood without some acquaintance with the texts; hence the importance of this anthology.
Grant, Frederick C. *Roman Hellenism and the New Testament.* Edinburgh and London: Oliver and Boyd, 1962.
Grant, Robert M. *Gnosticism and Early Christianity.* New York: Columbia University Press, 1959.

Nock, Arthur D. *Early Gentile Christianity and Its Hellenistic Background.* New York: Harper & Row, 1962.
_____. "Gnosticism." In *Essays on Religion and the Ancient World.* Oxford: Clarendon Press, 1972. Vol. 2, pp. 940–60.
By a notable authority; the best short account of Gnosticism available.
Wilson, R. McL. *Gnosis and the New Testament.* Oxford: Blackwell, 1968.

Chapter 2. The Earliest Believers

Goppelt, Leonhard. *The Apostolic and Post-Apostolic Times.* London: A. & C. Black, 1970.
A careful attempt at reconstruction of the developments in the early period.
Moule, Charles F. D. *The Birth of the New Testament.* 2nd ed. London: A. & C. Black, 1966.
A thorough-going attempt to get behind the New Testament and consider what it was like to be a Christian when there was no New Testament.
Weiss, Johannes. *Earliest Christianity.* 2 vols. New York: Harper & Row, Torch Books, 1959.
A classic, now happily again made available in paperback form.

Chapter 3. Paul

Lives of Paul

Bornkamm, Günther. *Paul.* New York: Harper & Row, 1971.
A rather limited Paul. Professor Bornkamm might have spread his net a little more widely than he has done.
Nock, Arthur D. *St. Paul.* London: Williams and Norgate, 1938.
Still the best introduction for the English reader, though some of Nock's judgments may be regarded as questionable.
Ogg, George. *The Chronology of the Life of Paul.* London: Epworth Press, 1968.
A thorough study of this tangled question.

The Pauline Theology

Cerfaux, Lucien. *Christ in the Theology of St. Paul.* New York: Herder, 1959.
_____. *The Church in the Theology of St. Paul.* 2nd ed. New York: Herder, 1959.
Two notably thorough and careful works on a major scale.
Davies, William D. *Paul and Rabbinic Judaism.* London: SPCK, 1948.
Deals adequately with one important aspect of Paul's teaching.
Furnish, Victor P. *Theology and Ethics in Paul.* Philadelphia: Westminster Press, 1968.
Holds together two aspects that are too often kept separate. On the whole the Roman Catholics have done a better job than the Protestants on general surveys of the Pauline theology.
Prat, Fernand, S. J. *The Theology of St. Paul.* 2 vols. London: Burns, Oates and Washburn, 1945.
An older book that still deserves attention.

The Pauline Epistles

Romans
Barrett, Charles K. *A Commentary on the Epistle to the Romans.* 2nd ed. London: A. & C. Black, 1962.
Barth, Karl. *The Epistle to the Romans.* Translated by Sir Edwyn Clement Hoskyns. Oxford and London: Humphrey Milford, 1933.
Interesting from the historical point of view and immensely influential in its day.
Bruce, Frederick F. *The Epistle of Paul to the Romans: An Introduction and Commentary.* London and Chicago: Inter-Varsity, 1963.

Cranfield, Charles E. *A Critical and Exegetical Commentary on the Epistle to the Romans.* The New International Critical Commentary. N.s., vol. 1. Edinburgh: T. and T. Clark, 1975.
For those with a knowledge of Greek. Most of the important theological work will appear in vol. 2.

Minear, Paul S. *The Obedience of Faith: A Study in Romans.* Studies in Biblical Theology No. 19, 2nd ser. Naperville: Allenson, 1970.
Pays special attention to the circumstances in which Romans was written and interprets the teaching in the light of that situation.

1 Corinthians

Barrett, Charles K. *A Commentary on the First Epistle to the Corinthians.* London: A. & C. Black, 1968.

Héring, Jean. *The First Epistle of Saint Paul to the Corinthians.* Translated by A. W. Heathcote and P. J. Allcock. London: Epworth Press, 1962.
Two very good theological commentaries, Héring representing the best continental scholarship.

2 Corinthians

Barrett and Héring have equally good commentaries on the Second Epistle. See Barrett, Charles K. *A Commentary on the Second Epistle to the Corinthians.* Black's Commentaries. London: A. & C. Black, 1973; Héring, Jean. *The Second Epistle of Saint Paul to the Corinthians.* Translated by A. W. Heathcote and P. J. Allcock. London: Epworth Press, 1967.

Galatians

Duncan, George S. *The Epistle of Paul to the Galatians.* London: Hodder and Stoughton, 1934.
The fullest English commentary of recent times; argues strongly in favor of the early date for Galatians.

Ridderbos, Herman N. *The Epistle of Paul to the Churches in Galatia.* Grand Rapids: Eerdmans, 1953.
By a Dutch scholar with a strongly Calvinistic outlook, but based on wide knowledge and deep theological thought.

Ephesians

Barth, Markus. *Ephesians.* 2 vols. New York: Doubleday, 1974.
Both Barth and Mitton (see below) support the view that Paul is the author of Ephesians.

Goodspeed, Edgar J. *The Key to Ephesians.* Chicago: University of Chicago Press, 1956.
American scholarship at its best.

Mitton, Charles L. *The Epistle to the Ephesians.* Oxford: Clarendon Press, 1951.

Robinson, J. Armitage. *The Epistle to the Ephesians.* 3rd ed. London: Macmillan & Co., 1922.
Nothing has yet taken the place of Robinson's book, which includes a superb exposition of the Epistle that requires no knowledge of Greek.
I have not been able to see the important works by Heinrich Schlier, *Brief an die Epheser.* Düsseldorf: Patmos, 1957; and E. Percy, *Die Probleme der Kolosser- und Epheserbriefe.* Lund, Sweden: Skrifter utgivna av kungl. Humanistika Vetenskapssamfundet, 1946—both of which accept the Pauline authorship.

Philippians

Beare, Francis W. *A Commentary on the Epistle to the Philippians.* London: A. & C. Black, 1959.
Takes the view that Philippians is by Paul but that a number of letters have been combined to make the Epistle as we have it.

Colossians and Philemon

Moule, Charles F. D. *Colossians and Philemon.* Cambridge Greek Testament. Cambridge, 1957.
Much in this excellent commentary can be used by those who do not know Greek.
Scott, Ernest F. *Epistles to Colossians and Philemon.* 2nd ed. London: Hodder and Stoughton, 1936.
This older commentary is still valuable.

1 and 2 Thessalonians

Best, Ernest. *A Commentary on the First and Second Epistles to the Thessalonians.* London: A. & C. Black, 1972.
The first major commentary in English for a considerable period. Thorough, and strong on the theological issues.
Whiteley, Denys E. H. *Thessalonians in the Revised Standard Version with Introduction and Commentary.* Oxford, 1969.
A smaller work, but careful and competent.

Chapter 4. Beginnings of Gospel-Writing

Mark
Commentaries

Nineham, Dennis E. *Saint Mark.* Harmondsworth, England: Penguin Books, 1963.
Stimulating, but gravely underestimates the historical element in Mark's account of Jesus.
Schweizer, Edward. *The Good News According to Mark.* London: SPCK, 1971.
Erudite, cautious, and well-balanced. As always, Schweizer is concerned about faith and not only about knowledge.

Theology

Lightfoot, Robert H. *The Gospel Message of St. Mark.* Oxford, 1950.
The work of a delicate and perceptive mind; beautifully written.
Marxsen, Willi. *Mark the Evangelist: Studies in the Redaction History of the Gospel.* Nashville: Abingdon, 1969.
A pioneer work. Redaction criticism really means no more than recognizing that each Evangelist is a great writer and a great theologian on his own account.

1 Peter
Commentaries

Kelly, John N. D. *The Epistles of Peter and Jude.* London: A. & C. Black, 1969.
Selwyn, Edward G. *The First Epistle of Peter.* Cambridge, 1946.
Some knowledge of Greek required. Supports an early date for the Epistle.

Theology

For the theology of the Epistle the student will have to go back to:
Bigg, Charles. *A Critical and Exegetical Commentary on the Epistles of St. Peter and St. Jude.* The International Critical Commentary. 2nd ed. Edinburgh: T. and T. Clark, 1902. Especially pp. 33–67.
For an entirely different type of exposition the reader might be interested in going back to:
Leighton, Robert, Archbishop of Glasgow. *First Peter.* Reprint. Grand Rapids: Kregel Publications, 1972.

Chapter 5. The Tradition of Israel

The Gospel of Matthew

There is no completely satisfactory commentary on Matthew in English. The best that is readily available is:

Filson, Floyd V. *The Gospel According to St. Matthew.* London: A. & C. Black, 1960.

Theology

Bornkamm, Günther; Barth, Gerhard; and Held, Heinz J. *Tradition and Interpretation in Matthew.* London: SCM Press, 1963.
Redaction criticism applied to Matthew's Gospel.
Davies, William D. *The Setting of the Sermon on the Mount.* Cambridge, 1964.
Kilpatrick, George D. *The Origins of the Gospel According to St. Matthew.* 2nd ed. Oxford, 1950.
Stendahl, Krister. *The School of Matthew.* 2nd ed. Philadelphia: Fortress, 1968.

The Epistle of James

Very little is available directly on the theology of this Epistle. See:
Blackman, Edwin C. *The Epistle of James.* London: SCM Press, 1957.
A slighter work than Mitton (see below), less conservative.
Mitton, Charles L. *The Epistle of James.* London: Marshall, Morgan and Scott, 1966.
A good modern commentary; supports the view that the author is James the brother of the Lord.

The Epistle to the Hebrews

Commentaries

Bruce, Frederick F. *Commentary on the Epistle to the Hebrews.* London: Marshall, Morgan and Scott, 1964.
Héring, Jean. *The Epistle to the Hebrews.* London: Epworth Press, 1970.
Manson, T. William. *The Epistle to the Hebrews.* 2nd ed. London: Hodder and Stoughton, 1953.
Attempts to place the Epistle historically and connects it with the witness of Stephen.
Montefiore, Hugh W. *A Commentary on the Epistle to the Hebrews.* London: A. & C. Black, 1964.
The viewpoint is original, the exposition excellent.

Theology

For detailed discussion of many points of theology the student still has to go back to:
Westcott, Brooke Foss. *The Epistle to the Hebrews.* Grand Rapids: Eerdmans, 1950.

Revelation

Commentaries

Beckwith, Isbon T. *The Apocalypse of John.* New York: Macmillan, 1919.
If this older American commentary is still available it will be found very useful.
Beasley-Murray, George R., ed. The Book of Revelation. The New Century Bible, based on the Revised Standard Version. London: Oliphants, 1975.
Well-informed, illuminating, cautious; an excellent complement to Caird's work (see below).
Caird, George B. *The Revelation of St. John the Divine.* London: A. & C. Black, 1966.
Thorough, straightforward, and easy to read. A useful chapter on the theology of Revelation.
Farrer, Austin. *The Revelation of St. John the Divine.* Oxford: Clarendon Press, 1964.
Some eccentric views but many original and valuable insights.

Theology

For extensive discussion of many theological points the student must go back to the very large work of:

Charles, Robert H. *A Critical and Exegetical Commentary on the Revelation of St. John.* The International Critical Commentary. 2 vols. Edinburgh: T. and T. Clark, 1920.

The theological sections of the Introduction are still of great value.

Chapter 6.   The Gospel for the Gentiles

Commentaries

Ellis, Edward E. *The Gospel of Luke.* London: Nelson, 1966.

The most recent commentary in English. Well-based on a wide knowledge of contemporary scholarship, moderate and well-balanced in judgment. A quite different type of exposition, both scholarly and devotional, is:

Moorman, John R. H. *The Path to Glory.* London: SPCK, 1964.

Theology

Barrett, Charles K. *Luke the Historian in Recent Study.* Philadelphia: Fortress Press, 1970.

An indispensable guide through the thickets of recent study, on the results of which a theological judgment on Luke so largely depends.

Conzelmann, Hans. *The Theology of St. Luke.* London: Faber and Faber, 1960.

One of the pioneer works of redaction criticism.

Flender, Helmut. *St. Luke, Theologian of Redemptive History.* Philadelphia: Fortress Press, 1970.

Marshall, Ian Howard. *Luke, Historian and Theologian.* Grand Rapids: Zondervan, 1971.

As against Conzelmann, stresses Luke's interest in salvation—a necessary corrective.

The Acts of the Apostles

Commentaries

Bruce, Frederick F. *The Acts of the Apostles.* Grand Rapids: Eerdmans, 1954.

Haenchen, Ernst. *The Acts of the Apostles, A Commentary.* Oxford: Blackwell, 1971.

This very large commentary takes a much more radical stance than Williams (see below) and takes a rather low view of Luke as a historian.

Williams, Charles S. *A Commentary on the Acts of the Apostles.* London: A. & C. Black, 1957.

Generally conservative in its approach.

Theology

There is very little directly on the theology of Acts. We may take:

Munck, Johannes. *Paul and the Salvation of Mankind.* London: SCM Press, 1959.

O'Neill, John C. *The Theology of Acts.* London: SPCK, 1970.

The wildness of some of the writer's views should not conceal the excellence of some of his observations.

Chapter 7.   The Johannine Literature

The literature is vast; any selection must be somewhat arbitrary.

Commentaries

Barrett, Charles K. *The Gospel According to St. John.* London: SPCK, 1955.

For those with a knowledge of Greek, still a standard work.

Brown, Raymond E., ed. *The Gospel According to St. John*. 2 vols. New York: Doubleday, 1966, 1970.
This is more than copious, but is so well set out that it is not difficult to use.
Lindars, Barnabas. S.S.F. *The Gospel of John*. London: Oliphants, 1972.
Lindars is especially interested in the traditions that lie behind the Gospel.
Schnackenburg, Rudolf. *The Gospel According to St. John*. Vol. 1. New York: Herder, 1968.
A welcome addition from the Roman Catholic side.

Theology

Most of the commentaries are theological. For special studies we turn to:
Dodd, Charles H. *The Interpretation of the Fourth Gospel*. Cambridge, 1953.
————. *Historical Tradition in the Fourth Gospel*. Cambridge, 1963.
Few adopt all Dodd's positions, but it is wise to have good reasons for rejecting them.

The Johannine Epistles

Commentaries

Bruce, Frederick F. *The Epistles of St. John*. London: Pickering and Inglis, 1970.
Dodd, Charles H. *The Johannine Epistles*. London: Hodder and Stoughton, 1946.

Theology

It is impossible to bypass:
Brooke, Alan England. *A Critical and Exegetical Commentary on the Revelation of St. John*. The International Critical Commentary. Edinburgh: T. and T. Clark, 1912.
Law, Robert. *The Tests of Life: A Study of the First Epistle of John*. 2nd ed. Edinburgh: T. and T. Clark, 1909.
For solid theological exposition nothing has surpassed this older book.

Chapter 8.   The Odds and Ends

Pastoral Epistles

Barrett, Charles K. *The Pastoral Epistles*. London: A. & C. Black, 1963.
Sees these Epistles in their present form as belonging to the second century.
Hanson, Anthony T. *Studies in the Pastoral Epistles*. London: SPCK, 1968.
Theological studies in the Epistles; difficult for those who do not know Greek.
Kelly, John N. D. *The Pastoral Epistles*. London: A. & C. Black, 1963.
Defends the Pauline authorship.

2 Peter and Jude

Green, Edward M. B. *Second Peter and Jude*. London: Tyndale Press, 1968.
Mainly on the critical questions, with little directly on the theology. See the highly critical essay of Ernst Käsemann referred to in the text of chapter 8.
Kelly, John N. D. See the work cited above on 1 Peter.

The Kingdom of God

Kümmel, Werner G. *Promise and Fulfilment: the Eschatological Message of Jesus*. London: SCM Press, 1957.
Kümmel takes seriously the eschatological element in the teaching of Jesus without going to extremes.
Ladd, George E. *Jesus and the Kingdom*. Grand Rapids: Eerdmans, 1974.
Perrin, Norman. *The Kingdom of God in the Teaching of Jesus*. Philadelphia: Westminster Press, 1963.
Ridderbos, Herman N. *The Coming of the Kingdom*. Translated by H. de Jongste. Philadelphia: Presbyterian and Reformed Publishing Company, 1962.

Perhaps the most thorough study of the subject in any language. The Dutch original (*De Komst van het Koningrijk Jesus' Prediking volgens de Synoptische Evangeliën*; Kampen: J. H. Kok) appeared in 1950.

The Historical Jesus

Keck, Leander E. *A Future for the Historical Jesus.* Nashville: Abingdon, 1971.
This most interesting work by a younger American scholar goes deeply into the question of the nature of history and the sense in which the term can be applied to the records concerning Jesus.

Mitton, Charles L. *Jesus: the Fact Behind the Faith.* Grand Rapids: Eerdmans, 1975.
Conservative, scholarly. The writer finds in the Gospels more factual information about Jesus than has been found by some others engaged in the quest.

Perrin, Norman. *Rediscovering the Teaching of Jesus.* New York: Harper & Row, 1967.

Rohde, Joachim. *Rediscovering the Teaching of the Evangelists.* London: SCM Press, 1969.
Careful studies of redaction criticism as practiced by a number of scholars, mainly German.

Resurrection

Fuller, Daniel P. *Easter Faith and History.* Grand Rapids: Eerdmans, 1968.
Critical methods here lead to conservative conclusions.

Fuller, Reginald H. *The Formation of the Resurrection Narratives.* New York: Macmillan Co., 1971.

Marxsen, Willi. *The Resurrection of Jesus of Nazareth.* Philadelphia: Fortress Press, 1970.

Pannenberg, Wolfhart. *Jesus, God and Man.* London: SCM Press, 1968.

Chapter 9. Back to Jesus of Nazareth

Jesus

Betz, Otto. *What Do We Know About Jesus?* London: SCM Press, 1968.
Generally conservative in approach; we know more of Jesus than so-called radical criticism would allow.

Dodd, Charles H. *The Founder of Christianity.* London: Collins, 1971.
The summing up of a lifetime of service to New Testament scholarship.

McArthur, Harvey K. *The Quest Through the Centuries.* Philadelphia: Fortress Press, 1966.
The quest is, of course, "the Quest of the Historical Jesus." The quest has moved forward since this book was written.

Muggeridge, Malcolm. *Jesus.* London: Collins, 1975.
This vivacious and at times infuriating evocation by a brilliant journalist might make a very good introduction to the study of Jesus. The illustrations alone are worth the price.

Schweizer, Edward. *Jesus.* London: SCM Press, 1968.
Gets to the heart of the matter on almost every question. The critical approach leads on to the questions of faith.

Vermés, Gezá. *Jesus the Jew: an Historian's Reading of the Gospel.* London: Collins, 1973.
This will take rank, I think, as an important book. The Jewish concern with Jesus is one of the most remarkable features of theological thought in this century.

The Titles of Jesus

Borsch, Frederick H. *The Son of man in Myth and History.* London: SCM Press, 1967.

Higgins, Angus J. B. *Jesus and the Son of man.* Philadelphia: Fortress Press, 1964.

Hooker, Morna D. *The Son of man in Mark.* London: SPCK, 1967.

Taylor, Vincent. *The Names of Jesus.* London: Macmillan & Co., 1953.
The only study known to me of all the names and titles of Jesus in the New Testament.

Tödt, Heinz E. *The Son of man in the Synoptic Tradition.* London: SCM Press, 1965.
Both Tödt and Higgins are rather negative as to the use of the term by Jesus himself.

Beginnings of Christology

Cullman, Oscar. *The Christology of the New Testament.* 2nd ed. London: SCM Press, 1963.

Fuller, Reginald H. *The Foundations of New Testament Christology.* New York: Scribners, 1969.

Hahn, Ferdinand. *The Titles of Jesus in Christology.* London: Lutterworth, 1969.
All three deal in different ways with the problem of finding the link between what Jesus thought about himself and what the church came to believe about him.

Indexes

Scriptural References

Old Testament (including Apocrypha and Pseudepigrapha)

New Testament

Names

Subjects

9972

DATE DUE

2 10 81	
JUN 1 5 1986	
MAR 0 1 89